AF880222

Houghton Mifflin Science

DiscoveryWorks

TEACHING GUIDE / 4

Classifying Living Things

Welcome

to Houghton Mifflin ***Science DiscoveryWorks*** — a science program that provides a balance of exciting hands-on activities and engaging content resources. ***Science DiscoveryWorks*** reflects our belief that effective science education gradually introduces students to the knowledge, methods, skills, and attitudes of scientists, while simultaneously recognizing and respecting the educational and developmental needs of all students.

HOUGHTON MIFFLIN

Boston • Atlanta • Dallas • Denver • Geneva, Illinois • Palo Alto • Princeton

Acknowledgments appear on pages A82, B70, C72, D82, E104, which constitute extensions of this copyright page.

Printed in the U.S.A.

Grade 4 One-Volume Teaching Guide	**ISBN 0-618-16758-7**	1 2 3 4 5 6 7 8 9 10 WEB 10 09 08 07 06 05 04 03 02 01
Grade 4 Modular Teaching Guides		
Unit A: Earth's Land	**ISBN 0-618-16876-1**	2 3 4 5 6 7 8 9 10 WEB 10 09 08 07 06 05 04 03
Unit B: Properties of Matter	**ISBN 0-618-16877-X**	2 3 4 5 6 7 8 9 10 WEB 10 09 08 07 06 05 04 03
Unit C: Classifying Living Things	**ISBN 0-618-16878-8**	2 3 4 5 6 7 8 9 10 WEB 10 09 08 07 06 05 04 03
Unit D: Magnetism and Electricity	**ISBN 0-618-16879-6**	3 4 5 6 7 8 9 10 WEB 10 09 08 07 06 05 04 03
Unit E: Weather and Climate	**ISBN 0-618-16880-X**	2 3 4 5 6 7 8 9 10 WEB 10 09 08 07 06 05 04 03

About the Program

THE AUTHORS

Coming From Diverse Backgrounds, Meeting on Common Ground

William Badders

Elementary Science Teacher,
Cleveland Public Schools, Cleveland, OH

A 1992 Presidential Award winner, Mr. Badders teaches science to students in Grades K through 6. He was a member of the Working Group on Science Assessment Standards. He is a member of the Board of Directors of the National Science Teachers Association. He specializes in the biological and physical sciences.

Dr. Lowell J. Bethel

Professor of Science Education,
The University of Texas at Austin, Austin, TX

Dr. Bethel recently served as Program Director for Teacher Enhancement at the National Science Foundation. He specializes in the biological and physical sciences, urban and multicultural education, constructivism, and the development and evaluation of in-service science programs.

Dr. Victoria Fu

Professor of Child Development and Early Childhood Education, Virginia Polytechnic Institute and State University, Blacksburg, VA

Dr. Fu has extensive experience in teaching child development and teacher education. She has been involved, nationally and internationally, in teacher education initiatives based on qualitative inquiry. Her current research and writings focus on young children as learners and inquirers.

Donald Peck

Director (retired), The Center for Elementary Science,
Fairleigh Dickinson University, Madison, NJ

Mr. Peck's extensive experience in science education includes conducting more than 500 hands-on science workshops for elementary school teachers. He also was a K–12 science supervisor for 23 years. He specializes in the physical and earth sciences.

Dr. Carolyn Sumners

Director of Astronomy and Physical Sciences,
Houston Museum of Natural Science, Houston, TX

Dr. Sumners directs the museum's Burke Baker Planetarium, Challenger Learning Center, and technology camps. She also curates the museum's Welch Chemistry Hall, Fondren Discovery Place, and Arnold Hall of Space Sciences. She is project director for the Toys in Space program at the Johnson Space Center and is a published author of children's books.

Catherine Valentino

Author-in-Residence – Houghton Mifflin,
West Kingston, RI

Ms. Valentino has extensive experience as a classroom teacher, a curriculum coordinator, and a director of elementary education. In her current position, she specializes in developing educational materials that integrate inquiry-based learning and problem-solving skills in all of the content areas. At the University of Rhode Island she serves as Curriculum Advisor for SMILE (Science and Math Investigative Learning Experiences), an after-school enrichment program for students in Grades 4–12.

Reading Consultant

Dr. Peter Dewitz

Educational Consultant
Charlottesville, VA

Dr. Peter Dewitz is a reading expert who specializes in the comprehension of informational text. He was an elementary school teacher in Los Angeles before moving to college teaching and research at the University of Toledo and most recently at the University of Virginia. Currently Dr. Dewitz is working with various school districts to restructure reading instruction.

Sheltered English Consultant

Ronald Rohac

Faculty Member,
California State University-Long Beach, Long Beach, CA

Ron Rohac has been a classroom teacher for 22 years, with extensive background and experience in working with Limited English Proficient students. Mr. Rohac is currently a faculty member at California State University, Long Beach, and is a well-known consultant who creates staff development programs, classroom strategies, and program design for state departments and school districts all over the United States.

We believe . . .

As individuals we come from a variety of backgrounds, but as educators we meet on common ground. We share a vision of effective science education for all children. Our vision is based on these principles.

Our Principles

- Students learn science concepts most effectively through a balance of hands-on activities and solid content knowledge. We provide students with many opportunities to use science process skills and the methods of science through hands-on activities. In addition, we provide solid content resources to help students understand their hands-on exploration.
- In a world that is growing increasingly dependent on the contributions of science, scientific literacy is an important educational goal for all students. In this program we teach students to use science process skills, critical-thinking skills, and scientific reasoning skills to help develop scientific literacy.
- Assessment is an ongoing process that should be used to guide instruction. The variety of assessment in ***DiscoveryWorks*** enables teachers to tailor assessment to student needs and abilities.
- Science education is enhanced when based upon reliable educational standards that guide student attainment, curriculum content, and teaching practices. ***Science DiscoveryWorks*** is based on the Benchmarks for Science Literacy prepared by Project 2061, a long-term educational reform project of the American Association for the Advancement of Science, and the National Science Education Standards prepared by the National Research Council.

The Authors

CONSULTANTS & REVIEWERS

National Advisory Board

Dr. Glenn Berkheimer
Retired Prof. of Science Ed.
Michigan State University
East Lansing, MI

Andrea Bermúdez
Dir., Research Ctr. for Language
University of Houston-Clear Lake
Houston, TX

Pat Bowers
Prof., Ctr. for Math and Science Education
University of North Carolina
Chapel Hill, NC

Bernard Bradley
Science Specialist
Newberry Math & Science Acad.
Chicago, IL

John Cunningham
Science Supervisor
East St. Louis School Dist. 189
East St. Louis, IL

Dr. Judy Dennison
K-12 Science Coordinator
Fulton County Schools
Atlanta, GA

Ronald Ellis
Assoc. Prof., City University of NY
Lehman College
Bronx, NY

Gilda Hester
Chap. 1 Math/Science Specialist
St. Louis Public Schools
St. Louis, MO

Carolyn Randolph
Science Supervisor
Lexington School District 2
West Columbia, SC

Josephine Scott
Supervisor, Multicultural Ed.
Columbus Public Schools
Columbus, OH

John Swang
Teacher
Mandeville Middle School
Mandeville, LA

Debbie Valdez
Teacher
Paul Revere Middle School
Houston, TX

Florencia R. Valenzuela
Technology Specialist
Cochise County Schools
Bisbee, AZ

Content Consultants

Dr. Carl Barrentine
Assoc. Prof., Humanities and Bio.
University of North Dakota
Grand Forks, ND

Dr. Nadine G. Barlow
Dir. of the Robinson Observatory
Physics Department
University of Central Florida
Orlando, FL

Dr. Glenn Berkheimer
Prof. Emeritus of Science Ed.
Michigan State University
East Lansing, MI

Dr. Bonnie Buratti
Jet Propulsion Lab
California Institute of Technology
Pasadena, CA

Dr. Dennis Cheek
Dir. of Info. Serv. and Research
Rhode Island Department of Ed.
Providence, RI

Dr. Linda Cronin-Jones
Assoc. Prof., Doctoral Faculty
University of Florida
Gainesville, FL

Dr. Thomas A. Davies
Research Scientist
Ocean Drilling Program
Texas A&M University
College Station, TX

Dr. Ruth Eshleman
Professor of Nutrition
University of Rhode Island
West Kingston, RI

David G. Futch, Ph.D.
Assoc. Prof., Dept. of Biology
San Diego State University
San Diego, CA

Dr. Orin G. Gelderloos
Department of Natural Sciences
University of Michigan-Dearborn
Dearborn, MI

Gretchen Gillis
Geologist
Maxus Exploration Company
Dallas, TX

Dr. John Gohagan
Early Detection Branch
National Cancer Institute
Rockville, MD

Dr. Fern Gotfried
Pediatrician
Cedar Knolls, NJ

Dr. Harry Hendon
NOAA/CIRES
Climate Diagnostic Center
Boulder, CO

Donald Lisowy
Manager of Teacher Programs
New York Botanical Gardens
New York, NY

Dr. Tom Murphree
Department of Meteorology
Naval Postgraduate School
Monterey, CA

Dr. Suzanne O'Connell
Department of Earth and Environmental Sciences
Wesleyan University
Middletown, CT

Dr. Wendell Potter
Department of Physics
University of California at Davis
Davis, CA

Dr. Betty Preece
Engineer and Physicist
Indialantic, FL

Dr. Yaakow Shecter
Professor, Department of Biological Sciences
City University of New York
Lehman College
Bronx, NY

Dr. Jennifer Specker
Prof. of Oceanography
Biological Sciences
University of Rhode Island
Narragansett, RI

Dr. Janet Sisterson
Cyclotron Laboratory
Harvard University
Cambridge, MA

Dr. Nina Surawicz
Director, Student Health Center
Arizona State University
Tempe, AZ

Dr. Beverly Taylor
Assistant Professor
Miami University, Hamilton
Hamilton, OH

Dr. Dominick Valentino
Professor of Psychobiology
University of Rhode Island
West Kingston, RI

Claudia Viehland
Biochemist, Research Technical Service
Sigma Chemical Company
St. Louis, MO

Dr. Sidney White
Dept. of Geological Sciences
Ohio State University
Columbus, OH

Multicultural Consultants

Eduardo Aparicio
Spanish Editor and Translator
Miami, FL

Albert Carranco
Honors Chemistry Teacher
Roy Miller High School
Corpus Christi, TX

Ronald Ellis
Associate Professor
City University of New York
Lehman College
Bronx, NY

John Kibler
InterAmerica Intercultural Training Institute
Des Plaines, IL

Chin Kim
LA Unified School District
Los Angeles, CA

Dr. Ngoc-Diep T. Nguyen
Director, Bilingual and Multicultural Program
Schaumburg, IL

Carolyn Randolph
Science Supervisor
Lexington School District 2
West Columbia, SC

Josephine Scott
Supervisor, Multicultural Ed.
Columbus Public Schools
Columbus, OH

Florencia R. Valenzuela
Technology Specialist
Cochise County Schools
Bisbee, AZ

Teacher Reviewers

Lisa Acy
Louis Agassiz Elementary Sch.
Cleveland, OH

Renee Addison
Northwestern Lehigh Middle Sch.
New Tripoli, PA

Leslie Armstrong
Laura S. Ward Elementary
Chicago, IL

Leslye Auerbach
Banyan Elementary
Sunrise, FL

Judith Ball
Coordinator for Math/Science/Health
School District U46
Elgin, IL

Karen R. Bishop
Ferron Elementary School
Ferron, UT

Jean Blackshear
Fred A. Toomer Elementary Sch.
Atlanta, GA

Frank A. Bodgen, Jr.
Carver Elementary
Henderson, NC

Bonnie Bohrer
Brookview Elementary School
Brook Park, OH

Robert L. Burtch
1990 Presidential Award winner
Batavia Middle School
Batavia, IL

Martha Christine
Calypso Elementary School
Bethlehem, PA

Mary Eve Corrigan
The Columbus Academy
Gahanna, OH

Patty Dadonna
Hollywood Elementary
Hollywood, FL

John S. Detrick
Emeritus Dept. Chair of Mathematics, holder of the McElroy Chair of Mathematics
The Columbus Academy
Gahanna, OH

Robert C. Dixon
National Center to Improve the Tools of Educators (NCITE)
University of Oregon, College of Education
Eugene, OR

Denise Pitts-Downing
James Elverson Middle School
Philadelphia, PA

Michaeline A. Dudas
Science and Math Instructional Support/Consultant
Northbrook, IL

William Dudrow
The Columbus Academy
Gahanna, OH

Terri Dyer
Lake Weston Elementary
Orlando, FL

Barbara Elliott
1990 Presidential Award winner
Ray E. Kilmer Elementary School
Colorado Springs, CO

Fred Fabry
Retired teacher of Geology and Biology
Deerfield High School
Deerfield, IL

Debbie Fitzpatrick
School 14
Clifton, NJ

Rhea Foster
Anderson Park Elementary Sch.
Atlanta, GA

Audrey Ann Fredrick
James Bowie Elementary
San Antonio, TX

Linda Froschauer
1993 Presidential Award winner
Weston Middle School
Weston, CT

Joanne Gallagher
Tamarac Middle School
Melrose, NY

Donna Green
Beauclerc Elementary
Jacksonville, FL

Marlene Gregor
Elem. Science Consultant
Bloomington, IL

Kim Grimme
Ponderosa Elementary
Sunnyvale, CA

Becca Stein Gutwirth
Florence M. Gaudineer School
Springfield, NJ

William L. Handy, Jr.
Parkland School District
Orefield, PA

Beverly Hanrahan
Franconia Elementary School
Souderton, PA

Renee Harris
Northwestern Lehigh Mid. Sch.
New Tripoli, PA

Patricia Heavens
Dunbar Elementary
East St. Louis, IL

Rhonda Hicks
James Elverson Middle School
Philadelphia, PA

Sr. Marie Patrice Hoare, S.L.
Loretto Middle School
El Paso, TX

Nancy Hronkin
Forest Park Elementary
Crystal Falls, MI

Gail Hurst
Dr. Philips Elementary
Orlando, FL

Lester Y. Ichinose, Ph.D.
Evanston, IL

Mace A. Ishida, Ph.D.
Diversity and Ed. Consultant
Blacklick, OH

Kristine D. Jackson
Belleville, IL

Pearline A. James
W. F. Slaton Elementary School
Atlanta, GA

Evette Jones
Grover Cleveland Elementary
Philadelphia, PA

Charlene Kalinski
Gilvert Cuellar Elementary
Dallas, TX

Sr. Sharon Kassing, S.L.
St. Pius Catholic School
Kirkwood, MO

Jill Kersh
Bullock Elementary
Garland, TX

Gail Kirkland
Hiawassee Elementary
Orlando, FL

John Kibler
InterAmerica Intercultural Training Institute
Des Plaines, IL

Jennifer Kimble
Rogers Elementary
Dallas, TX

Diane Landschoot
John N. C. Stockton Elementary
Jacksonville, FL

Bonnie Lawhorn
Evening Street Elementary
Worthington, OH

Sharon Lempner
R. G. Jones School
Cleveland, OH

Barbara Leonard
1992 Presidential Award winner
Heritage Elementary School
Pueblo, CO

Gus Liss
Young Elementary School
Burlington, NJ

Jo Ann Liss
Intervale School
Parsippany, NJ

Marlenn Maicki
1990 Presidential Award winner
Detroit Country Day School
Bloomfield Hills, MI

Lynn Malok
Spring Garden Elementary Sch.
Bethlehem, PA

Barbara Mecker
Rockwood South Middle Sch.
St. Louis, MO

Leonardo Melton
Fred A. Toomer Elementary Sch.
Atlanta, GA

Bonniejean Meyer
Tremont Elementary School
Cleveland, OH

Laura Mobbett
Huff School
Mountain View, CA

Dr. Suzanne Moore
L. L. Hotchkiss Elementary Sch.
Dallas, TX

Kathy Morton
Christ the King School
Atlanta, GA

Debora Multisano
Clair-Mel Elementary
Tampa, FL

Dr. Ngoc-Diep T. Nguyen
Director, Bilingual and Multicultural Program
Schaumburg, IL

Michael O'Shea
R. G. Jones School
Cleveland, OH

Wendy Peterson
Harvey Rice Elementary School
Cleveland, OH

Filomena Poli-Aleman
Clifton Public School #4
Clifton, NJ

Alexandra Pond
Science Coordinator
North Shore School
Chicago, IL

Herb Quon
Spangler Elementary
Milipitas,CA

Terry Ramirez
Lackland City Elementary
San Antonio, TX

José Salas
Hooper Ave. School
Los Angeles, CA

Erika Silverman
Public School 41
Bronx, NY

Debi Sitkoski
Forest Park Elementary
Crystal Falls, MI

Chris Spigarelli
Forest Park Elementary
Crystal Falls, MI

Christine Spinner
Parkview Elementary
Parma, OH

Jean Ann Strillacci
Kennedy Elementary School
Succasunna, NJ

Laura Swanson
WATTS Intermediate School
Burlington City, NJ

Arthur F. Tobia
Public School 41
Bronx, NY

Laura Turner
Clover Flat Elementary
Boulevard, CA

Nancy Vibeto
1993 Presidential Award winner
Jim Hill Middle School
Minot, ND

Kathy Westbrook
Bluffsview Elementary
Columbus, OH

Sandra Wilson
McKinley Elementary School
Abington, PA

Bonita Wylie
Minnewashta Elementary
Excelsior, MN

THE SCOPE OF THE PROGRAM

An Overview of Concepts and Themes

	KINDERGARTEN	GRADE 1	GRADE 2
Life Science	**UNIT A Characteristics of Living Things** Classification of objects as living or nonliving; basic needs and stages of growth of living things **Themes:** *Systems, Constancy and Change*	**UNIT A Kinds of Living Things** The similarities and differences between plants and animals; classifying plants and animals according to one characteristic; life cycles of plants and animals **Theme:** *Systems*	**UNIT A Interactions of Living Things** The needs of living things; plant and animal adaptations to various habitats; the effect of living things and natural forces on environments **Themes:** *Constancy and Change, Models*
	**UNIT E Body Parts** Identification of internal and external body parts; the functions and importance of individual body parts, including the hands, bones, muscles, heart, stomach, and brain **Themes:** *Systems, Models*	**UNIT E Keeping Fit and Healthy** The importance of good nutrition, exercise, sleep, and proper hygiene; the food pyramid and a healthful diet **Themes:** *Systems, Constancy and Change*	**UNIT E What Makes Me Sick** How germs cause illness; how illnesses spread; prevention of illnesses and injuries; how to stay healthy **Themes:** *Systems, Scale*
Physical Science	**UNIT B Exploring With the Senses** Using the senses to observe the physical characteristics of objects; grouping objects by their physical characteristics **Theme:** *Systems*	**UNIT C Magnets** The properties of magnets; magnetic force; magnetic fields; temporary magnets; magnets and compasses **Themes:** *Systems, Scale*	**UNIT B Energy and Motion** Characteristics of light; measuring motion; how forces affect motion; sound waves, pitch, and volume; heat energy and uses of natural resources for heat **Themes:** *Constancy and Change, Scale*
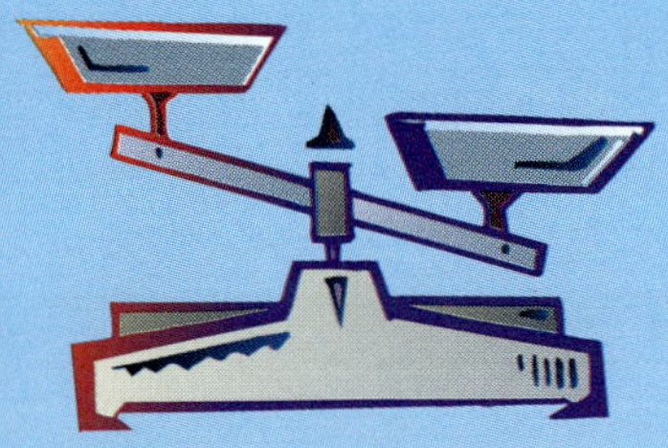	**UNIT D Pushes and Pulls** Different ways things move; pushes and pulls; surfaces; directional motion **Themes:** *Systems, Models*	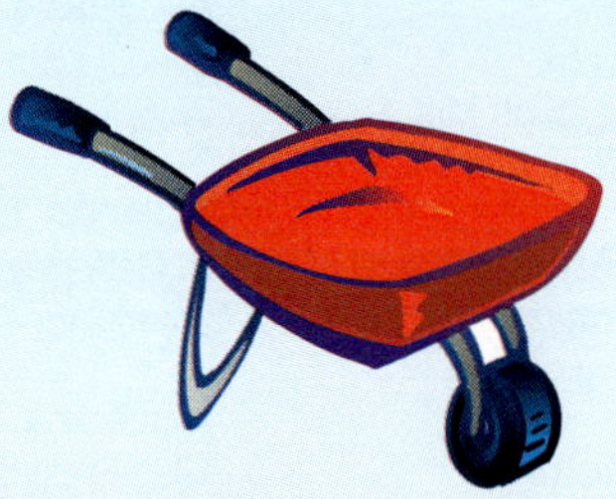	**UNIT D Solids, Liquids, and Gases** Properties of solids, liquids, and gases; the changing of materials from one state to another **Theme:** *Constancy and Change*
Earth Science	**UNIT C Looking at the Earth and Sky** Landforms; daytime sky and the sun; changing seasons and the weather; the moon and the stars **Themes:** *Constancy and Change, Scale*	**UNIT B Weather and Seasons** Factors that affect the weather; seasonal weather changes; how people, plants, and animals respond to weather conditions **Theme:** *Constancy and Change*	**UNIT C Changes Over Time** Characteristics of different dinosaurs; how trace fossils and fossil remains provide clues about the earth's history; changes in the day and night sky; daily and seasonal weather patterns **Themes:** *Models, Scale, Constancy and Change*
		**UNIT D Earth's Land and Water** Properties of soil and rocks; how water and soil mix; how water flows; recycling soil, water, and rocks **Themes:** *Systems, Models*	

> *The science that all students are expected to learn is defined so that students have sufficient time to develop a deep understanding of essential scientific ideas rather than superficial acquaintance with many isolated facts.*
>
> *National Science Education Standards*

GRADE 3	GRADE 4	GRADE 5	GRADE 6
UNIT A Life Cycles Stages in the life cycles of animals and plants; changes in animals and plants as they mature; inherited traits; ways that animals and plants survive **Theme:** *Models*	**UNIT C Classifying Living Things** Classification of living things; characteristics of different animal and plant groups; basic needs of living things; adaptations that help living things meet their needs. **Theme:** *Systems*	**UNIT A Systems in Living Things** Life processes of plants and animals; structure of plant and animal cells; human digestive, respiratory, circulatory, and excretory systems; life cycles of plants and animals **Theme:** *Systems*	**UNIT A Cells and Microbes** Structure and life processes of cells, including mitosis; protists and fungi; bacteria and viruses **Theme:** *Models*
UNIT E Roles of Living Things The needs of living things in relation to their environments; how living things adapt to their environments, change them, and respond to them **Theme:** *Constancy and Change*		**UNIT D Populations and Ecosystems** Dynamic interactions of living and nonliving things in an ecosystem; how energy and matter flow through an ecosystem; biomes; biodiversity **Theme:** *Systems*	**UNIT D Continuity of Life** Asexual reproduction; sexual reproduction, including meiosis; inherited and acquired traits; evolution, including evidence for evolution and evolutionary processes **Theme:** *Constancy and Change*
UNIT C Matter, Energy, and Forces Properties, states, and changes in matter; forms of energy and how heat energy moves and changes matter; forces and machines **Theme:** *Systems*	**UNIT B Properties of Matter** Physical properties; states; effects of heat loss or gain and of physical and chemical changes **Theme:** *Scale*	**UNIT C Matter and Energy** Properties of matter; states of matter; elements, compounds, and mixtures; forms of energy; energy transfer; changes in energy; changes in matter **Theme:** *Models*	**UNIT C The Nature of Matter** Physical and chemical properties; elements, compounds, mixtures; physical and chemical changes; acids and bases; atomic structure **Theme:** *Scale*
	**UNIT D Magnetism and Electricity** Properties of magnets; forms of electrical energy; electric circuits; sources of electric current; how electric current is changed into useful energy **Theme:** *Models*	**UNIT F Light and Sound** Properties of light; lenses and their uses; color; properties of sound; the sense of hearing; controlling, recording, and transmitting sound **Theme:** *Models*	**UNIT F Forces and Motion** Characteristics of motion; gravity; measuring changes in motion; friction; action-reaction forces; how forces affect the motion of objects **Theme:** *Scale*
UNIT B Sun, Moon, and Earth The physical features of the Sun and Moon; the rotation and revolution of Earth and the Moon; planets of the solar system; Earth's seasonal changes; eclipses **Theme:** *Scale*	**UNIT A Earth's Land** How moving water, wind, and ice shape the land; natural resources and conservation efforts; consequences of producing and disposing of trash **Theme:** *Constancy and Change*	**UNIT B The Solar System and Beyond** The night sky; how astronomers learn about space; the solar system; stars and galaxies; survival in space **Theme:** *Scale*	**UNIT B The Changing Earth** Theory of plate tectonics; the movement of continents; the formation of mountains; earthquakes and volcanoes **Theme:** *Models*
UNIT D Earth's Resources The importance of air, water, and land; renewable, nonrenewable, and inexhaustible resources; uses and protection of Earth's air, water, and land; forces that change Earth's surface; properties of soils **Theme:** *Constancy and Change*	**UNIT E Weather and Climate** Earth's atmosphere; effects of changes in the air on weather; the water cycle; weather patterns and predictions; seasonal weather changes and climate **Theme:** *Constancy and Change*	**UNIT E The Solid Earth** Properties and uses of minerals and rocks; the rock cycle; Earth's structure; fossils as clues to the age of rocks; the formation of crustal features, such as mountains **Theme:** *Constancy and Change*	**UNIT E Oceanography** Contents and properties of ocean water; features and exploration of the ocean floor; currents, waves, and tides; resources from the ocean; ocean pollution **Theme:** *Systems*

TEACHING MODEL

Flexibility is an important feature of the **Science DiscoveryWorks** ***program. Although the*** **Teaching Guide** ***suggests ways in which you can use the program components to organize and guide each lesson, you can adapt these suggestions or develop your own teaching strategies. The model shown here is one way of teaching a unit.***

Unit Opener

The *Unit Opener* headline and photograph highlight a scientific phenomenon that occurs in a real-world setting. The opener can be used to engage students' interest in the topic to be studied.

Introduction Have students read the introductory paragraph and discuss what they know about the science topic.

Think Like a Scientist Have students review some of the questions they will investigate in the unit and then have them suggest some of their own questions.

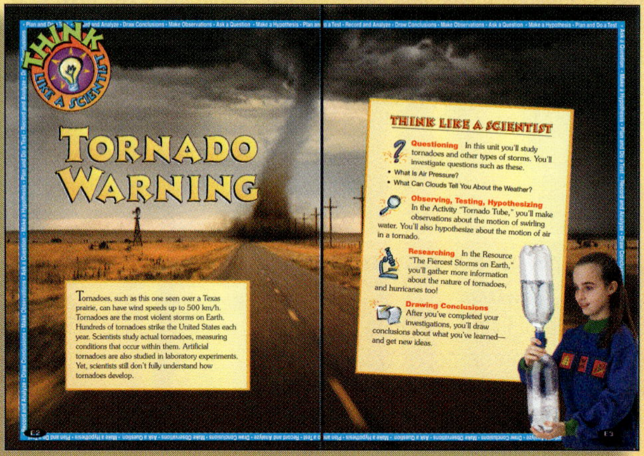

Chapter Opener

The *Chapter Opener* photograph and introductory text focuses on people using science and the role of science in culture and the arts. The photo and text can be used as a discussion starter for the chapter topics.

Warm-up Activity Use the suggested activity in the *Teaching Guide* to motivate interest.

Home-School Connection Extend science learning to the home with easy-to-do activities.

Investigations

The *Investigations*, which form the heart of the ***Science DiscoveryWorks*** program, are made up of two types of student pages—*Activities* and *Resources*.

Baseline Assessment Use the Baseline Assessment in the Teaching Guide as the starting point for the Investigation.

- The Baseline Assessment helps identify the level of prior knowledge for the concept.
- Both individual and whole-class strategies are used in the Baseline Assessment.

Baseline Assessment Blow up a balloon. Suggest students push gently on its sides. Ask: **What is air pressure? How does it affect you or the weather?** Save responses for Following Up.

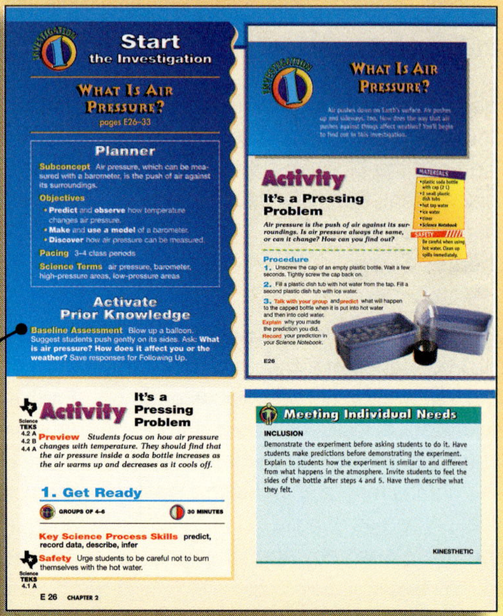

Activities Provide hands-on experiences for students that make subsequent readings more meaningful. These experiences form the basis for conceptual development.

- Have students record their observations, data, and responses in their *Science Notebooks* as they do the Activities.
- Have students go beyond the basic Activities, using suggestions found in *Investigate Further* boxes. These suggestions include both hands-on and CD-ROM activities.

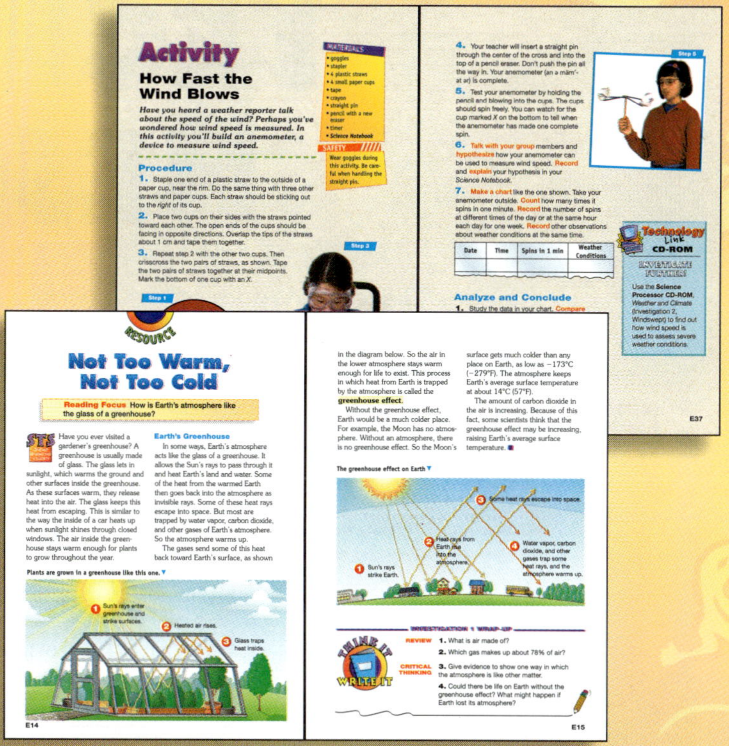

Resources Provide solid science content that reinforces and extends the concepts that students explored in the Activities.

- In addition to regular text material, these resources use a variety of approaches that include Time Capsules; How It Works; Science, Technology & Society; and Global Views.
- Use the *Unit Project Links* and the associated *Science Notebook* pages to provide students with an opportunity to apply their knowledge and understanding.

Close the Investigation Assess student understanding of key science concepts and vocabulary.

- Have students write the answers to the *Think It–Write It* questions in their *Science Notebooks*.
- Use the *Investigation Review* found in the *Assessment Guide* as additional assessment.

Following Up/Baseline Assessment Return to students' Baseline Assessments and use the suggested strategy in the Teaching Guide.

- Allow students to discuss their initial ideas and to "update" their knowledge.
- Students can see for themselves how their conceptual understanding has grown.

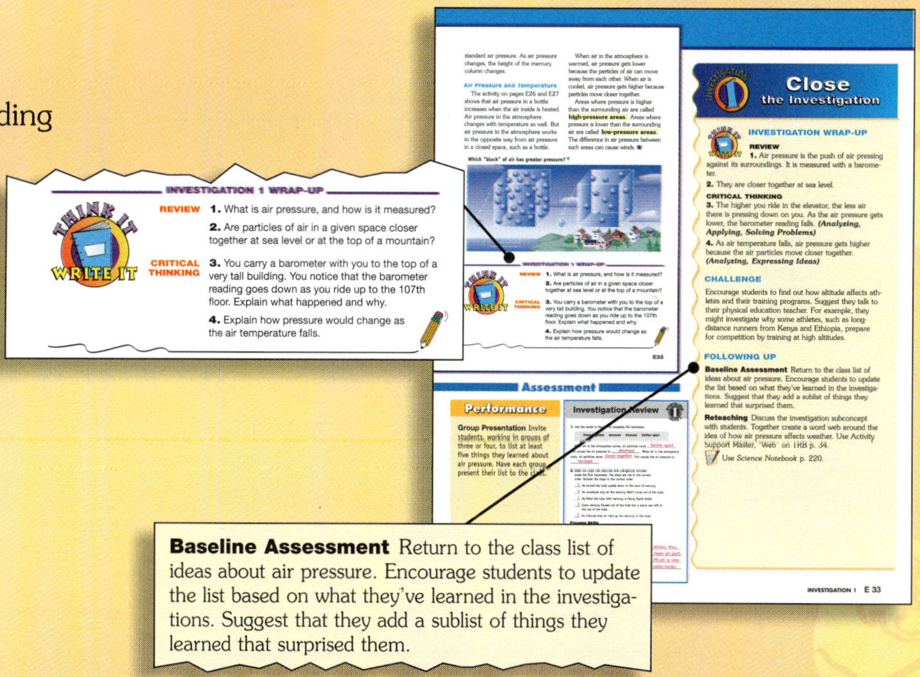

Reflect and Evaluate

The *Reflect and Evaluate* page at the end of each chapter helps students reinforce and review the concepts developed in the chapter.

- Have students reflect on their understanding by answering the questions in their *Science Notebooks*.
- Use the *Performance Assessment* suggestion, with accompanying scoring rubric, found in the *Teaching Guide,* to further assess student understanding.

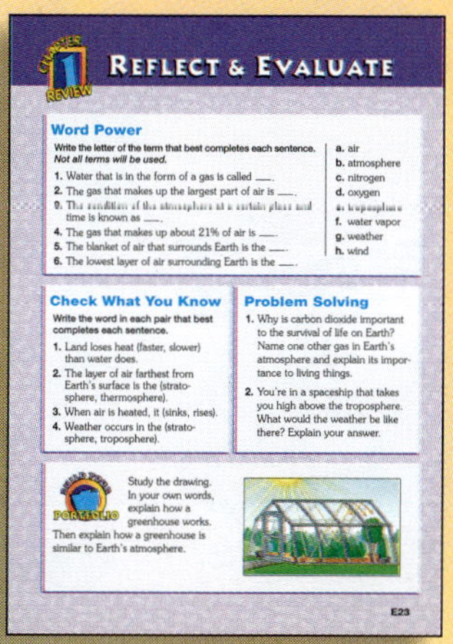

TECHNOLOGY RESOURCES

Science DiscoveryWorks *offers a wide variety of technology resources that provide alternative ways of presenting and developing science concepts. These resources also provide students with opportunities to use technological tools and to develop an understanding of how technology contributes to advances in science.*

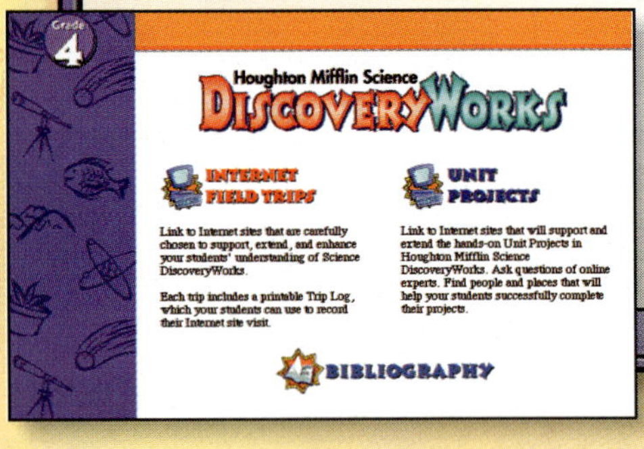

www.eduplace.com

Visit Houghton Mifflin's Web site, Education Place, to access a rich environment of interactive on-line teacher resources and student activities. Internet Field Trips and Unit Project Links referenced in the Student Edition are supported by up-to-date links. Also included are professional development resources, Science Library Adventures, the Discussion Forum, and Best of the Net.

Science Processor CD-ROM

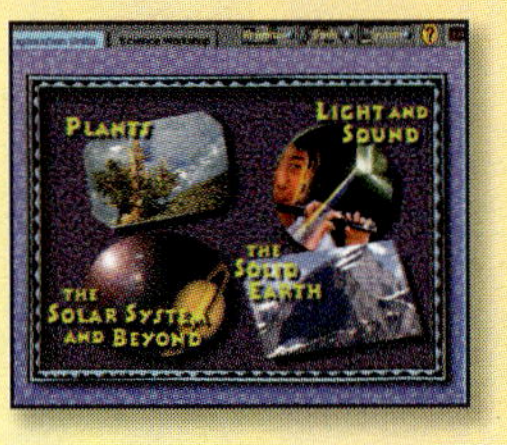

This software provides an interactive, child-centered learning approach. The CD-ROM provides Investigations that replace or enhance the Investigations in the student book. On-screen tools include a Spreadsheet, a Grapher, a Writer, a Painter, a Calculator, and a Timer.

DiscoveryWorks Test Generator

This CD-ROM contains ready-made chapter, unit, and standardized-format tests, in English and Spanish, that can be easily customized to meet your needs. Choose from multiple-choice and free-response questions.

Best of the Net

This CD-ROM program provides guided Internet experiences in Life Science, Earth Science, Physical Science, and the Human Body. It requires no Internet connection.

Videotapes

"Bill Nye the Science Guy" videos are correlated to units throughout *Science DiscoveryWorks*. Ways to use these exciting videos to enhance or extend science concepts are suggested on the Using Technology page that precedes each unit.

Books on Tape

Audiotapes in English and Spanish enable students to follow along as the Student Edition is read aloud. These tapes help meet the individual needs of auditory learners, bilingual and ESL students, and challenged readers.

Activity Video Lab

Video demonstrations aid you in preparing, conducting, and concluding activities from *Science DiscoveryWorks*.

MEETING INDIVIDUAL NEEDS

We know that classroom educators today are very conscious of trying to meet the needs of a diverse student population. Houghton Mifflin Science DiscoveryWorks *provides varied activities throughout the program designed to help you meet these needs.*

Students Acquiring English

These activities are intended for use with students who are just learning the English language.

Gifted and Talented

These activities are appropriate for students who can think creatively and work independently on more challenging tasks.

Inclusion

These activities are intended for students with mental or physical disabilities who might benefit from alternative learning strategies.

Early Finishers

These activities can be used with students who complete the basic material earlier than the rest of the students.

For Extra Help

These activities provide additional help for students who are having difficulty understanding the concept of the lesson.

Learning Styles

Additionally, we realize that learning styles vary from student to student and even vary for a given student on different topics. Therefore, we have provided Activities that use the following learning styles to enable students to learn in ways that are most comfortable to them.

- **LINGUISTIC**
- **VISUAL/SPATIAL**
- **LOGICAL/MATHEMATICAL**
- **KINESTHETIC**
- **AUDITORY**

CONCEPT MAPS

Helping Students Organize Data

Houghton Mifflin *Science DiscoveryWorks* uses concept maps throughout the program to help students identify, organize, and process science information. These maps can be used to enhance student understanding by presenting processes and relationships visually.

KWL Chart

KWL charts help students form purposes for reading. The name of the concept being studied goes at the top of the chart. The first column is for recording what students know about the concept, and the second column is for recording what they want to know about it. In the last column, students record what they've learned after they have completed the unit.

Topic The Solar System		
K What you know	W What you want to know	L What you learned
Earth revolves around the Sun. There are other planets in our solar system.	What are the other planets? Do other planets have moons?	

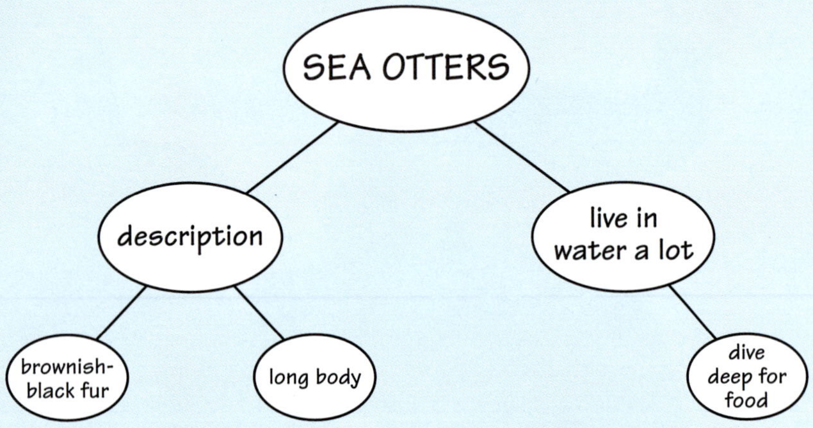

Webs

Webs can be used to show main ideas and subordinate ideas as well as part-whole relationships. The central large circle is for showing the main idea or concept. Smaller circles are for showing subordinate ideas.

Venn Diagram

A Venn diagram is an excellent way to compare and contrast things, such as a robin and a cardinal. Characteristics both birds share, such as wings and feathers, are listed in the overlapping parts of the two circles. Unique characteristics are listed in the non-overlapping parts of the circles.

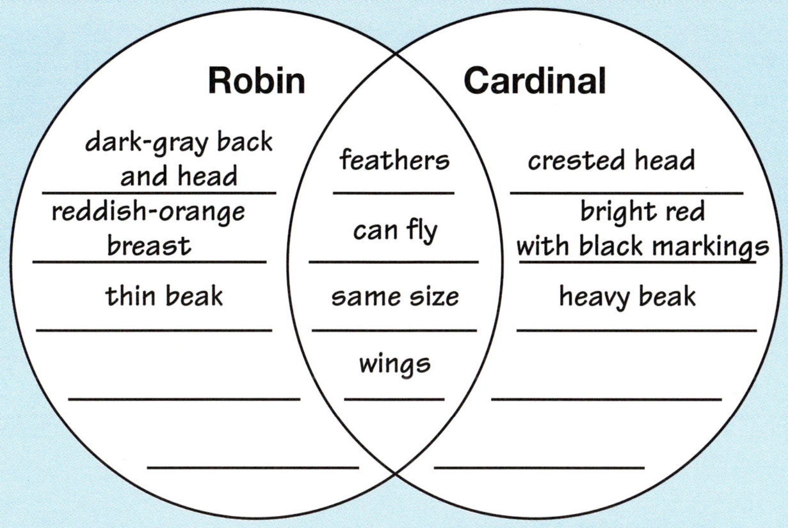

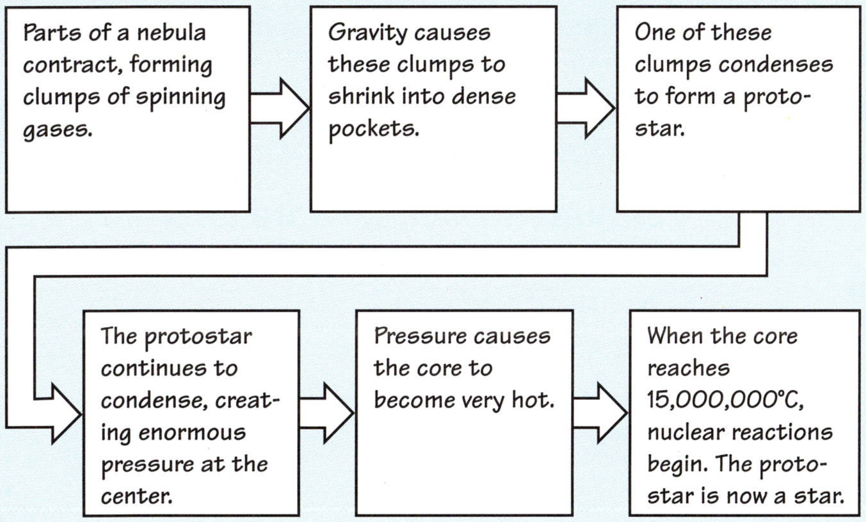

Sequence Chart

A sequence chart can be used to clarify the steps of a process or a chain of events. Each step is recorded in its own box, and the boxes are connected by arrows. In some cases, the last step in a process leads back to the first step. The chart then becomes a representation of a cycle.

Cause and Effect

A cause-and-effect chart shows the relationship between causes and effects. Sometimes you may want to show how multiple causes lead to one effect. At other times you may want to show how one cause leads to several effects. You may also want to show a chain of causes and effects.

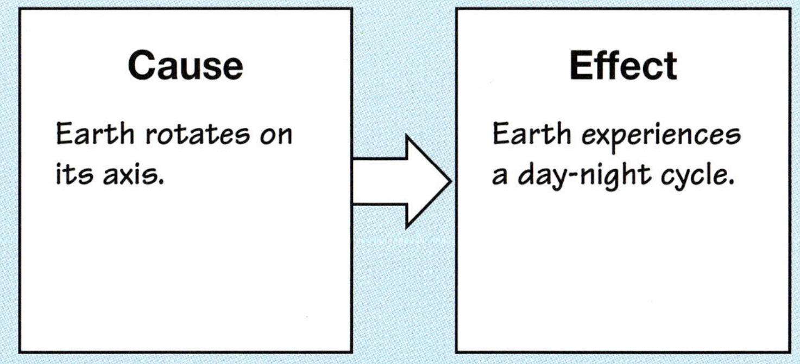

Reading in the Content Area

Houghton Mifflin's Science DiscoveryWorks *helps make science concepts and informational text accessible to all students by providing students with opportunities to practice and apply reading skills and strategies.*

Improving Reading Comprehension

Science DiscoveryWorks recognizes that students can sometimes have difficulty reading informational text. Therefore, the development of *DiscoveryWorks* focused on creating a program that helps students read purposefully and strategically.

Features to Build Prior Knowledge

- **Concept Map Transparencies** preview important chapter ideas and their relationships.
- **Support Terms** (words that present problems for some students, especially those acquiring English) are identified in the *Teaching Guide* so that you can help students before they begin reading.
- **Concrete Hands-on Activities** help students understand concepts before they read.

Features to Make Reading Purposeful

- **KWL Activities** at the start of each unit help students inquire as they read and study.
- The **Reading Focus** question at the beginning of each Resource helps set a purpose for reading.

Features to Maximize Comprehension

- **Key science terms** are highlighted and explained in context.
- **Subheads** within each Resource divide the text into manageable sections.
- **Photos, illustrations,** and **charts** present concepts, processes, and relationships graphically.

Features to Consolidate Learning

- **Completed Concept Maps** help students integrate and study new ideas.
- **Vocabulary Masters** provide additional support for the chapter science terms.

Using Reading Skills Pages

At the end of each unit, a *Using Reading Skills* page gives students an additional opportunity to apply and practice a particular reading skill, using science informational text. The table below shows the set of skills that are developed across Grades 3 through 6 in *Science DiscoveryWorks*.

Unit	Grade 3	Grade 4	Grade 5	Grade 6
Unit A	Finding the Main Idea	Main Idea and Details	Main Idea and Details	Detecting the Sequence
Unit B	Drawing Conclusions	Cause and Effect	Drawing Conclusions	Main Idea and Details
Unit C	Detecting the Sequence	Compare and Contrast	Cause and Effect	Drawing Conclusions
Unit D	Cause and Effect	Drawing Conclusions	Summarizing	Cause and Effect
Unit E	Compare and Contrast	Detecting the Sequence	Detecting the Sequence	Compare and Contrast
Unit F			Compare and Contrast	Summarizing

INTEGRATING SCIENCE & MATH

Since mathematics frequently supports or forms the basis for scientific ideas, students often use their math skills as they study science.* Science DiscoveryWorks*, therefore, provides a variety of opportunities for students to apply, practice, and improve their math skills and knowledge.

Applying and Practicing Math Skills

It is often helpful to know exactly where math can be found in a science lesson. The icons below, which appear in the Student Edition, will help you and your students see and better use the connections that naturally exist between science and math.

Using Math You will find the *Using Math* feature throughout the Resources. This feature is usually a special "math caption" that asks students to use the data presented in drawings, graphs, or other visuals. For example, students may be asked to use computational skills, compare data, estimate, and apply other math skills.

Math Hint This feature is found throughout the Activities. These hints are included in procedural steps in Activities to assist students with the math that is needed in order to do the Activity successfully.

Science and Math Toolbox This section of the Student Edition provides instruction in using science equipment and reviews the math skills that are needed to do the Activities successfully. The Science and Math Toolbox varies by grade level so that skills and tools may be introduced at the appropriate time. Students can use these pages to review measurement techniques, graphs, calculators, and other skills and tools. The Toolbox is referenced in Activities where a particular skill or tool is needed.

Using Math Skills Pages

At the end of each unit, a *Using Math Skills* page gives students an additional opportunity to apply and practice a particular math skill in the context of science content. The table below shows the set of skills that are developed across Grades 3 through 6 in *Science DiscoveryWorks*.

Unit	Grade 3	Grade 4	Grade 5	Grade 6
Unit A	Analyze Data	Circle Graph	Line Graph	Analyze Data
Unit B	Time Measurement	Volume	Analyze Data	Bar Graph
Unit C	Bar Graph	Analyze Data	Equations and Formulas	Line Graph
Unit D	Circle Graph	Bar Graph	Circle Graph	Analyze Data
Unit E	Analyze Data	Line Graph	Bar Graph	Circle Graph
Unit F			Analyze Data	Equations and Formulas

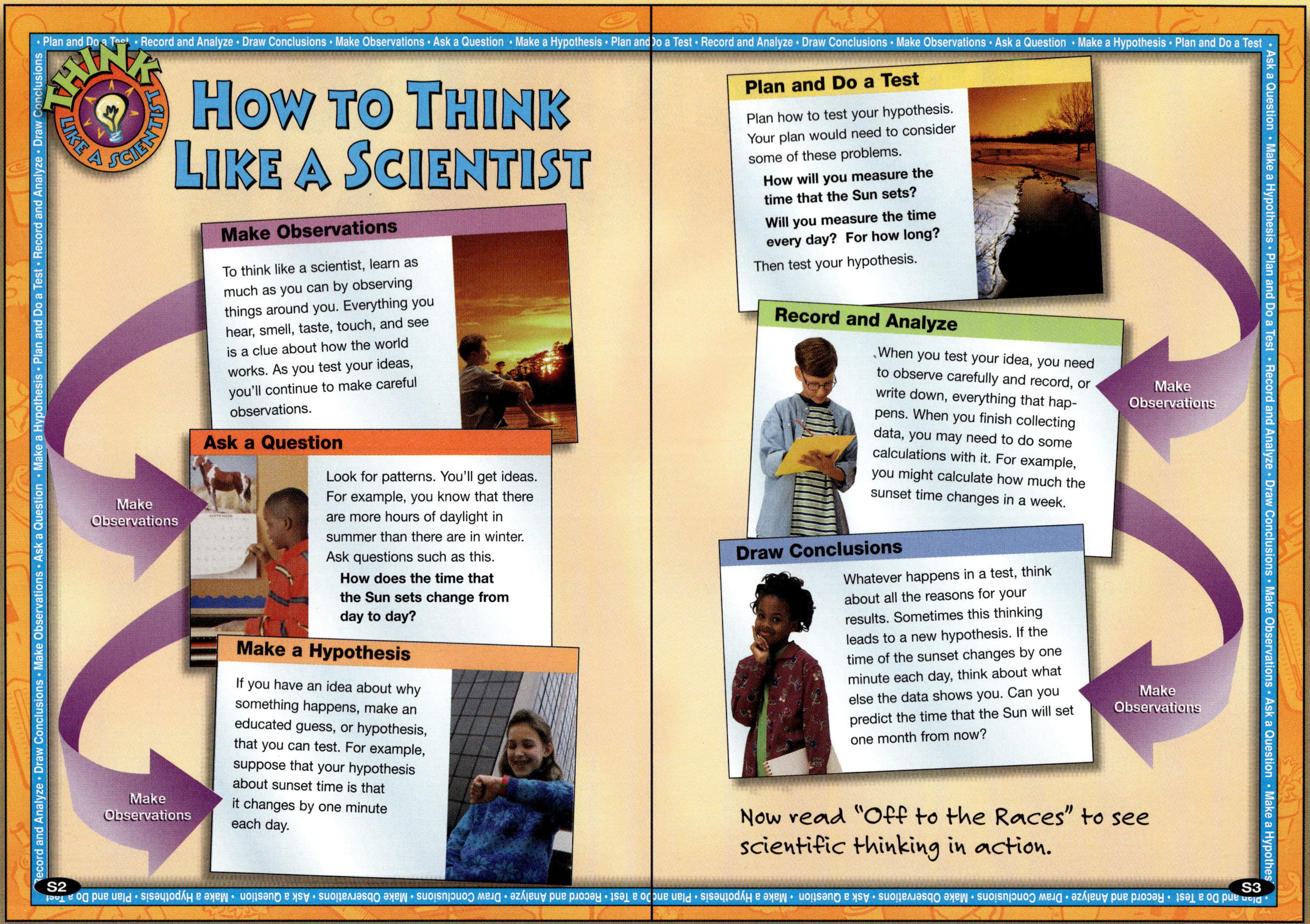

How to Think Like a Scientist

Make Observations

To think like a scientist, learn as much as you can by observing things around you. Everything you hear, smell, taste, touch, and see is a clue about how the world works. As you test your ideas, you'll continue to make careful observations.

Make Observations

Ask a Question

Look for patterns. You'll get ideas. For example, you know that there are more hours of daylight in summer than there are in winter. Ask questions such as this.

How does the time that the Sun sets change from day to day?

Make Observations

Make a Hypothesis

If you have an idea about why something happens, make an educated guess, or hypothesis, that you can test. For example, suppose that your hypothesis about sunset time is that it changes by one minute each day.

Plan and Do a Test

Plan how to test your hypothesis. Your plan would need to consider some of these problems.

How will you measure the time that the Sun sets?

Will you measure the time every day? For how long?

Then test your hypothesis.

Make Observations

Record and Analyze

When you test your idea, you need to observe carefully and record, or write down, everything that happens. When you finish collecting data, you may need to do some calculations with it. For example, you might calculate how much the sunset time changes in a week.

Make Observations

Draw Conclusions

Whatever happens in a test, think about all the reasons for your results. Sometimes this thinking leads to a new hypothesis. If the time of the sunset changes by one minute each day, think about what else the data shows you. Can you predict the time that the Sun will set one month from now?

Now read "Off to the Races" to see scientific thinking in action.

S2 S3

How Do Scientists Study Nature?

What discoveries and inventions have had the greatest impact on people's lives? Antibiotics? Cell biology? The structure of matter? The printing press? Computer technology? Although all of these would be nominated, most people would not identify scientific thinking as a great invention. Yet this unique process for building knowledge has led to many discoveries. What makes this process such a powerful tool?

Exploring Nature

Until the seventeenth century, most people accepted untested explanations of events in nature. Myths and superstitions were often part of such explanations. Most people thought that Earth was at the center of the universe. They believed that the Sun, Moon, planets, and stars circled Earth. Although some scientists had hypothesized that Earth circled the Sun, it took an invention—the telescope—and the inquiring mind of a great scientist, Galileo Galilei, to provide evidence that supported this hypothesis.

Scientific Revolution

In 1609, Galileo peered through his primitive telescope at the planet Jupiter and *observed* what appeared to be tiny "stars" in a straight line near the giant planet. As he studied the planet for many nights, he was amazed to discover that the stars moved, yet stayed close to Jupiter. He *questioned* what these points of light could be. After *recording* the position of the stars each night and *analyzing* his records, Galileo *concluded* that the tiny lights must be Jupiter's moons. Galileo's discovery contradicted the common thinking of the day—that all heavenly bodies orbited Earth. And his evidence paved the way for popular acceptance of a revolutionary new way of understanding nature—scientific thinking.

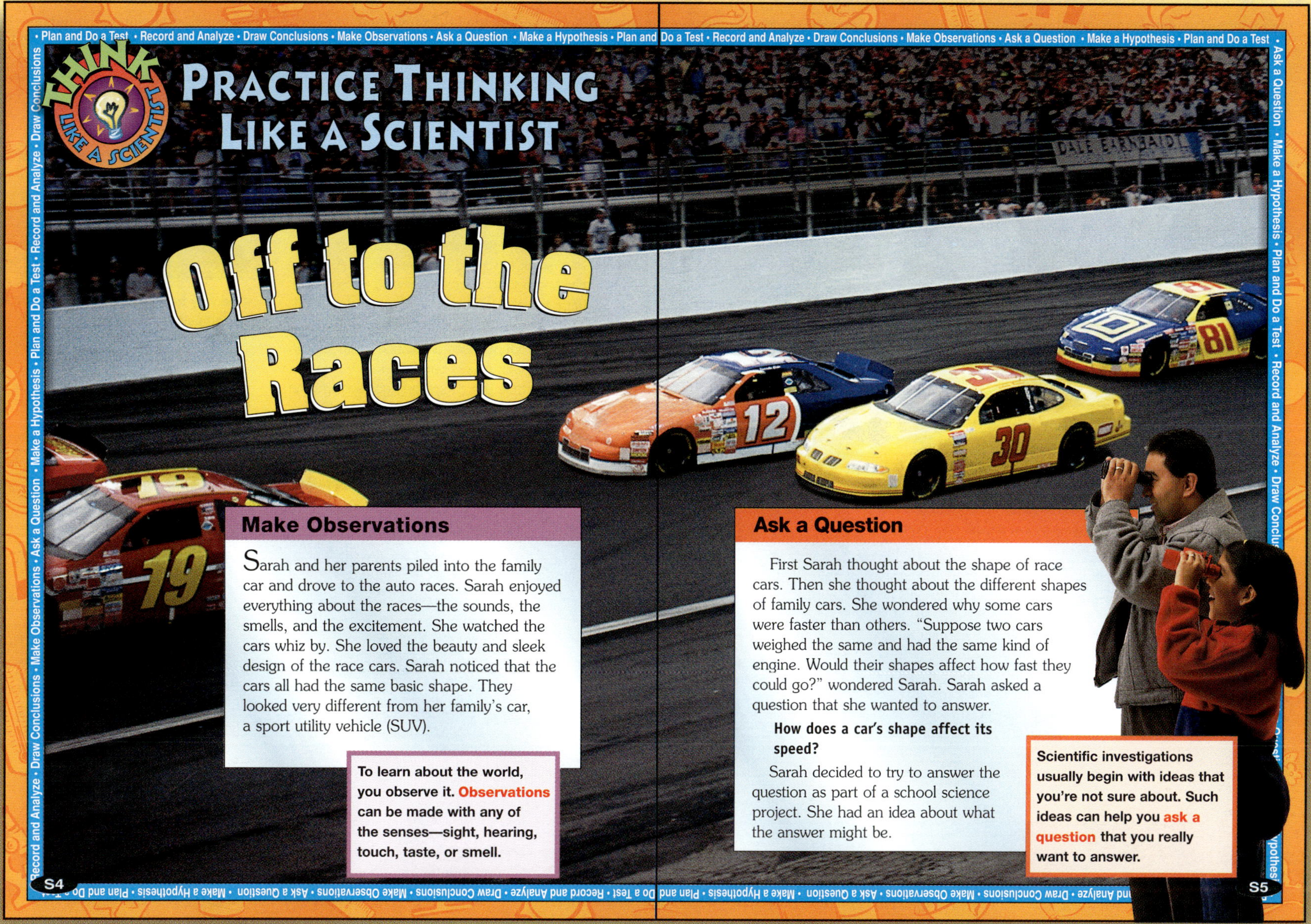

Plan and Do a Test • Record and Analyze • Draw Conclusions • Make Observations • Ask a Question • Make a Hypothesis

THINK LIKE A SCIENTIST

PRACTICE THINKING LIKE A SCIENTIST

Off to the Races

Make Observations

Sarah and her parents piled into the family car and drove to the auto races. Sarah enjoyed everything about the races—the sounds, the smells, and the excitement. She watched the cars whiz by. She loved the beauty and sleek design of the race cars. Sarah noticed that the cars all had the same basic shape. They looked very different from her family's car, a sport utility vehicle (SUV).

To learn about the world, you observe it. Observations can be made with any of the senses—sight, hearing, touch, taste, or smell.

Ask a Question

First Sarah thought about the shape of race cars. Then she thought about the different shapes of family cars. She wondered why some cars were faster than others. "Suppose two cars weighed the same and had the same kind of engine. Would their shapes affect how fast they could go?" wondered Sarah. Sarah asked a question that she wanted to answer.

How does a car's shape affect its speed?

Sarah decided to try to answer the question as part of a school science project. She had an idea about what the answer might be.

Scientific investigations usually begin with ideas that you're not sure about. Such ideas can help you ask a question that you really want to answer.

S4

S5

WHAT IS SCIENTIFIC THINKING?

Scientific thinking, also commonly called "scientific inquiry" or "the scientific method," is not a single method with a set number of orderly steps. It is a flexible process for both asking and answering questions about nature. Scientific thinking involves:

- Using all of the senses to make careful observations
- Asking specific questions about those observations that can be answered by using the tools of science
- Forming hypotheses that explain what is observed
- Testing these hypotheses through experiments and other tests and gathering and recording data
- Analyzing and drawing conclusions from the data
- Asking new questions, making new observations, and forming new hypotheses based on those findings

In school, students can learn how to use the process of scientific thinking in their daily lives. Students can also discover the vast body of knowledge that scientists, using that same process, have uncovered.

Scientific inquiry is dependent on critical-thinking skills. Scientists analyze nature in their attempts to understand and explain how nature works. This often involves breaking a phenomenon down (mentally and physically) into smaller and smaller parts to understand how the parts relate. Scientists also employ synthesis in their work—putting together pieces of the puzzle that is nature.

Scientific thinking also involves keeping an open mind about ideas. A tendency to want to investigate for oneself, rather than to accept the explanations of others, also characterizes scientific thinking.

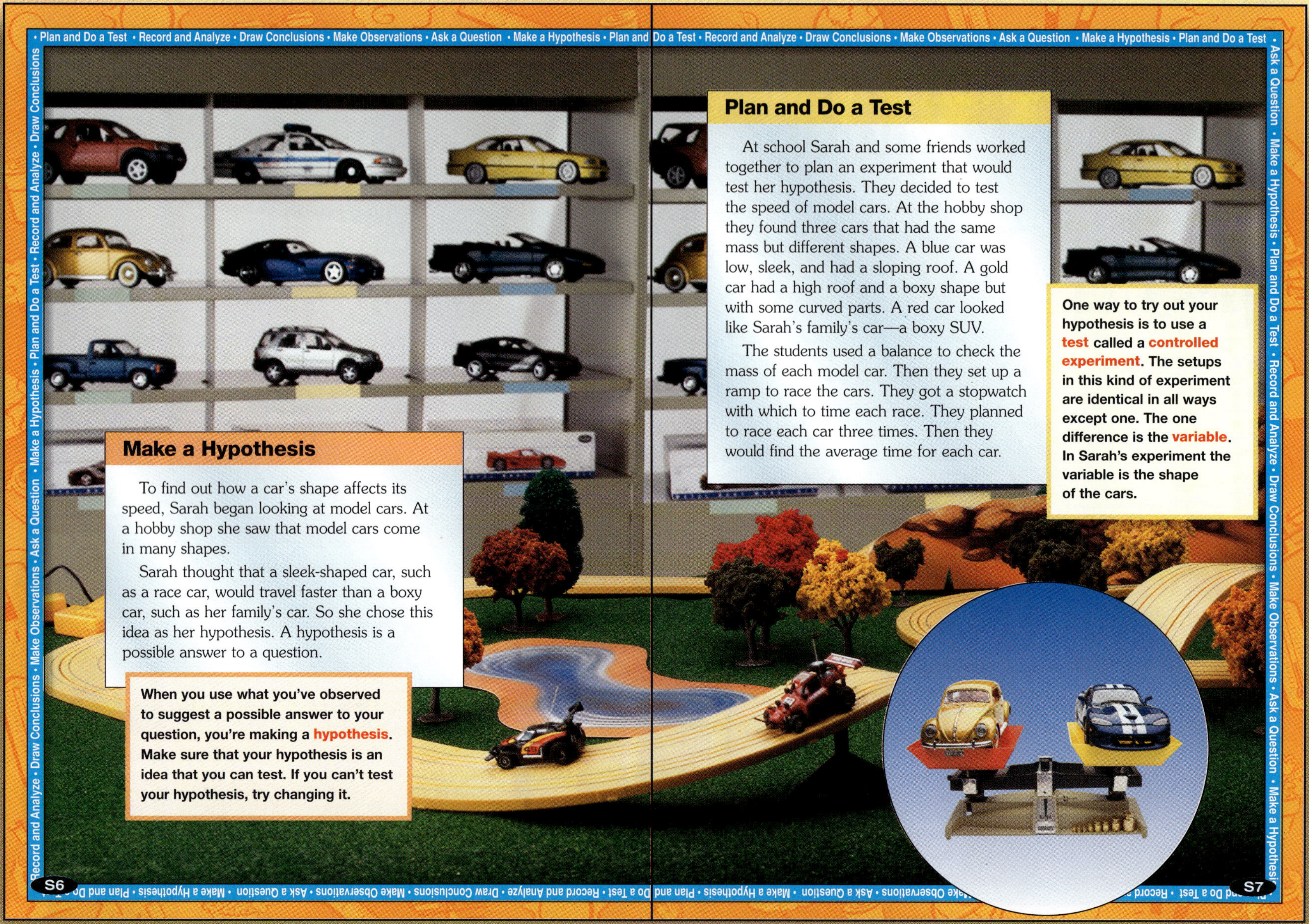

Make a Hypothesis

To find out how a car's shape affects its speed, Sarah began looking at model cars. At a hobby shop she saw that model cars come in many shapes.

Sarah thought that a sleek-shaped car, such as a race car, would travel faster than a boxy car, such as her family's car. So she chose this idea as her hypothesis. A hypothesis is a possible answer to a question.

When you use what you've observed to suggest a possible answer to your question, you're making a hypothesis. Make sure that your hypothesis is an idea that you can test. If you can't test your hypothesis, try changing it.

Plan and Do a Test

At school Sarah and some friends worked together to plan an experiment that would test her hypothesis. They decided to test the speed of model cars. At the hobby shop they found three cars that had the same mass but different shapes. A blue car was low, sleek, and had a sloping roof. A gold car had a high roof and a boxy shape but with some curved parts. A red car looked like Sarah's family's car—a boxy SUV.

The students used a balance to check the mass of each model car. Then they set up a ramp to race the cars. They got a stopwatch with which to time each race. They planned to race each car three times. Then they would find the average time for each car.

One way to try out your hypothesis is to use a test called a controlled experiment. The setups in this kind of experiment are identical in all ways except one. The one difference is the variable. In Sarah's experiment the variable is the shape of the cars.

S6 S7

Where Is the Evidence?

With which of the following statements would your students agree? *Friday the 13th is an unlucky day. In a championship game, the home team has an advantage. Studying with the television on doesn't affect learning. If five coin tosses in a row show heads, the next toss is more likely to be tails.* To a scientist, each of these statements can be considered a testable *hypothesis.*

Gathering Data

Which hypotheses are supported by evidence and which are just unsupported opinions? There are many ways to test a hypothesis. Some involve gathering data and analyzing it. For example, is Friday the 13th really an "unlucky" day? A scientist would start by carefully defining certain terms and gathering information. What does the word *unlucky* mean in measurable terms? How many times has Friday occurred on the 13th of the month? Are there more unlucky events on Friday the 13th than on the 13th day of the month when that day doesn't land on a Friday? By analyzing this data, a scientist could draw reasonable conclusions about whether the data supported the hypothesis that Friday the 13th was "unlucky."

A Controlled Test

Sometimes a hypothesis is best tested in a carefully controlled experiment. To discover if studying with the television on affects grades, scientists would compare students' learning scores under two conditions—an experimental condition in which the television is on and a control condition in which it is not. Again, data would be gathered and analyzed to determine if the hypothesis is supported or not. And the experiment would be repeated to verify the results.

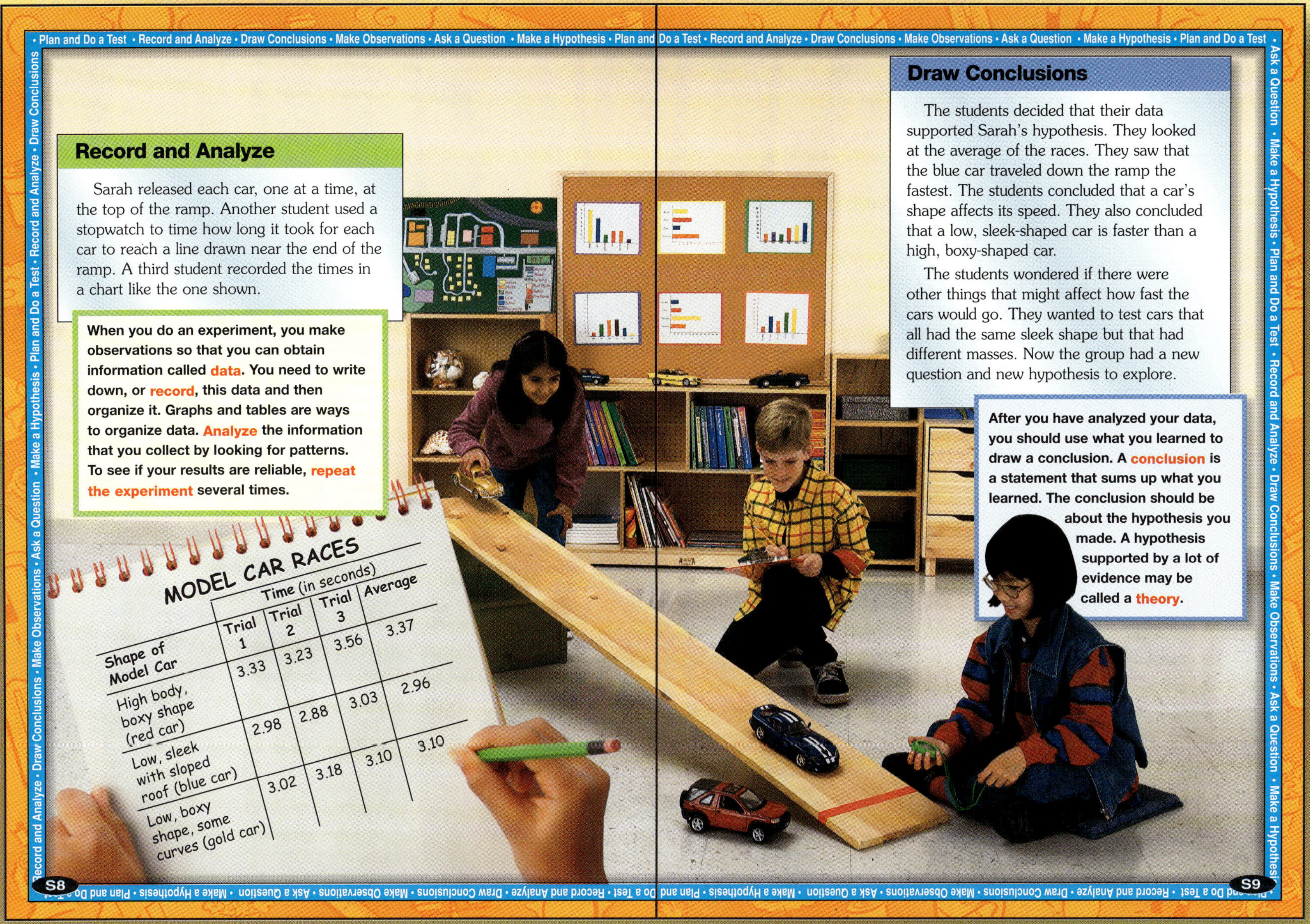

Record and Analyze

Sarah released each car, one at a time, at the top of the ramp. Another student used a stopwatch to time how long it took for each car to reach a line drawn near the end of the ramp. A third student recorded the times in a chart like the one shown.

When you do an experiment, you make observations so that you can obtain information called data. You need to write down, or record, this data and then organize it. Graphs and tables are ways to organize data. Analyze the information that you collect by looking for patterns. To see if your results are reliable, repeat the experiment several times.

MODEL CAR RACES

Shape of Model Car	Time (in seconds) Trial 1	Trial 2	Trial 3	Average
High body, boxy shape (red car)	3.33	3.23	3.56	3.37
Low, sleek with sloped roof (blue car)	2.98	2.88	3.03	2.96
Low, boxy shape, some curves (gold car)	3.02	3.18	3.10	3.10

Draw Conclusions

The students decided that their data supported Sarah's hypothesis. They looked at the average of the races. They saw that the blue car traveled down the ramp the fastest. The students concluded that a car's shape affects its speed. They also concluded that a low, sleek-shaped car is faster than a high, boxy-shaped car.

The students wondered if there were other things that might affect how fast the cars would go. They wanted to test cars that all had the same sleek shape but that had different masses. Now the group had a new question and new hypothesis to explore.

After you have analyzed your data, you should use what you learned to draw a conclusion. A conclusion is a statement that sums up what you learned. The conclusion should be about the hypothesis you made. A hypothesis supported by a lot of evidence may be called a theory.

S8 S9

How Do Scientists Build Knowledge?

The power of scientific thinking becomes evident when scientists share their data, analyses, and results at national and international meetings and in specialized science journals. This communication and teamwork is important because it serves as a way to collect and disseminate scientific findings. Because scientists may draw different conclusions from the same data, it also allows other scientists to challenge, retest, and verify or refute the findings of other researchers.

Scientific Theories

When a hypothesis about natural phenomena is strongly supported by evidence and widely accepted by the scientific community, the hypothesis is called a *theory.* A theory usually explains a broader range of phenomena than does a hypothesis. Also, a theory often includes a demonstrable model of how ideas fit together. New theories can replace older ones as more data is gathered. For example, Copernicus's theory of a heliocentric (Sun-centered) universe replaced Ptolemy's geocentric (Earth-centered) theory when Galileo and others demonstrated conclusively that all objects in the universe did not orbit Earth.

Scientific Laws

Descriptions of natural phenomena are referred to as *scientific laws.* Such descriptions are often mathematical and have great predictive value. Sir Isaac Newton's laws of motion and law of universal gravitation are examples of scientific laws.

Using Science Process Skills

Observing involves gathering information about the environment through your five senses—seeing, hearing, smelling, touching, and tasting.

Classifying is grouping objects or events according to common properties or characteristics. Often you can classify in more than one way.

Measuring and using numbers involves the ability to make measurements (including time measurements), to make estimates, and to record data.

Communicating involves using words, both speaking and writing, and using actions, graphs, tables, diagrams, and other ways of presenting information.

Inferring means coming to a conclusion based on facts and observations you've made.

Predicting involves stating in advance what you think will happen based on observations and experiences.

S10

Collecting, recording, and interpreting data all involve gathering and understanding information. This skill includes organizing data in tables, graphs, and in other ways. Interpretation includes finding patterns and relationships that lead to new questions and new ideas.

Identifying and controlling variables involves determining the effect of a changing factor, called the variable, in an experiment. To do this, you keep all other factors constant, or unchanging.

Defining operationally means to describe an object, an event, or an idea based on personal observations. An operational definition of a plant might be that it is a green living thing that is attached to soil and that does not move around.

Making a hypothesis is suggesting a possible answer to a question or making an educated guess about why something happens. Your hypothesis should be based on observations and experiences.

Experimenting is testing your hypothesis to collect evidence that supports the hypothesis or shows that it is false.

Making and using models includes designing and making physical models of processes and objects, or making mental models to represent objects and ideas.

S11

How Can Scientific Thinking Be Applied?

The importance of learning to think scientifically beginning in elementary school cannot be underestimated. Every aspect of home and career in the twenty-first century will require students to apply science process skills. The following activities can be used throughout the year to reinforce the wealth of opportunities *Science DiscoveryWorks* integrates into each Investigation.

Testing Ideas

On a self-stick note or on an index card, have each student write a science question he or she is curious about but can't answer. Have each student describe an observation that prompted the question. On a bulletin board, arrange the notes in the shape of a large question mark. Divide the students into groups. Ask each group to select a question that students in the group think they already know something about or one they are confident they can answer with a little library research or experimentation. Explain that each group must write a testable hypothesis to answer the question and identify the science process skills they would need to use in answering it. Encourage them to list other questions that occur to them.

What's the Best Money Can Buy?

What brands of supplies should your school purchase? Have students apply science process skills, beginning with observations and questions they have about the supplies they use in school each day, such as crayons, paper, pencils, washroom soap, paper towels and so on. Ask students to choose a product, ask questions about it, and design tests to compare it to other brands. Provide an opportunity to submit the findings to school administrators and board members.

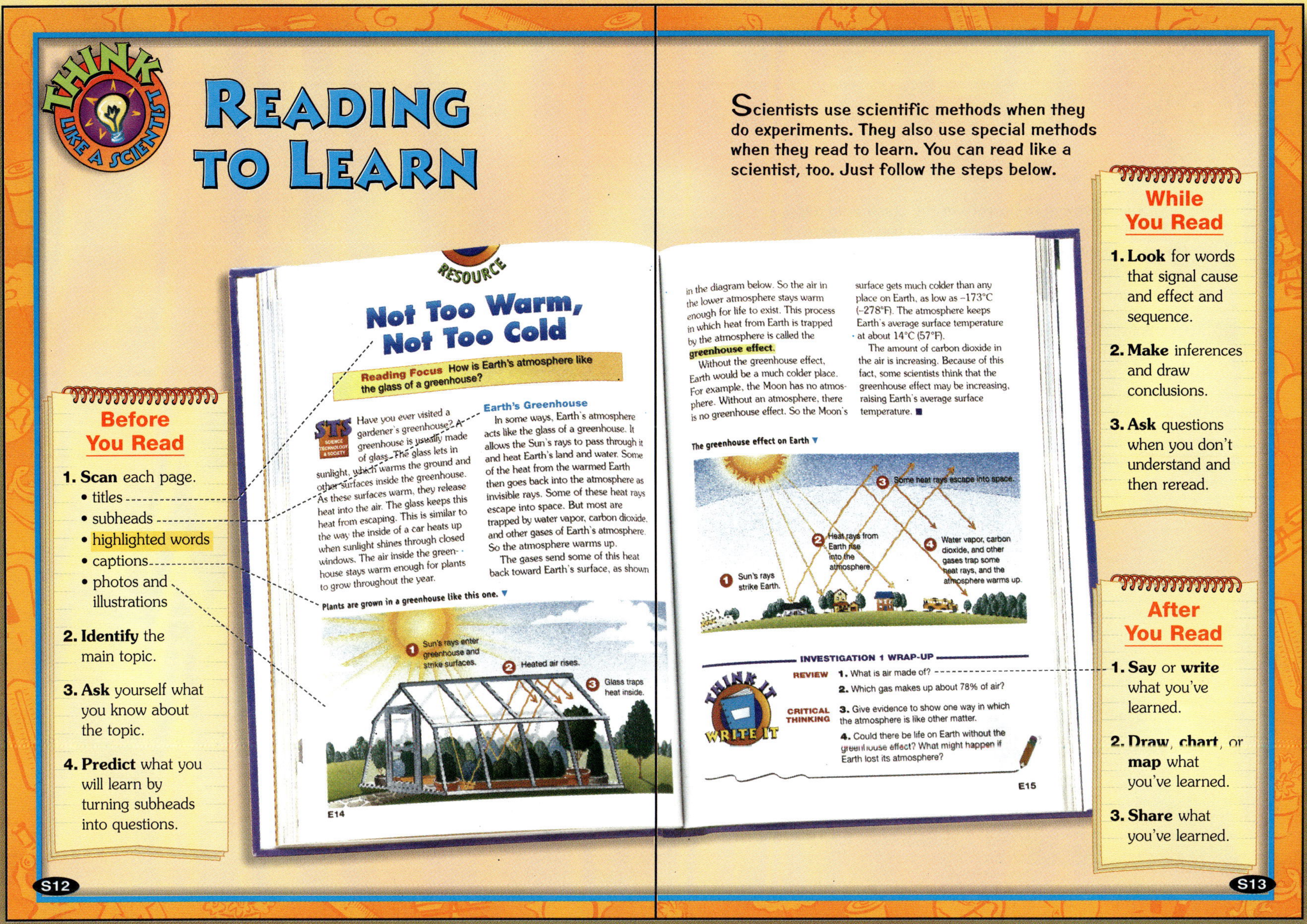

THINK LIKE A SCIENTIST

READING TO LEARN

Scientists use scientific methods when they do experiments. They also use special methods when they read to learn. You can read like a scientist, too. Just follow the steps below.

Before You Read

1. **Scan** each page.
   - titles
   - subheads
   - highlighted words
   - captions
   - photos and illustrations
2. **Identify** the main topic.
3. **Ask** yourself what you know about the topic.
4. **Predict** what you will learn by turning subheads into questions.

RESOURCE

Not Too Warm, Not Too Cold

Reading Focus How is Earth's atmosphere like the glass of a greenhouse?

STS SCIENCE TECHNOLOGY & SOCIETY

Have you ever visited a gardener's greenhouse? A greenhouse is usually made of glass. The glass lets in sunlight, which warms the ground and other surfaces inside the greenhouse. As these surfaces warm, they release heat into the air. The glass keeps this heat from escaping. This is similar to the way the inside of a car heats up when sunlight shines through closed windows. The air inside the greenhouse stays warm enough for plants to grow throughout the year.

Earth's Greenhouse

In some ways, Earth's atmosphere acts like the glass of a greenhouse. It allows the Sun's rays to pass through it and heat Earth's land and water. Some of the heat from the warmed Earth then goes back into the atmosphere as invisible rays. Some of these heat rays escape into space. But most are trapped by water vapor, carbon dioxide, and other gases of Earth's atmosphere. So the atmosphere warms up.

The gases send some of this heat back toward Earth's surface, as shown in the diagram below. So the air in the lower atmosphere stays warm enough for life to exist. This process in which heat from Earth is trapped by the atmosphere is called the **greenhouse effect**.

Without the greenhouse effect, Earth would be a much colder place. For example, the Moon has no atmosphere. Without an atmosphere, there is no greenhouse effect. So the Moon's surface gets much colder than any place on Earth, as low as –173°C (–278°F). The atmosphere keeps Earth's average surface temperature at about 14°C (57°F).

The amount of carbon dioxide in the air is increasing. Because of this fact, some scientists think that the greenhouse effect may be increasing, raising Earth's average surface temperature. ■

Plants are grown in a greenhouse like this one. ▼

1 Sun's rays enter greenhouse and strike surfaces.
2 Heated air rises.
3 Glass traps heat inside.

E14

The greenhouse effect on Earth ▼

1 Sun's rays strike Earth.
2 Heat rays from Earth rise into the atmosphere.
3 Some heat rays escape into space.
4 Water vapor, carbon dioxide, and other gases trap some heat rays, and the atmosphere warms up.

INVESTIGATION 1 WRAP-UP

THINK IT WRITE IT

REVIEW
1. What is air made of?
2. Which gas makes up about 78% of air?

CRITICAL THINKING
3. Give evidence to show one way in which the atmosphere is like other matter.
4. Could there be life on Earth without the greenhouse effect? What might happen if Earth lost its atmosphere?

E15

While You Read

1. **Look** for words that signal cause and effect and sequence.
2. **Make** inferences and draw conclusions.
3. **Ask** questions when you don't understand and then reread.

After You Read

1. **Say** or **write** what you've learned.
2. **Draw**, **chart**, or **map** what you've learned.
3. **Share** what you've learned.

S12

S13

READING TO LEARN

Before Students Read

Discuss each numbered feature with students and explain how each will help them read more effectively.

- Guide students to preview the reading by scanning titles and heads.
- Have students use the Reading Focus question to set a purpose for reading.
- Point out that asking questions helps students engage their interest in the topic.
- Suggest that students look ahead at illustrations and captions to predict what they will find in the reading.

While Students Read

Explain how the numbered strategies can help students while they read.

- Show students how signal words like *first*, *next*, *so*, and *because* identify important relationships such as sequence and cause and effect.
- Help students draw conclusions and make inferences by thinking about what they are reading.
- Have students self-monitor their reading by asking themselves questions as they read.

After Students Read

Encourage students to review what they have read and to assess their understanding by using these strategies.

- Have students restate or write down main ideas and important details to help remember information.
- Show students how using graphic aids such as charts or diagrams help them organize information.
- Point out that sharing what they read helps students summarize what they have read.

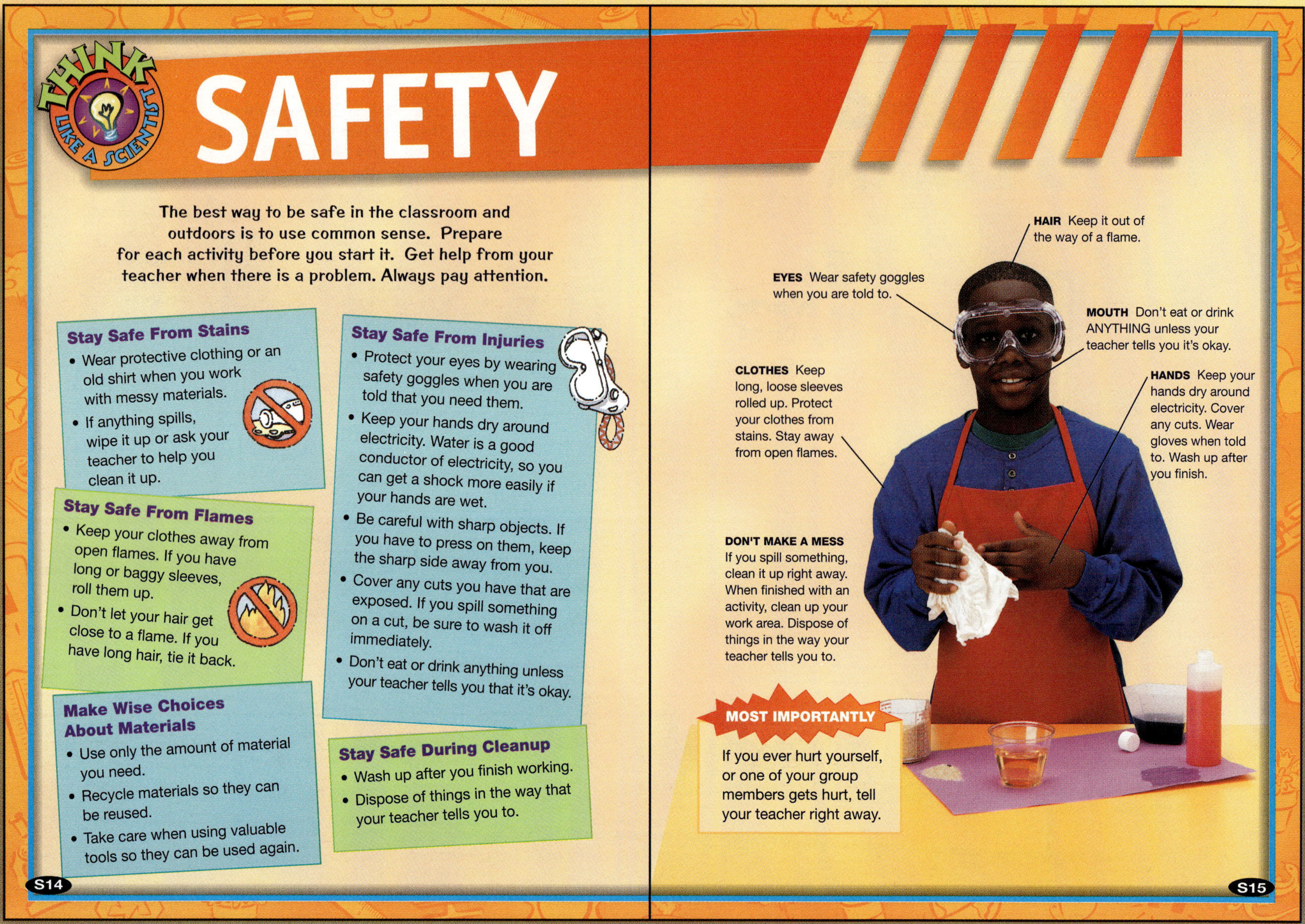

SAFETY

THINK LIKE A SCIENTIST

The best way to be safe in the classroom and outdoors is to use common sense. Prepare for each activity before you start it. Get help from your teacher when there is a problem. Always pay attention.

Stay Safe From Stains

- Wear protective clothing or an old shirt when you work with messy materials.
- If anything spills, wipe it up or ask your teacher to help you clean it up.

Stay Safe From Flames

- Keep your clothes away from open flames. If you have long or baggy sleeves, roll them up.
- Don't let your hair get close to a flame. If you have long hair, tie it back.

Make Wise Choices About Materials

- Use only the amount of material you need.
- Recycle materials so they can be reused.
- Take care when using valuable tools so they can be used again.

Stay Safe From Injuries

- Protect your eyes by wearing safety goggles when you are told that you need them.
- Keep your hands dry around electricity. Water is a good conductor of electricity, so you can get a shock more easily if your hands are wet.
- Be careful with sharp objects. If you have to press on them, keep the sharp side away from you.
- Cover any cuts you have that are exposed. If you spill something on a cut, be sure to wash it off immediately.
- Don't eat or drink anything unless your teacher tells you that it's okay.

Stay Safe During Cleanup

- Wash up after you finish working.
- Dispose of things in the way that your teacher tells you to.

MOST IMPORTANTLY

If you ever hurt yourself, or one of your group members gets hurt, tell your teacher right away.

S14 S15

Safety

In order for students to develop respect for safety, they need to understand exactly what is meant by safe and unsafe behavior and what the rationale is behind safety rules. Through your teaching, students can develop the "safe science" attitudes and skills that are essential both in school and at home.

General Safety Guidelines

- Post an easy-to-read list of safety rules in a prominent place in the classroom. Review it with students on a regular basis.
- Become familiar with the safety procedures that are necessary for each activity before introducing it to your students.
- Discuss specific safety precautions with students before beginning every hands-on science activity.
- Always act as an exemplary model of safe behavior.
- Have students wear protective aprons, goggles, and gloves whenever these items will prevent injury.
- Keep safety equipment, such as extinguishers, readily accessible and know how to use it.
- Prepare students for emergencies by having them practice leaving the classroom quickly and safely.
- Show students how to obtain help in an emergency by using the telephone, an intercom, or other available means of communication.
- Never leave students unattended while they are involved in science activities.
- Provide ample space for activities that require students to move about and handle materials.
- Keep your classroom and all science materials in proper condition. Check their condition regularly.
- Tell students to report injuries to you immediately.

UNIT C

Classifying Living Things

Overview This unit examines how the classification of plants and animals is based upon their physical and behavioral characteristics. Through activities and resources in this chapter, students will discover the survival needs that animals share and how their physical structure and behavioral characteristics help them to meet these needs.

Theme Your students may be familiar with different systems for organizing the contents of their closet at home. For instance, some students tend to group, or classify, the contents of their closet by the type of clothing. Similarly, scientists may classify plants or animals by appearance, hereditary or evolutionary relationships, where an animal lives, and an animal's learned and instinctive behavior.

The Big Idea

Animals can be grouped by the presence or absence of a backbone. Plants can be grouped by the presence or absence of seeds.

Tracing Major Concepts

CHAPTER 1 **Animals and plants are classified by their structure and behavior; animals are further classified by the absence or presence of a backbone and plants by the absence or presence of seeds.**

Subconcepts

- All living things, called *organisms,* can be classified into five large categories—the plant, animal, fungus, protist, and moneran kingdoms. The presence or absence of a backbone is one characteristic used to classify members of the animal kingdom.
- Animals with backbones are called vertebrates. Vertebrate groups are distinguished by how they maintain their body temperature, how they breathe, and their body coverings.
- Animals without backbones are called invertebrates. Different groups of invertebrates are classified by body structures, feeding behaviors, and methods of locomotion.
- Plants can be classified by whether or not they reproduce through seeds. Seed plants are classified further by whether they produce flowers or cones. Plants are a valuable tool for treating diseases.

CHAPTER 2 **All animals share certain basic survival needs, which they must satisfy by using both their body parts and behavior.**

Subconcepts

- All animals share the need for food, water, and shelter, as well as the need to maintain body temperature within certain ranges.
- Structural and behavioral adaptations help animals meet their needs and contribute to a species' survival.

Contents

DiscoveryWorks Correlations

1. Organisms have basic needs. . . . Organisms can survive only in environments in which their needs can be met. The world has many different environments, and distinct environments support the life of different types of organisms. ***(Entire Unit)***

2. Each plant or animal has different structures that serve different functions in growth, survival, and reproduction. ***(Ch. 1; Ch. 2, Inv. 2)***

3. The behavior of individual organisms is influenced by internal cues . . . and by external cues. . . . Humans and other organisms have senses that help them detect internal and external cues. ***(Ch. 2, Inv. 2)***

4. Many characteristics of an organism are inherited from the parents of the organism, but other characteristics result from interactions with the environment. . . . ***(Ch. 2, Inv. 2)***

5. All animals depend on plants. Some animals eat plants for food. Other animals eat animals that eat the plants. ***(Entire Unit)***

6. An organism's patterns of behavior are related to the nature of that organism's environment, including the kinds and numbers of other organisms present, . . . and the physical characteristics of the environment. When the environment changes, some plants and animals survive and reproduce, and others die or move to new locations. ***(Ch. 1, Inv. 2 and 3; Ch. 2)***

7. Environments are the space, conditions, and factors that affect an individual's and a population's ability to survive and their quality of life. ***(Ch. 2)***

---

1. A great variety of kinds of living things can be sorted into groups . . . to decide which things belong to which group. ***(Ch. 1)***

2. Features used for grouping depend on the purpose of the grouping. ***(Ch. 1)***

3. For any particular environment, some kinds of plants and animals survive well, some survive less well, and some cannot survive at all. ***(Ch. 2)***

4. Over the whole earth, organisms are growing, dying, and decaying, and new organisms are being produced by the old ones. ***(Ch. 1, Inv. 1)***

5. Scientific investigations may take many different forms, including observing . . . , collecting specimens for analysis, and doing experiments. Investigations can focus on physical, biological, and social questions. ***(Entire Unit)***

NSES Standards are based on *National Science Education Standards* (© 1996) published by The National Research Council.
Project 2061 Benchmarks are based on *Benchmarks for Science Literacy* (© 1993) published by The American Association for the Advancement of Science.

CURRICULUM INTEGRATION

An integrated approach to the teaching of science will help students understand how science connects to other school subjects as well as to technology and to literature. The chart below indicates where to find the activities in this unit that connect to other disciplines.

CONNECTING SCIENCE TO

THE SCIENCES
- Earth Science, page C20
- Earth Science, page C27
- Earth Science, page C35
- Physical Science, page C45
- Physical Science, page C54
- Earth Science, page C58

LITERATURE
- Animal Tales, page C10
- *Eyewitness Living Earth*, page C37
- *Snakes and Other Reptiles*, page C57

MATH
- Time Lines, page C12
- Vertebrate Pie Graph, page C18

WRITING
- Wild Kingdom, page C8
- Animal Stories, page C22
- Feeding the Stars, page C28
- Leaf Pictionary, page C34
- Write Stories, page C56
- Report Writing, page C59

SCIENCE AROUND THE WORLD
- Making a Map, page C36
- Arctic Life, page C44

SOCIAL STUDIES
- Native American Studies, page C11
- Different Feet, page C14
- Dinosaur Treasure Map, page C19
- Pet Therapy, page C26
- Map Making, page C48

TECHNOLOGY & SOCIETY
- Soak It Up, page C29
- A Zoo Habitat, page C46

THE ARTS
- Kingdom Mural, page C9
- Animal Waltz, page C21
- Making a Model, page C37
- Collage Making, page C57

SCIENCE BACKGROUND

A Planet Full of Living Creatures

by Orin G. Gelderloos

Orin Gelderloos is a Professor of Biology and Director of Natural Areas at the University of Michigan–Dearborn. He lives in a city and studies the plants and animals of urban places. He has also been a camp counselor and camp director.

Classifying Earth's Organisms

People have been studying and counting the kinds of creatures on Earth for years. Even after counting all over the planet, we are still very uncertain of the number of creatures. All we can do is make a reasonable estimate. Scientists now estimate that there may be tens of millions of species on Earth. Scientists who study and classify living things are called taxonomists.

Why don't we know the exact number of living things on Earth? It is easy to count the kinds of mammals, birds, or reptiles because they are big enough to be seen by people. But counting the number of different kinds of insects or snails is extremely difficult. Many of these creatures are very small and live in places where humans cannot get to easily. Some insects spend their entire lives in the tops of tall trees or under the ground in remote places on Earth.

Scientists speculate that Earth is full of organisms that have not yet been identified. Many people are involved in making a list of the creatures on our planet. If a person is a sharp observer of nature and keeps looking for differences among organisms, he or she may discover a new species—one which no other person has ever seen. Often the new species is named after the person who discovers it.

Many years ago, a plant or animal was named only after it had been studied extensively and a great deal had been learned about it. Then the name was very meaningful. A famous naturalist often said, "When you name something, the learning stops." She meant that if you look at living organisms and just make a list of the ones you see, you will not know very much about them. But if you study an organism very carefully, even though you do not know its name, you will be much richer and more knowledgeable.

In this unit, Classifying Living Things, your students will learn the names of many organisms. They will also learn that each organism is adapted to live in its environment, get its food, and behave in special ways. Scientists study these adaptations of organisms to find out how they survive or why they are becoming extinct. These studies are fascinating because they show many ways by which organisms manage to stay alive. In studying how living things are classified, your students will learn about many of the adaptations that help living things survive.

These bees are instinctively social animals. This adaptation helps the hive survive by giving each bee a specific job for the overall good of the community.

Tips from Teachers

Try This!

For an artistic life-science emphasis, we make animal portraits entirely out of once-living things. One student made a memorable butterfly out of flowers, pine needles, and seeds. We have displayed some beautiful creations from kitchen goods alone – bread dough, rice, and different-shaped pastas. Once-living things are everywhere, and part of the fun is in recognizing the materials that compose each portrait. Students who wish can also write a short report about the natural habitat and behaviors of the featured animal. We display the works for the rest of the school and for parents.

Jean Harris
Webster Groves, Missouri

Try This!

Plan a simulated bird watch. Use coloring-book pages, or student or teacher drawings of birds from your region. Make the colors as accurate as possible. Laminate the pictures, mount each one on an ice-cream stick, and place them along the edge of a field or lot. Then, using binoculars and a Peterson field guide, let the class identify the birds. Even if birds aren't scarce in your area, this activity brings out everyone's best observation skills.

Roy Boyle
DuBois, Pennsylvania

Try This!

Students are fascinated by odd locomotion strategies. You can make use of one of the most unusual means of getting around by holding snail races. Mark off an aluminum pie pan in centimeters from the center to the edge. Put snails in the center and either have them race each other to the edge or time their progress to various centimeter marks. Keep the arena moist with an occasional misting from a spray bottle. You can get snails at pet shops and supply houses. Snails are also common house and garden dwellers. Small land snails are commonly found in leaf litter along building foundations and will emerge if you give the leaves a good soaking with a garden hose.

Morris Chestang
Lakeland, Florida

SKILLS FOR SCIENTIFIC LITERACY

Science DiscoveryWorks helps students develop scientific literacy by providing activities and resources that challenge students to use process skills, critical thinking skills, and scientific reasoning skills. Students develop process skills as they ask questions and investigate to discover the answers. They develop critical thinking skills and scientific reasoning skills as they respond to thought-provoking questions about their investigations and in on-going assessment.

Science Process Skills

Science process skills provide a framework in which ideas can be conceptualized, tested, and evaluated. The processes listed here are developed through a wide range of hands-on experiences.

Activities	Page	Observing	Classifying	Measuring/ Using Numbers	Communicating	Inferring	Predicting	Collecting, Recording, and Interpreting Data	Identifying and Controlling Variables	Defining Operationally	Making Hypotheses	Experimenting	Making and Using Models
Animals Are Different	C6	•	•			•		•					
Cold Fish	C16	•		•				•	•			•	
Worming Their Way Home	C24	•				•	•	•				•	
Looking at Leaves	C32	•	•			•		•					
Needs in Common	C42	•			•	•	•						
Feather Feats	C50	•			•	•		•				•	
Tap, Tap, Tap	C52	•			•		•	•			•	•	

Critical Thinking Skills

Critical thinking skills are embedded in the questioning strategies throughout the program. The chart below summarizes the processes assessed in the Think It/Write It sections that end each investigation.

Process	Description	C15	C23	C31	C38	C49	C60
Analyzing	Studying something to identify constituent elements or relationships among elements	•	•	•	•	•	•
Synthesizing	Using deductive reasoning to pull together key elements	•	•	•	•	•	•
Evaluating	Reviewing and responding critically to materials, procedures, or ideas and judging them by purposes, standards, or other criteria			•	•		
Applying	Using ideas, processes, or skills in new situations	•	•		•	•	•
Generating Ideas	Expressing thoughts that reveal originality, speculation, imagination, a personal perspective, flexibility in thinking, invention, or creativity					•	•
Expressing Ideas	Presenting ideas clearly and in logical order, while using language that is appropriate for the audience and occasion	•					
Solving Problems	Using critical thinking processes to find solutions to a problem			•	•		

Scientific Reasoning Skills

Scientific reasoning skills are developed and reinforced through the science process skills and critical thinking skills.

Reasoning Skill	Description
Longing to Know and Understand	The desire to probe, find information, and seek explanations
Questioning of Scientific Assumptions	The tendency to hold open for further verification of presented assumptions, encounters, and ideas
Searching for Data and Its Meaning	The propensity to collect information and to analyze it in context
Demand for Verification	The inclination to repeat and replicate findings and studies
Respect for Logic	The inclination to move from assumptions to testing and data collection to conclusions
Consideration of Premises	The tendency to put into context the reason for a particular point of view
Consideration of Consequences	The tendency to put into perspective the results of a particular point of view
Respect for Historical Contributions	The inclination to understand and learn from the contributions of earlier ideas, studies, events, and so on

ONGOING ASSESSMENT

Houghton Mifflin Science DiscoveryWorks *provides a variety of ongoing assessment tools to help you monitor student growth.*

Written Reviews and Tests

Written reviews and tests throughout the program help assess student learning.

In the Student Edition

- Analyze & Conclude questions at end of each Activity
- Think It/Write It questions at end of each Investigation
- Reflect & Evaluate questions at end of each chapter

In the Teacher Resource Book

- Investigation Reviews
- Chapter Tests/Unit Tests
- Chapter and Unit Tests in standardized test format

Performance Assessment

Performance Assessment tasks allow students to demonstrate their learning through hands-on activities.

In the Teaching Guide Performance tasks appear at end of specific investigations and end of each chapter.

In the Teacher Resource Book A Unit Performance Task, with accompanying rubric, appears in each unit.

Portfolio Assessment

Portfolios of student work can be used to holistically assess student progress. Portfolio support material is provided in the Ongoing Assessment section of the TRB.

In the Student Edition A Portfolio suggestion appears at end of chapter.

In the Teaching Guide Portfolio tasks appear at end of specific investigations.

Chapter 1
Assessment Options

Investigation 1 Review

Label the drawing of each animal below as a vertebrate or an invertebrate.

1. vertebrate
2. vertebrate
3. invertebrate

4. invertebrate
5. vertebrate
6. invertebrate

Draw a line to match each living thing with its kingdom.

7. bacteria	Animal
8. paramecium	Plant
9. mushroom	Fungus
10. maple tree	Moneran
11. horse	Protist

Process Skills
Classifying

You observe a many-celled organism. It does not have a structure for moving from place to place. It absorbs food from other organisms. It is not a protist. In which kingdom would you classify the organism and why?

The organism is a fungus. It is not a moneran because it is many-celled. It does not move from place to place, so it is not an animal. It does not make its own food, so it is not a plant.

Ongoing Assessment, TRB p. 93

Investigation 2 Review

Use the words in the box to label the vertebrates shown.

amphibian	fish	mammal	bird	reptile

1. fish
2. reptile
3. amphibian
4. mammal
5. bird

Next to each vertebrate group, write two traits of that group.

6. fish live in water; get oxygen through gills; most have fins; many have scales

7. amphibian live on land and in water; grow legs; lose gills and form lungs; body temperature varies with environment

8. reptile dry, scaly skin; eggs have tough, leathery shells; body temperature varies with that of environment

9. mammal have hair or fur; feed milk to their young; most give birth to live young

10. bird have bodies covered with feathers; have wings; eggs have hard outer shells

Process Skills
Classifying

Elephants, lions, tigers, bears, dogs, and horses often appear in circuses. Name two groups to which all these animals belong. List the characteristics of the groups.

Vertebrates—animals that have a backbone; mammals—animals that have hair or fur, feed milk to their young, and in most cases give birth to live young.

Ongoing Assessment, TRB p. 94

Investigation 3 Review

Circle the word or words that complete each sentence.

1. (Sponges, Corals) look like plants but are actually animals with soft, tubelike bodies.

2. As an arthropod grows, it molts or sheds its (exoskeleton, wings).

3. A jellyfish catches food with its (muscular foot, tentacles).

4. Complete the diagram about the traits of arthropods by listing some defining characteristics of each subgroup.

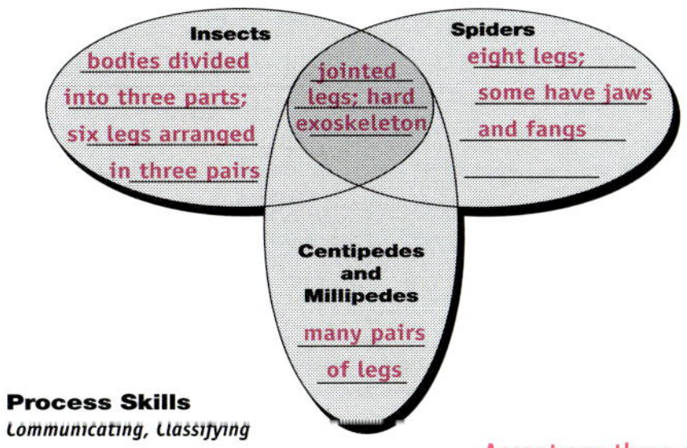

Process Skills
Communicating, Classifying

Name three different groups of invertebrates. List one trait that only that group has.

Accept any three of the following groups—sponges, the coral and jellyfish group, worms, the starfish and sea urchins group, mollusks, or arthropods. Students should list an accurate characteristic for each invertebrate group chosen.

Ongoing Assessment, TRB p. 95

Investigation 4 Review

Use the words in the box to complete each sentence.

mosses	conifers	ferns	flowers

1. Small nonseed plants that lack true roots, stems, and leaves are called mosses.

2. Before the dinosaurs lived, giant ferns covered much of Earth.

3. Huge forests of conifers cover much of the northern part of the world today.

4. Seed plants are plants that have cones or flowers.

Draw a line to match each plant with its trait.

5. pine tree	netted veins
6. liverwort	nonseed plant
7. corn	monocot
8. dicot	conifer

Processing Skills
Communicating, Classifying

List three traits of mosses. List one way in which mosses differ from ferns.

Three traits are as follows: mosses are nonseed plants; mosses lack true roots, stems, and leaves; mosses grow only in moist places. Mosses differ from ferns in that they do not have roots, stems, or leaves.

Ongoing Assessment, TRB p. 96

Chapter Test

Check What You Know Each item is worth 15 points.

1. Circle the letter of the characteristics that the animals shown at the right share.

(a.) have a backbone; breathe air

b. have no backbone; live in water after hatching from an egg

c. give birth to live young; have hollow bones

d. have a body made of segments; have smooth, moist skin

2. If you saw an earthworm on a sidewalk, you could correctly conclude that ____.

a. the sidewalk is its shelter

b. it stopped to look for food

c. it is shedding its exoskeleton

(d.) it is heading toward a dark, moist area

3. Complete the diagram about traits of plants and animals. Sample answers are shown.

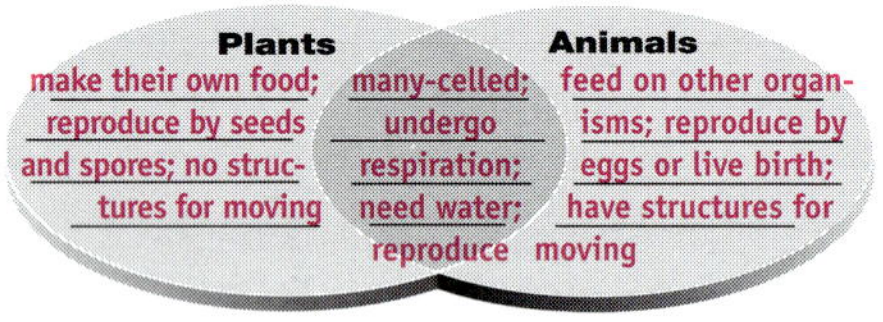

Ongoing Assessment, TRB p. 97

Chapter Test

Problem Solving Each item is worth 15 points.

4. Jake kept a goldfish in an unheated fish bowl. No fresh air was pumped into the water. He fed the fish and cleaned the bowl regularly. Jake's fish became sick and died. Hypothesize why Jake's fish became sick and died.

Possible answers are that cold water may have lowered the fish's body temperature too much and there may not have been enough air (oxygen) in the water.

5. Complete the chart describing the groups of vertebrates.

	Amphibian	Reptiles	Birds	Mammals
Type of body covering	some have smooth, moist skin	dry, scaly skin	feathers	fur or hair
How it breathes	lungs	lungs	lungs	lungs
How its young are produced	hatch from jelly-coated eggs	hatch from eggs with leathery shell	hatch from hard-shelled eggs	most are born live

Word Power Each item is worth 5 points.

Use the words in the box to complete each sentence.

exoskeleton vertebra dicot invertebrate organisms seeds

6. Each bone that makes up a backbone is called a _vertebra_.

7. Conifers reproduce by forming _seeds_.

8. The hard _exoskeleton_ of an arthropod protects it.

9. All kinds of living things are called _organisms_.

10. A _dicot_ is a flowering plant that produces seeds that have two sections.

Ongoing Assessment, TRB p.98

Pressed for Time Test

Check What You Know Each item is worth 10 points.

For questions 1–5, circle the letter of the correct answer.

1. An animal that lives in water after hatching from an egg but lives on land as an adult is a(n)

a. reptile **(b.)** amphibian **c.** bird **d.** marsupial

2. Every living thing on Earth is a(n) _____.

a. dicot **b.** spore **(c.)** organism **d.** vertebrate

3. Spore-forming plants that have roots, stems, and leaves are called _____.

(a.) ferns **b.** conifers **c.** monocots **d.** mosses

4. A lima bean plant is an example of a _____ .

(a.) dicot **b.** moss **c.** fern **d.** fungus

5. All living things are classified into one of five groups called _____.

a. species **b.** communities **c.** mammals **(d.)** kingdoms

Word Power Each item is worth 10 points.

Write the letter of the term that best matches the definition.

_e_ **6.** an animal that doesn't have a backbone

_a_ **7.** an egg-laying vertebrate with dry, scaly skin

_d_ **8.** a vertebrate with hollow bones

_c_ **9.** an animal that has hair or fur and feeds milk to its young

_b_ **10.** a nonseed plant without true roots, stems, and leaves

a. reptile

b. liverwort

c. mammal

d. bird

e. invertebrate

Ongoing Assessment, TRB p. 99

Chapter 2
Assessment Options

Investigation 1 Review

Use the words in the box to complete each sentence.

environment food temperature water

1. The living and nonliving things that surround and affect an animal make up its _environment_.

2. In some animals, body _temperature_ changes as the surroundings get hotter or colder.

3. Seeds and cactus pulp supply food and _water_ for the kangaroo rat.

4. Grasses in an African savanna are a source of _food_ for zebras.

5. Complete the chart by writing the type of food and shelter you would provide for a pet bird and a pet dog. Possible answers are shown.

	Bird	Dog
Food	seeds and insects	meat, dog food
Shelter	dry, warm cage	dry, warm house

Process Skills
Communicating

Choose two animals that live on the African savanna. Explain how one animal meets its need for food and how the other meets its need for shelter. Write your answer on another sheet of paper.

Answers may vary. A possible response is: Giraffes meet their need for food by eating the leaves of the acacia tree. Weaverbirds meet their need for shelter by making nests of woven grass.

Ongoing Assessment, TRB p. 100

Investigation 2 Review

Use the words in the box to complete each sentence.

temperature	shelter	adaptation	behavior

1. A body part or a behavior that helps an animal survive in its environment is a(n) adaptation.

2. Wings, large ears, feathers, and fat are adaptations that help maintain an animal's body temperature.

3. Shells and sharp claws for digging tunnels provide many animals with shelter.

4. A young wolf is born with deer-chasing behavior.

Write below each picture whether it shows a learned or instinctive behavior.

5. instinctive **6.** instinctive **7.** learned **8.** learned

Process Skills
Classifying

Describe how the terms *extinct* and *endangered* are different. List one extinct species and one endangered species.

Extinct means the species has died out completely. *Endangered* means the species is scarce and may be near extinction. Students may name any of several extinct species and endangered species.

Ongoing Assessment, TRB p. 101

Chapter Test

Check What You Know Each item is worth 10 points.

For questions 1–4, circle the letter of the correct answer.

1. Which of these statements can be said about the pine tree pictured?

a. It is a conifer. (circled)
b. It is a nonseed plant.
c. It is a flowering plant.
d. It is a dicot.

2. The body parts of the elephant that enable it to dig to underground water are its ____.

a. ears **b.** eyes **c.** tusks (circled) **d.** feet

3. What kind of behavior is a parrot showing when it says its own name?

a. instinctive **b.** learned (circled) **c.** basic **d.** suitable

4. Doris has a pet hamster. She just received a pet salamander for her birthday. Which of the following needs will she have to provide for both the hamster and the salamander?

a. food, water, shelter, and the proper temperature (circled)
b. food, water, and shelter only
c. food and water only
d. food and shelter only

Ongoing Assessment, TRB p. 102

Chapter Test

Problem Solving Each item is worth 20 points.

5. List the four basic needs of living things and describe one way a bird might meet each of these needs. Possible answers are shown.

a. Getting food—catching insects or worms, finding seeds
b. Getting water—drinking rain as it falls, drinking from puddles or ponds
c. Finding shelter—building nests, perching in trees or bushes
d. Maintaining body temperature—fluffing feathers to keep in body heat, bathing to cool off

6. The crab spider can change colors to blend in with its surroundings. How might this adaptation help it survive?

It protects the crab spider from its enemies because they may have trouble seeing it.

Word Power Each item is worth 5 points.

Write the letter of the term that best completes the sentence.

b **7.** A savanna is a type of ____.	**a.** learned behavior
c **8.** An elephant's tusk is a(n) ____.	**b.** environment
d **9.** A shivering cat is showing ____.	**c.** adaptation
a **10.** A circus dog doing tricks is showing ____.	**d.** instinctive behavior

Ongoing Assessment, TRB p. 103

Pressed for Time Test

Check What You Know Each item is worth 10 points.

For questions 1–5, circle the letter of the correct answer.

1. Polar bears survive because they are well suited for ____.
a. living far away from water **c.** protecting their eggs
b. living in very hot lands **d.** living in their environment (circled)

2. A circus dog doing tricks is showing ____.
a. learned behavior (circled) **c.** an adaptation
b. instinctive behavior **d.** a survival technique

3. An elephant's tusk is a(n) ____.
a. learned behavior **c.** breathing tool
b. environment **d.** adaptation (circled)

4. A reading of 98.6°F is a(n) ____ body temperature for a person.
a. high **b.** unusual **c.** normal (circled) **d.** low

5. Of all Earth's living things, very few can survive without ____.
a. eggs **b.** backbones **c.** fur **d.** water (circled)

Word Power Each item is worth 10 points.

Use the words in the box to complete each sentence.

extinct	environment	behavior
learned behavior	instinctive behavior	

Every day, people show different types of behavior, or ways to act. Sandra is a newborn baby, who often eats and sleeps. Eating is a(n) instinctive behavior. Sandra may cry because she hears a startling sound in her environment while she's sleeping. Sandra cannot read yet, because reading is a(n) learned behavior. Sandra's mother is a biologist who studies why certain animals have died out, or have become extinct.

Ongoing Assessment, TRB p. 104

End-of-Unit
Assessment Options

Unit Test

Analyze Information Each item is worth 5 points.

For items 1–4, circle the letter of the correct answer.

1. Helen and Ricardo made a chart of their observations of two animals they saw in the zoo. Circle the letter of the sentence that tells about the types of animals they observed.

Animal	How It Moves	Type of Body Covering	Number of Legs	Backbone	Where It Lives
A	leaps	smooth, moist skin	four	yes	water and land
B	wiggles	segmented skin	none	no	moist soil

a. Animal *A* is an amphibian, and Animal *B* is a worm.
b. Animal *A* is a reptile, and Animal *B* is a sponge.
c. Animal *A* is a fish, and Animal *B* is a sea anemone.
d. Animal *A* is a mammal, and Animal *B* is a coral.

2. Study the picture. The girl is checking on which of the fish's needs?

a. food **c.** shelter
b. water **d.** maintaining proper body temperature

Ongoing Assessment, TRB p. 109

Unit Test

3. Look at the picture. What role does the cone of a conifer have?

a. It collects rainwater for the thirsty tree.
b. It protects seeds located between its scales.
c. It provides cool shade from the sun.
d. It distracts insects from the needles of the tree.

4. Predict what you think the earthworm is most likely to do next.

a. lie on top of the rock **c.** find a dark, damp area
b. swim in the pond **d.** climb up a flower stalk

5. Look at the picture of the aardvark. Identify the body part(s) the animal uses to help meet its need for food.

a. snout **c.** tail
b. claws **d.** ears

6. It's time for the keeper in the picture to feed the fish. For the past two weeks, he has tapped on the tank just before feeding time. What kind of behavior are the fish showing? How do you know?

Learned behavior; the fish learned that tapping means feeding time.

Ongoing Assessment, TRB p. 110

Unit Test

Problem Solving Each item is worth 6 points.

7. Jeannie is trying to determine if an organism is an animal or a plant. Which of the following characteristics, if present, will help her to decide?
a. It has many cells.
b. It absorbs food from other organisms.
c. It has a whiplike part that moves it through water.
d. It reproduces by seeds.

8. Roy put his hand on an animal and felt separate bones up and down its back. The animal he is touching is most likely a ________.
a. centipede **b.** squid **c.** flatworm **d.** dog

9. While at the zoo, Olivia wanted to see an animal with characteristics most similar to her pet cat. Which animal should she visit?
a. an ape **b.** a salamander **c.** a tortoise **d.** a spider

10. How might the study of leeches help people who are at risk for heart attacks? Blood clotting can lead to heart attacks. Knowledge about the chemicals in a leech's saliva that prevent clotting might be beneficial.

Sample answers are shown. Accept reasonable responses. Each item is worth 6 points.

For items 11–15, list three major characteristics of each group.

11. fish "breathe" through gills; swim; many are covered with scales; most have fins; most have same body temperature as environment

Ongoing Assessment, TRB p. 111

Unit Test

12. amphibians use gills when young and lungs as adults; lay jelly-coated eggs; some have smooth, moist skin

13. reptiles lay eggs with leathery shells on land; breathe with lungs; body temperature varies with environment

14. birds have feathers and wings; lay hard-shelled eggs; have a skeleton that is light in weight

15. mammals have hair or fur; feed milk to their young; young of most are born live

Word Power Each item is worth 4 points.

Circle the word or words that best complete each sentence.

16. A grassland found in tropical climates is a (savanna, burrow).

17. A starfish and a lobster are (vertebrates, invertebrates).

18. A chimpanzee that uses sign language to talk to its keeper is demonstrating (instinctive, learned) behavior.

19. A wasp and a lobster both have (vertebras, exoskeletons).

20. Animals, plants, fungi, monerans, and protists are all (organisms, reptiles).

Ongoing Assessment, TRB p. 112

Pressed for Time Test

Check What You Know Each item is worth 5 points.

For questions 1–6, circle the letter of the correct answer.

1. An animal with bones up and down its back is a(n) _____ .
   a. invertebrate (b.) vertebrate c. exoskeleton d. dicot
2. All monerans are made up of one _____ .
   a. frond b. tissue c. spore (d.) cell
3. A great percentage (97%) of the animal kingdom is made up of _____ .
   (a.) invertebrates b. mammals c. fish d. humans
4. A ladybug and a lobster both have _____.
   a. vertebras (b.) exoskeletons c. pincers d. wings
5. Animals, plants, fungi, monerans, and protists are all _____ .
   a. reptiles b. arthropods (c.) organisms d. mammals
6. A starfish and a lobster are _____ .
   a. vertebrates b. fish (c.) invertebrates d. mammals

For questions 7–12, fill in the blank with the correct word or phrase.

7. A shivering bird is showing __instinctive__ behavior.
8. Unlike plants, animals cannot make their own __food__.
9. Whales, cats, and horses are all examples of the vertebrates called __mammals__.
10. Fur traps a layer of __air__ near an animal's body, which helps keep it warm.
11. Flat, round, and segmented are terms used to describe __worms__.
12. Everything, both living and nonliving, that surrounds and affects an animal is its __environment__.

Ongoing Assessment, TRB p. 113

Pressed for Time Test

Word Power Each item is worth 5 points.

For questions 13–18, write the letter of the term that best matches the definition.

__b__ 13. individual bone in a backbone

__d__ 14. seed plant that reproduces with cones

__c__ 15. a vertebrate that has fur and feeds milk to its young

__e__ 16. any animal or plant that is scarce

__f__ 17. body parts or behaviors that help a living thing survive in an environment

__a__ 18. the hard outer covering that supports and protects an animal

a. exoskeleton
b. vertebra
c. mammal
d. conifer
e. endangered species
f. adaptations

Problem Solving Each item is worth 5 points.

19. Why are hollow bones important to a bird's survival? Explain your answer.
    A bird's hollow, lightweight bones allow it to fly. Flying allows birds to find food, escape predators, and build safe homes high in trees.
20. Why have laws been passed about the hunting of Asian elephants? Explain your answer.
    Asian elephants are an endangered species. Humans were killing them at a much faster rate than the elephants could reproduce. Laws were passed to protect the remaining elephant population.

Ongoing Assessment, TRB p. 114

Additional Unit Support Material

Science Notebook Masters
See *Science Notebook,* TRB pp. 25–59.

Support Masters for Unit Activities
See Teacher Resource Book pp. 14–15.

Support Masters for Unit Project
See Teacher Resource Book pp. 16–21.

Letters and Activities to send home
See Teacher Resource Book pp. 2–5.

Support Masters for vocabulary development
See Reading Support Book.

Reading Transparencies for concept development
See Reading Support Transparencies.

Chapter and Unit Tests in Standardlzed Test Format
See Standardized Test Practice pp. 121–136.

UNIT PROJECT

Making a Field Guide to Local Plants or Animals

Students collect and compile information about local plants or animals.

Getting Ready

Groups of 4 to 6 students

Have each group gather information about local plants or animals and then make a field guide. For activities in which groups work independently, each group should have an opportunity to compare its efforts with those of other groups.

Materials

For Research

- Books and magazines about plants or animals
- Field guide to regional plants or animals in the United States

For Models and Presentations

- Construction paper, white paper, crayons, markers, glue, scissors, hole punch, yarn or other bookbinding materials

Other Materials

- Unit Project Masters 1–6, TRB pp. 16–21
- *Science Notebook,* TRB pp. 31, 38, 49, 55
- Transparency 13
- Transparency 14
- Transparency 15
- Transparency 16

Plan Ahead

Gather the materials needed for research and for making the field guides. Prepare an area of the classroom for students to store their field guides for the duration of the unit.

Building the Project

Through Project Links

LINK 1

Chapter 1, p. C13 Groups brainstorm and make a list about which plants or animals to include in their field guides. Have students decide what information should be given about the animals they decide to include in the field guides. For example, they might choose to give information such as color, size, and habitat. Students may use *Science Notebook,* TRB, p. 31 to help them create their field guides.

Assessing Student Progress: Observe how well student groups work together and determine if each member participates in the group effort.

LINK 2

Chapter 1, p. C31 Students brainstorm how to classify the plants or animals they have decided to include in their field guides. Have students decide how to organize the information they have gathered. Students may use *Science Notebook,* TRB, p. 38 to help them organize the information.

Assessing Student Progress: Determine if students' field-guide plans reflect an understanding of plant or animal classification systems.

LINK 3 **Chapter 2, p. C47** Students explore the body parts and behaviors of animals that they have decided to include in their field guides. Students can try to determine how these adaptations help the animals meet their needs. Students may use *Science Notebook,* TRB, p. 49 to help them analyze adaptations.

Assessing Student Progress: Evaluate whether or not the students make appropriate connections between an organism's needs and specific body parts or behaviors.

LINK 4 **Chapter 2, p. C53** Students decide on a format they want to use to present the information they have gathered. Each group thinks about whether they want to compile booklets, make bulletin board displays, make audiotapes, or use another format. Students may use *Science Notebook,* TRB, p. 55 to help them plan their presentation.

Assessing Student Progress: Evaluate each group's cooperative effort in deciding on a format and assess how well the format chosen presents the information.

Technology Link

You can have students visit our Web site at **www.eduplace.com** to access additional content-related resources, locate agencies that can help with the Unit Projects, and link to experts. You can download Unit Project Masters and obtain a scoring rubric. Classes can also share the results of their projects on-line.

Wrapping Up the Project

A Safari Day

Once students have decided which format they would like to use to present their materials, they can put together their field guides. When the field guides have been completed, have students present their materials. Then lead a discussion in which students share the information they have included and interesting facts they have discovered about local plants or animals. Have students plan field trips for a Safari Day for trying out their field guides. Invite family and friends to attend and participate. Following the Safari Day, other classes can be invited to see the bulletin-board displays. Booklets or audiotapes can be placed in the class library for reference. Use *Science Notebook,* TRB, p. 59.

People to Contact

In Person

- Ask a local veterinarian to describe to the class procedures for taking good care of pets.
- Ask a local nursery to explain the way they meet the needs of their plants.

By Mail

- **American Society for the Prevention of Cruelty to Animals,** 424 E. 92nd Street, New York, NY 10128
- **Center for Plant Conservation,** P.O. Box 299, St. Louis, MO 63166

USING TECHNOLOGY

BILL NYE the Science Guy

There's no one better than scientist-comic-author-former engineer Bill Nye to show students how "Science Rules!"

Invertebrates

Use this episode with Chapter 1.

This spine-tingling episode exposes the unique characteristics of the members of the group that makes up over 90% of the world's animals. Watch a crab get under its own skin in a segment on molting. Bill explains that some invertebrates can regenerate body parts. In *No Backbone, No Problem,* observe how an octopus gets into a tight spot in a spineless bid for a meal, exhibiting one reason that invertebrates are so successful at survival.

Video Features

Nifty Home Experiment: Chock Full of Worms
Using a big jar of moist soil, black paper, food scraps, and a few worms, observe how earthworms really dig squirming around in the dirt.

Check It Out! In an old-growth forest, children catch and group invertebrates, which they subsequently send to scientists for studying.

Consider the Following How do invertebrates know what to do if they don't have a spine and a central nervous system? Bill explains how nerve nets allow many invertebrates to get along without a brain.

Club Invertebrate This disco is where kids dance like they have no backbone as they "Squirm, Baby, Squirm."

Try This Observe a long water balloon both in water and on dry land to understand why the largest invertebrates live in the sea.

Follow-up Questions

1. What percentage of all animals on earth do not have backbones? (About 90% of all animals)
2. Are all insects invertebrates? (Yes)
3. Can certain invertebrates grow their legs back if they break off? (Yes, for example, crabs and lobsters)

▲ The way cool Science Guy proves that "science rules!"

To order this or other Bill Nye videos, call Disney Educational Productions at 1-800-295-5010.

Science Processor

An Interactive CD-ROM

The CD-ROM investigations for this unit enable students to explore how plants and animals meet their needs in various habitats. Students learn about adaptations and the skeletal structure of vertebrates.

Animals

Unit Opening: It's Alive!

(Beginning the Unit)

Students observe a tropical rain forest. They identify which inhabitants of the rain forest are plants and which are animals. They use the Animal Data Pack to explore the differences between amphibians, birds, fish, mammals, and reptiles and record their observations in their *Science Notebook*. They click on different organisms to animate them and compare how these organisms meet their needs for food, water, and shelter.

Investigation 1: Feed Me!

(Enhances or replaces Chapter 2, Inv. 2)

How can body structures help animals meet their needs for food? Students investigate the heads of different insects to determine which types of foods each insect is best adapted to eat. Then they watch a video to observe how mammals use body parts to meet their needs. Students can further study adaptive body structures in the Mammals Data Pack and use their Science Notebook to record their observations.

Investigation 2: Skin and Bones

(Enhances or replaces Chapter 1, Inv. 2)

How are vertebrates' skeletal structures similar? Students click on various animals to explore similarities in skeletal structure. They watch a video about vertebrates and how a backbone is useful. Students use Data Packs to classify amphibians, birds, fish, reptiles, and mammals. Students also explore body temperatures of different groups of animals. They record their findings in their *Science Notebook* and a Spreadsheet.

Other Technology Resources

Additional Video

Bill Nye the Science Guy – Amphibians Bill examines how this group of smoothies found niches in their ecosystems with adaptations that have given them a special way to survive for the past 400 million years. Use with Chapter 1.

Books on Tape

Grade 4, Unit C Auditory learners and students acquiring English can strengthen their learning by listening to the Student Edition read aloud.

Internet Field Trip

Throughout the unit, have students go on-line at **www.eduplace.com** for links to content-related sites.

UNIT PROJECT LINK

Students can go on-line at **www.eduplace.com** to link to additional resources for completing their unit projects.

TEACHER-TESTED ACTIVITIES

Every Activity in Houghton Mifflin Science DiscoveryWorks *was author written, teacher reviewed, and student tested.*

Developed and Tested by Authors

The Activities in Houghton Mifflin *Science DiscoveryWorks* were developed by the program authors, and have been used by them in their own classrooms. Many of the Activities have also been used in teacher-training programs sponsored by the Center for Elementary Education at Fairleigh Dickinson University. All the Activities related to astronomy and space science have been used by students at the Houston Museum of Natural Science.

Reviewed by Teachers

All lessons and chapters in Houghton Mifflin *Science DiscoveryWorks* have been reviewed by **practicing classroom teachers**. One aspect of that review was to verify that procedures are clearly written and understandable to students and that questions are appropriate and focus on the concepts being developed. Teacher reviewers provided valuable input into the Activities, including suggestions for the type of support to provide in the Teaching Guides. A list of teacher reviewers appears at the beginning of this Teaching Guide.

Field-Tested by Students

In addition to being reviewed by teachers, all Activities in Houghton Mifflin *Science DiscoveryWorks* have been field-tested by classroom teachers in their classrooms. More than 90 teachers at 9 schools across the nation worked with the program development team during these field tests. Each Activity was tested by at least two teachers in different school districts. A list of the school districts that participated in the field tests is shown below.

Science DiscoveryWorks Field-Test Sites

- Cranford Public Schools
Cranford, NJ
- Education Center
Dumont, NJ
- Gateway School District
Monroeville, PA
- Dr. Charles R. Drew
Magnet School, PS #59
Buffalo, NY
- Mount Laurel-Hartford
School
Mount Laurel, NJ
- Gwinnett County Schools
Lawrenceville, GA
- Mountain Park School
Berkeley Heights, NJ
- Woodward School
Saint George, UT
- Muscogee County
School District
Columbus, GA

MATERIALS LIST

Following is a list of materials needed for activities in this unit. Quantities are for a class of 30 students working in groups of 5. Quantities are also listed for those materials included in the Unit Kit. Additional kit options are available. Contact your sales representative for details.

Materials	Class Quantity Needed	Unit Kit Quantity	Pressed For Time Kit Quantity	Activity Page
Consumable Materials				
bags, plastic sealable	75	50		C32
cardboard boxes	6			C24
feathers, down	6 bags	1 pkg (about 200)	★	C50
feathers, tail or wing	6	1 pkg (6)	★	C50
fish food	1 pkg	1 pkg	★	C52
gloves, plastic	30 pairs	1 pkg (50 pairs)		C32
ice cubes	as needed			C16
leaves, dry (or shredded newspaper)	as needed			C24
paper, sheets	75			C32
pencils	15			C32, C52
sand	3 lb	1 bag (2.5 kg)	★	C24
soil	6 lb	3 bags (12 lb)	★	C24
Nonconsumable Materials				
animals for observation	3 (shared)			C6
earthworms	6	1 coupon (24 worms)	★	C24
fish tanks	6	6	★	C52
goggles	30	Safety Kit		C24
goldfish	12	1 coupon (12 fish)	★	C16, C52
hand lenses (magnifiers)	6	6	★	C6, C24, C50
jars, plastic (large)	6	6	★	C16
sow bugs	6	1 coupon (12 bugs)	★	C6
thermometers	6	6	★	C16
timers (stopwatches)	6	6	★	C16, C24

★ *Included in the Pressed for Time Kit.*

UNIT C

Classifying Living Things

Overview

In this unit, students will be learning about the classification of plants and animals. Students will investigate vertebrate and invertebrate animals, plants, and the basic needs of all living things.

Reading to Learn

Unit Preview Display the KWL transparency from the *Reading Support Package*.

- Ask students what they know about living things and record their thoughts in the **K** column.
- Ask students what they want to know about living things. Record their questions in the **W** column. Be sure to include the following questions:

  How many kinds of living things are there?

  What do all living things need?

- You may wish to have students complete their own KWL chart using the TRB master found on TRB page 9. Have them fill in the **L** column of the chart when they complete the unit.

Warming Up

Explain that the photo shows a school of fish. Stimulate discussion with these questions:

What is a school of fish?

Why do some fish travel in schools?

Tell students that as they work through this unit, they'll find answers to these and other questions.

Use *Science Notebook,* TRB pp. 25–26.

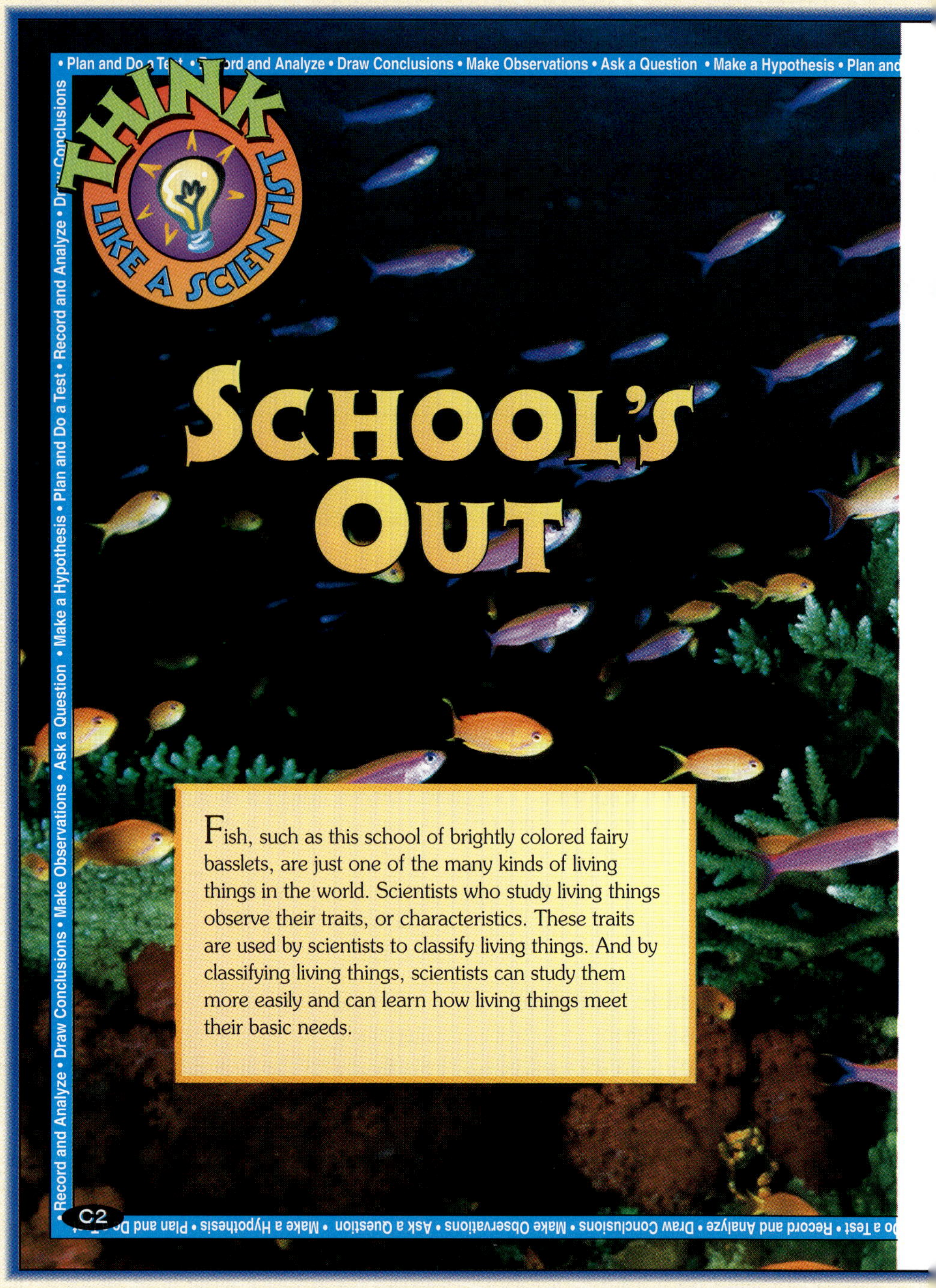

Fish, such as this school of brightly colored fairy basslets, are just one of the many kinds of living things in the world. Scientists who study living things observe their traits, or characteristics. These traits are used by scientists to classify living things. And by classifying living things, scientists can study them more easily and can learn how living things meet their basic needs.

C2

Home-School Connection

The Opening Letter at the beginning of the unit introduces family members to the topic of living things. Distribute the Opening Letter (TRB p. 2) at the beginning of the unit.

Opening Letter

Dear Family,

If you have a pet at home, what things would you need to do for your pet before you leave for a weekend? What needs do all animals have in common? How might animals be grouped based on their physical traits, or characteristics? In our science class, we will be investigating living things for the next few weeks.

You can help bring science from the classroom into your home by talking with your child about the basic needs of food, water, and shelter that all animals share. Visit your local zoo or a pet shop and look for ways that animals are alike. Also talk about how a bird is different from a frog or how a chicken is different from a horse.

For this unit, we will be using the following materials. Can you donate any of these items? If so, we will need to receive them by ________.

- *cardboard boxes*
- *dry leaves*
- *blue cloth and green cloth*
- *large plastic jars*
- *soil or sand*
- *down feathers*
- *blue, green, red, and yellow pipe cleaners*
- *sealable plastic bags*

Do you or any family members have a special interest in living things? Can you help with activities? If so, please fill out the form below and have your student return it to class.

Thank you for your help!

Opening Letter
Classifying Living Things

Your name ________ Student's name ________

Home phone ________ Work phone ________

Do a Test • Record and Analyze • Draw Conclusions • Make Observations • Ask a Question • Make a Hypothesis • Plan and Do a Test

THINK LIKE A SCIENTIST

Questioning In this unit you'll study fish and many other living things. You'll investigate questions such as these.

- How Can Living Things Be Classified?
- How Do Living Things Meet Their Needs?

Observing, Testing, Hypothesizing In the Activity "Animals Are Different," you'll make observations about the traits of three different animals. You'll also infer how body parts help each animal survive.

Researching In the Resource "Variety of Life on Earth," you'll gather more information about how animals and other living things are classified.

Drawing Conclusions After you've completed your investigations, you'll draw conclusions about what you've learned—and get new ideas.

C3

THINK LIKE A SCIENTIST

Before starting this unit, you may wish to have your students review scientific methods on pages S2–S9 found at the beginning of their book.

Refer students to the two questions listed at the end of the *Questioning* section on page C3 of their book. Tell them that these questions are the titles of some of the Investigations in this unit.

Have students select one of the questions and form a hypothesis that might answer that question.

Ask students: **What other questions would you like to ask about living things?** You may wish to write student questions on the chalkboard. At the end of the unit have students determine whether or not each question has been answered.

Science in Literature

The following two books, which are featured in this unit, can be used to spark student interest in living things.

Eyewitness Living Earth
by Miranda Smith
DK Publishing, 1996

Snakes and Other Reptiles
by Mary Elting
Illustrated by Christopher Santoro
Simon and Schuster, 1987

Books and Articles for Teachers

Bill Nye the Science Guy's Consider the Following by Bill Nye and Ian Saunders (Disney Press, 1995). Presents articles and experiments about mammals, reptiles, fish, giant ants, ocean life, and plants.

Bird by David Burnie (Eyewitness Books, Alfred A. Knopf, 1988). Covers body structures, feathers and flight, adaptation of beaks and feet for feeding, courtship, and nests and eggs.

Insect by Laurence Mound (Eyewitness Books, Alfred A. Knopf, 1990). A wealth of information about insects—their bodies, life cycles, senses—including beautiful close up photos.

The Random House Book of How Nature Works by Steve Parker (Random House, 1993). Packed with pictures and clear explanations related to living things. Topics include classification, food for life, reproduction, predator and prey, hibernation, and migration.

CHAPTER 1

ALL KINDS OF LIVING THINGS

Subconcepts	Activities	Materials
Investigation 1 How Can Living Things Be Classified? pp. C6–C15		
All living things, called *organisms*, can be classified into five large categories—the plant, animal, fungus, protist, and moneran kingdoms. *Suggested Pacing: 4–5 class periods* **National Standards** See page C 1c, numbers 1, 2, 5, and 6. **Project 2061 Benchmarks** See page C 1c, numbers 1, 2, 4, and 5.	**Animals Are Different,** p. C6 *Science Process Skills:* observe, collect and record data, infer	**Animals Are Different** hand lens *, 3 animals for observation, *Science Notebook,* TRB pp. 29–30
Investigation 2 How Do Vertebrates Differ? pp. C16–C23		
Animals with backbones are called vertebrates. *Suggested Pacing: 4 class periods* **National Standards** See page C 1c, numbers 1, 2, 5, and 6. **Project 2061 Benchmarks** See page C 1c, numbers 1, 2, and 5.	**Cold Fish,** p. C16 *Science Process Skills:* observe; measure; collect, record, and interpret data	**Cold Fish** goldfish in large plastic jar *, thermometer *, timer *, ice cubes, *Science Notebook,* TRB pp. 33–34
Investigation 3 How Do the Groups of Invertebrates Differ? pp. C24–C31		
Animals without backbones are called invertebrates. *Suggested Pacing: 3 class periods* **National Standards** See page C 1c, numbers 1, 2, 5, and 6. **Project 2061 Benchmarks** See page C 1c, numbers 1, 2, and 5.	**Worming Their Way Home,** p. C24 *Science Process Skills:* predict, observe, describe, infer	**Worming Their Way Home** goggles *, cardboard box, dry soil *, damp soil *, sand *, dry leaves or shredded newspaper, hand lens *, earthworm *, timer *, *Science Notebook,* TRB pp. 36–37
Investigation 4 How Are Plants Classified? pp. C32–C38		
Plants can be classified by whether or not they reproduce through seeds. *Suggested Pacing: 3 class periods* **National Standards** See page C 1c, numbers 1, 2, and 5. **Project 2061 Benchmarks** See page C 1c, numbers 1, 2, and 5.	**Looking at Leaves,** p. C32 *Science Process Skills:* observe, describe, classify, infer, collect and interpret data	**Looking at Leaves** gloves *, 5 sheets of paper, pencil, 5 sealable plastic bags *, Leaf Characteristics and Classification Table on Activity Support Masters 1–2 (TRB pp. 14–15), *Science Notebook,* TRB pp. 40–41

Overview

In this chapter students investigate the characteristics of animals and plants.

Chapter Concept

Animals and plants are classified by their structure and behavior; animals are further classified by the absence or presence of a backbone and plants by the absence or presence of flowers.

Theme: Systems

The system for classifying living things has five large categories known as kingdoms. These are Plants, Animals, Fungi, Monerans, and Protists. Each kingdom has various subgroups. For example, animals are subdivided into a group with backbones and a group without backbones.

Advance Preparation	Resources/ Vocabulary	Assessment
Animals Are Different Get three animals for the students to observe.	**Variety of Life on Earth** **Vocabulary:** organisms **Classifying—Past and Present** **Classification of Animals** **Vocabulary:** vertebra, vertebrates, invertebrates, exoskeleton	**Chapter 1 Baseline Assessment:** TRB pp. 27–28 **Investigation 1 Baseline Assessment:** TG p. C6 **Investigation 1 Review:** TRB p. 93 **Think It/Write It:** p. C15; TRB p. 32 **Following Up on Baseline Assessment:** TG p. C15 **Performance:** TG p. C15
Cold Fish Get goldfish and put them in aquarium or aged water. Get 2–3 ice cubes per group.	**Swim, Leap, and Slither** **Vocabulary:** fish, gills, amphibian, reptile **Fly, Dive, and Gallop** **Vocabulary:** birds, mammals	**Investigation 2 Baseline Assessment:** TG p. C16 **Investigation 2 Review:** TRB p. 94 **Think It/Write It:** p. C23; TRB p. 35 **Following Up on Baseline Assessment:** TG p. C23 **Portfolio:** TG p. C23
Worming Their Way Home Have four boxes per group. Have enough dry soil, damp soil, leaves or shredded newspaper, and earthworms to supply all the groups.	**Lifesaving Leeches** **Nothing Much in Common** **Vocabulary:** molts	**Investigation 3 Baseline Assessment:** TG p. C24 **Investigation 3 Review:** TRB p. 95 **Think It/Write It:** p. C31; TRB p. 39 **Following Up on Baseline Assessment:** TG p. 31 **Portfolio:** TG p. C31
Looking at Leaves Before distributing copies of the "Leaf Characteristics and Classification" table, review the table carefully to be prepared for any explanation you think the students might need in using the chart. Explain that the term *parallel veins* refers to veins that run side by side down the length of a leaf.	**Plants to the Rescue** **All Kinds of Plants** **Vocabulary:** nonseed plants, seed plants, mosses, liverworts, ferns, horsetails, conifers, monocot, dicot	**Investigation 4 Baseline Assessment:** TG p. C32 **Investigation 4 Review:** TRB p. 96 **Think It/Write It:** p. C38; TRB p. 42 **Performance:** TG p. C38 **Following Up on Baseline Assessment:** TG p. 38 **Chapter 1 Summative Assessment** Reflect and Evaluate, p. C39 Chapter 1 Review/Test: TRB pp. 97–98 *Science Notebook,* TRB pp. 43–44

*Materials in the Equipment Kit TG= Teaching Guide TRB= Teacher Resource Book

CHAPTER 1 Chapter Overview

Concept Preview

You may wish to use Transparency C1 to introduce some of the important concepts of the chapter. Students can add to the map as they complete each Activity and Resource. Then they can use the completed map as a study guide.

Vocabulary Development

Use Vocabulary Master C1 at any point in the chapter for additional vocabulary support.

Common Misconceptions

Most of the animals that students see are vertebrates, and they may falsely conclude that most animals are vertebrates. Vertebrates account for only 3% of the entire animal kingdom.

Introducing the Chapter

Warm-Up Activity

Ask the students to form groups of 3–4. Tell each group they have one minute to name all the animals they can. After one minute, ask each group to read their list. Determine how many, if any, were invertebrates. Let them try again for one minute, this time only naming invertebrates.

Use *Science Notebook,* TRB pp. 27–28.

Discussion Starter

Initiate a discussion about students' current understanding of characteristics of animals.

- **How many characteristics of animals can you think of? Do these characteristics apply to many animals or just a few?** Students may name such characteristics as size, color, how animals move, what they eat, and so on.
- **What is your favorite animal? Why is it your favorite?** Students' responses will vary. Encourage them to discuss characteristics of their favorite animal.

CHAPTER 1

ALL KINDS OF LIVING THINGS

What's your favorite plant or animal? Are there other plants or animals that are similar to it? In this chapter you'll learn about many kinds of living things. As you explore, think about ways that living things are similar and different.

PEOPLE USING SCIENCE

Field Biologist You may have seen a macaw (mə kô′) at the zoo, a pet store, or in someone's home. These large parrots live in the tropical rain forests of South America. Macaws nest in trees more than 31 m (100 ft) off the ground.

Eduardo Nycander is a field biologist. He studies wild macaws at a research station in the Amazon forest of Peru. He discovered that macaws have a hard time finding hollow tree trunks that can serve as suitable places to build nests.

Eduardo Nycander now works at providing macaws with plastic nests. The nests are hollow tubes about 35.6 cm (14 in.) wide and 2.4 m (8 ft) long. Nycander climbs high above the ground and straps the nests to the tree trunks. The birds love them! The nests look like hollow tree trunks. What would you ask Eduardo Nycander about his work?

C4

Concept Preview

Transparency

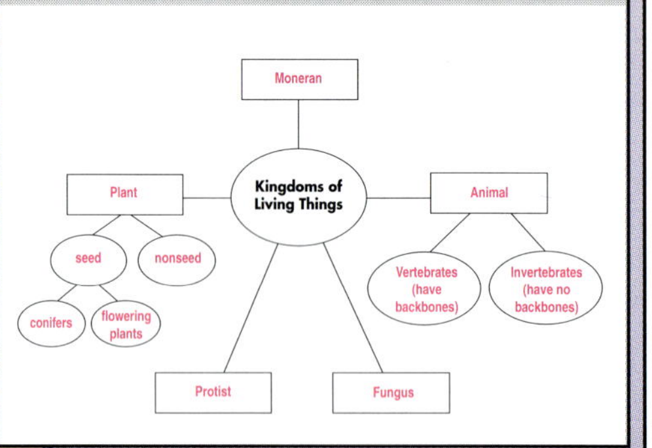

▲ **Reading Support Book**
Transparency C1

Vocabulary Development

Vocabulary Master

Use the clues and the words in the box to help you unscramble the letters of each word.

exoskeleton	vertebrates	vertebra	birds
organisms	invertebrates	reptile	gills
amphibian	mammals	molts	fish

Clues

1. Each bone that makes up the backbone	betravre	vertebra
2. Vertebrate that usually lives in water after hatching from an egg, but as an adult can live on land	iipabahmn	amphibian
3. Living things	ssmnaogir	organisms
4. Animals with no backbones	setarbetrevni	invertebrates
5. The feathery parts on each side of a fish's head	lglsi	gills
6. A vertebrate that has dry, scaly skin and lays eggs that have leathery shells	pelitre	reptile
7. Vertebrate that lives in water and uses gills for breathing	sihf	fish
8. Vertebrates that feed milk to their young and have hair or fur	aamlmsm	mammals
9. Animals that have backbones	sebtaerrevt	vertebrates
10. Periodically sheds its exoskeleton	smtol	molts
11. Vertebrates that have wings and are covered with feathers	dirbs	birds
12. A hard outer covering that protects or supports an animal's body	soxnoteelke	exoskeleton

▲ **Reading Support Book**
Vocabulary Master C1

Coming Up

◄ Field biologist Eduardo Nycander checks on a macaw chick 31 m (100 ft) above the ground.

C5

Chapter Road Map

Investigation 1 How Can Living Things Be Classified?

Activities Animals Are Different*

Resources Variety of Life on Earth*, Classifying—Past and Present, Classification of Animals*

Investigation 2 How Do Vertebrates Differ?

Activities Cold Fish*

Resources Swim, Leap, and Slither*, Fly, Dive, and Gallop*

Investigation 3 How Do Groups of Invertebrates Differ?

Activities Worming Their Way Home*

Resources Lifesaving Leeches, Nothing Much in Common*

Investigation 4 How Are Plants Classified?

Activities Looking at Leaves*

Resources Plants to the Rescue*, All Kinds of Plants*

* Pressed for Time?

If you are pressed for time, focus on the Activities and Resources identified by this clock.

Home-School Connection

Distribute the Explore at Home Activity "Animal Rummy" (Teacher Resource Book, page 3) to students after they have completed the chapter.

Technology Link

CD-ROM

Science Processor ***Animals***

To enhance or replace Investigation 2, use **Skin and Bones.**

Students on an expedition to a pond determine the characteristics of the types of vertebrates and subgroups found there. They observe the external structures of the animals and then "click" to see the skeletal systems of each. A video explains the importance of animals' backbones. Next, they classify the vertebrates into groups—mammals, birds, fish, reptiles, or amphibians—by listening to a description and dropping a label onto each animal. They "probe" body temperatures of animals and the temperatures of the air and water.

Start the Investigation

How Can Living Things Be Classified?

pages C6–C15

Planner

Subconcept All living things, called *organisms,* can be classified into five large categories—the plant, animal, fungus, protist, and moneran kingdoms. The presence or absence of a backbone is one characteristic used to classify members of the animal kingdom.

Objectives

- **Identify** and **record** similarities and differences among animals.
- **Describe** how organisms are classified.

Pacing 4–5 class periods

Science Terms organisms, vertebra, vertebrates, invertebrates, exoskeleton

Activate Prior Knowledge

Baseline Assessment Ask students to find their backbone and draw a picture of what they think it looks like. Save drawings for use in Following Up.

Investigation 1: How Can Living Things Be Classified?

Suppose you made a list of all the living things that you could think of. How would you classify them to make it easy to study them? Find out in this investigation how scientists classify living things.

Activity

Animals Are Different

Which animal is a cat more like—a catfish or a dog? How would you decide? In this activity you'll make observations that could be used to classify animals.

MATERIALS

- hand lens
- 3 animals for observation
- *Science Notebook*

SAFETY

Do not touch the animals unless you have your teacher's permission.

Procedure

1. Your teacher will give your group three different animals to observe. As you **observe** the animals, look for ways that they are alike and ways that they are different.

Step 1

C6

Activity: Animals Are Different

Preview *Students observe how three or more animals are alike and different, and record their observations.*

Advance Preparation *See p. C4b*

1. Get Ready

GROUPS OF 4–6 | 45 MINUTES

Key Science Process Skills observe, collect and record data, infer

Meeting Individual Needs

STUDENTS ACQUIRING ENGLISH

Go over the data table and the heading "Traits." Be sure students understand the term and each of the items in the column. Use a model to define each trait. Be sure students recognize that they are able to respond to each category with simple responses (single words or phrases). Encourage students to think of more observable traits to add to the data table.

VISUAL/SPATIAL

2. In your *Science Notebook*, **make a chart** like the one shown below. Add as many different traits, or characteristics, as you can think of. **Record** your observations under the column for each animal.

Traits	Animal 1	Animal 2	Animal 3
How It Moves			
Type of Body Covering			
Number of Legs/Description			
Number of Eyes			
Number of Ears			
Where It Might Live			

Step 4

3. **Record** the ways you think these living things are alike and the ways they are different.

4. You may want to use a hand lens to **observe** some animals more closely. **Record** any further observations you make. **Infer** where each animal might live and **record** your inference.

See SCIENCE *and* MATH TOOLBOX *page H2 if you need to review* ***Using a Hand Lens****.*

Analyze and Conclude

1. Are there any traits that all the animals share? If so, what are they?

2. **Infer** how each animal's body parts help it survive.

3. **Infer** which of the animals might have a backbone. Give reasons for your inferences.

Meeting Individual Needs

GIFTED AND TALENTED

Have students create a fourth column in their charts to include an animal that was not observed in the classroom. Have them research an animal of their choice in order to complete the new column in their chart. Students should include the same information for the fourth animal that they included for the animals observed in class.

LINGUISTIC

Collaborative Strategy Allow half of the groups to observe one set of three animals, while the other half observes a different set of animals. Groups can share information.

Materials Hints Provide students with live animals, such as an earthworm, snail, goldfish, hamster, or bird. Some parents may be willing to bring a family pet to school for this activity. If goldfish and earthworms are used, save goldfish for the Activity on p. C16; save earthworms for the Activity on p. C24.

Safety Review safety precautions with students. Be aware of student allergies prior to bringing animals into the class. Do not allow students to handle animals.

2. Guide the Procedure

- Ask students to think of other traits to add to their chart.
- **What traits do you share with each of the animals?** Students may mention traits such as two eyes, a mouth to eat with, and the ability to move.

Have students record their observations and inferences, and answer questions on *Science Notebook,* TRB pp. 29–30.

Science Processor Students can use the CD-ROM Data Table to organize and display their data.

3. Assess Performance

Process Skills Checklist

- Did students **observe** the animals and **record** their similarities and differences?
- Did students **infer** where each animal might live, whether or not they have backbones, and how their body parts help them survive? Were students able to give reasonable explanations for their inferences?

Analyze and Conclude

1. Students might note that all of the animals move about, use food, have the same type of body covering, or share other traits.
2. Students may infer that an animal's legs, eyes, and ears help it escape predators or find food. A body covering may protect an animal from enemies, keep it warm, or prevent it from drying out.
3. Students may infer from pictures, skeletons, or relationships to other vertebrates whether an animal has a backbone or not.

RESOURCE

Variety of Life on Earth

Reading Focus Suggest that students ***use the graphics*** in the resource to answer the Reading Focus question.

1. Get Ready

Vocabulary

Science Term organisms

Support Terms classify, kingdom, traits, life processes

Background

- Some classification systems divide bacteria into two separate kingdoms—Archaebacteria and Eubacteria. Archaebacteria, or "ancient" bacteria, live in harsh conditions with little sunlight or oxygen. Examples of such places include hot sulfur springs, extremely salty water such as the Great Salt Lake, and oxygen-free environments such as sewage, some swamps, and thermal vents on the ocean floor. Eubacteria, or "true" bacteria, live everywhere life can exist and have thick, rigid cell walls.

Discussion Starter

- Play a shortened version of charades. Ask a student to demonstrate the actions of a particular animal for the class to guess. **After a few different animals have been demonstrated, ask students why an animal's actions might help scientists to classify it.** Students might answer that an animal's movements might tell us where it lives, how it gets its food, or what physical traits it might have.
- **What are some living things that are not plants or animals?** Write students' ideas on an overhead or on the chalkboard. As you read this section, have students try to fit each list item into the appropriate kingdom.

RESOURCE

Variety of Life on Earth

Reading Focus Into what large groups can organisms be classified?

How many kinds of living things could there be on Earth—hundreds? thousands? The answer is millions! Millions of kinds of **organisms** (ôr′gə niz əmz), or living things, exist on Earth.

Living things can be found in oceans, forests, deserts, mountains, soil, air—almost everywhere on Earth. And incredibly, many scientists classify, or group, all organisms into just five large groups, called kingdoms.

Organisms placed in the same kingdom share certain traits, or characteristics. Scientists use the different traits of living things to classify them. The number of cells, the basic units that make up all organisms, is just one trait used to classify living things. Other traits include life processes, such as how an organism gets food or reproduces. Study the table and the pictures on the next page to see the general traits shared by living things in each kingdom.

How many kinds of living things can you find in this picture? ▼

C8

Science & Writing

WILD KINGDOM

What to Do In five groups students can plan and write a story like *The Wizard of Oz* about a boy and a girl who want to meet the Wizard but must first visit five kingdoms—animal, plant, fungus, protist, and moneran—under the wizard's rule. Each group is assigned a different kingdom. Each group's story should include information about organisms in that kingdom and have an inventive title.

What's the Result? Ask students to read their stories aloud. As they read, list organisms they mention, as well as traits of organisms in the kingdom. Use the lists to review the kingdoms.

Multi-Age Classroom Each student in the group should contribute an idea for their fantasy story.

Kingdoms of Living Things

Kingdom	Examples	Traits
Animal	horse, dog, bird, fish, spider, worm, starfish, coral	• many-celled • most have structures for moving from place to place • feed on other organisms • reproduce by eggs or live birth
Plant	pine tree, cactus, tulip, tomato, ivy, maple tree	• many-celled • no structures for moving from place to place • make their own food • reproduce by seeds or spores
Fungus	yeast, slime mold, mushroom, mold	• many-celled; some one-celled • most don't have structures for moving from place to place • absorb food from other organisms
Protist	amoeba, paramecium, diatom, algae	• most one-celled; some many-celled • can make their own food or feed on other organisms • some have structures for moving from place to place
Moneran	bacteria	• very simple cells • some make their own food; some feed on other organisms • some have structures for moving from place to place

C9

Science & the Arts

KINGDOM MURAL

What You Need large butcher paper; scraps of materials such as cardboard, sponges, cotton balls, paper, clay, sand, and toothpicks

What to Do Have students make a mural of a place where they may find the kingdoms of living things. Students can work in groups, each making part of the landscape and adding a variety of organisms. Tell students to label each organism with its name and the kingdom to which it belongs.

What's the Result? What does your mural show? Students may respond that their mural shows that all kingdoms of organisms live in a variety of places.

2. Guide the Discussion

Choose from the following strategies to facilitate discussion.

Transparency 13 and 14: Visual/Spatial Activity Use "Variety of Life in a Deciduous Forest (base)," and "Variety of Life in a Deciduous Forest (overlay)," to reinforce the concept of the diversity of life on Earth.

Connecting to the Activities

- ***Animals Are Different, p. C6***
- **Why are the animals we observed part of the animal kingdom? What makes them different from organisms in the other four kingdoms?** Students may respond that animals can move from place to place, they are all consumers, they reproduce by eggs or live births, and they are many-celled organisms.
- **What traits did you use to classify the animals you observed?** Students may have used shape, numbers of legs, outer covering, or other traits for classifying their animals.
- **Why would an organism's environment not be a useful method for classifying organisms?** Students may respond that this method is unreliable because many kinds of very different animals may live in the same environment.

Meeting Individual Needs

Students Acquiring English In your pre-reading scheme students will find it helpful if you go over the key terms, *organism, trait, classify, kingdom*. It is important for students to see that the classification system is based on similarities and not differences.

Making Inferences

- **Why do you think scientists today classify living things into more than two or three kingdoms?** Students may infer that many organisms have traits that are too different to be grouped in just two or three kingdoms.

Identifying and Solving Problems

- **How can scientists be sure that all living things can be classified into a certain number of kingdoms?** Students might say that so far many scientists have been able to classify all the organisms they know of into five kingdoms. If some organisms are discovered that do not have the traits of any of the kingdoms, scientists might decide that there should be more than five kingdoms. Explain that some scientists have proposed different ways to classify organisms currently known.

Thinking About the Data

- **Which characteristic do you think is the most important in telling the difference between a plant and an animal?** A plant makes its own food. An animal cannot make its own food. It feeds on other organisms.
- **How are protists different from monerans?** The cells of monerans are simpler than those of protists.

Meeting Individual Needs

Gifted and Talented Ask students to choose one kingdom from the chart on page C9 and use the information on the chart to write a paragraph about that kingdom.

Transparency 15: Visual/Spatial Activity
Use "Kingdoms of Living Things" to help students learn the traits of each kingdom.

ANIMAL KINGDOM The clownfish and the orangutan look very different from one another. But they are both members of the animal kingdom. Like most kinds of animals, they move from place to place, often in search of food.

▼ orangutan

▲ clownfish

PLANT KINGDOM The largest members of the plant kingdom are trees. Trees, like other plants, use the Sun's energy to make food in their leaves. An oak tree can produce over a million leaves in a single year!

oak tree ▶

C10

Science & Literature

ANIMAL TALES

What to Do Ask students to look in the library or at home to find titles of stories about animals. Compile a class list. Encourage students to find stories about vertebrates and/or invertebrates. You might suggest *Charlotte's Web, Aesop's Fables,* or *The Bookstore Mouse* as examples.

What's the Result? Make a chart of the stories on posterboard. Have students list the animals that appear in each story. Discuss how animals that are depicted as humans may be different from animals in real life.

Multi-Age Classroom Provide animal stories in trade books at varying levels of reading difficulty. Students can work in small groups to construct their lists of animal stories.

FUNGUS KINGDOM You might think these mushrooms look like plants, but they're not plants. They belong to a different kingdom—the fungus kingdom. Unlike plants, mushrooms can't make their own food. Most mushrooms get their food from the dead plant material on which they grow.

mushroom ▶

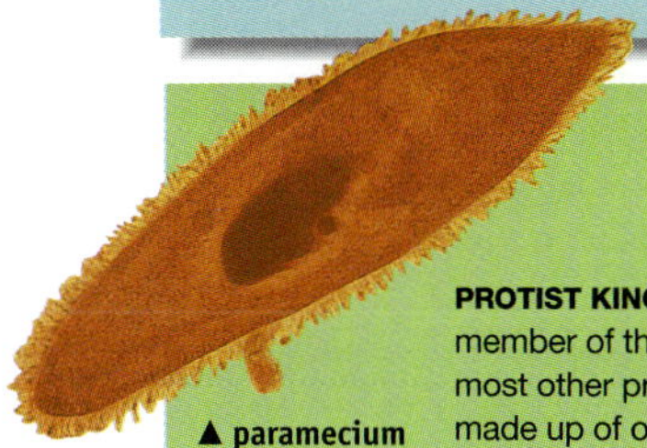

▲ paramecium

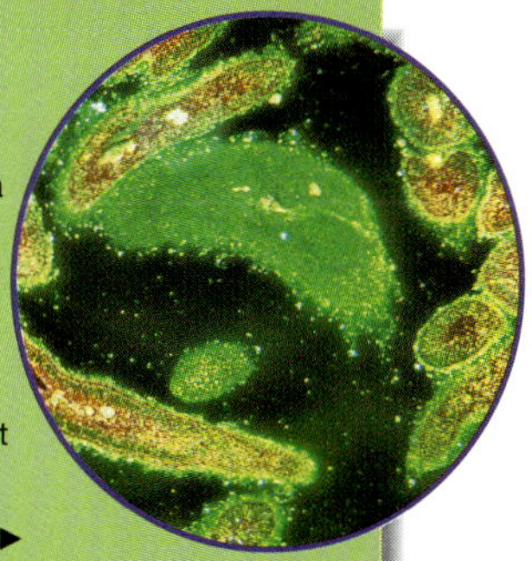

PROTIST KINGDOM A paramecium is a member of the protist kingdom. Like most other protists, the paramecium is made up of one cell and so is microscopic. Some protists have structures for moving from place to place. The paramecium has hairlike parts that pull it through the water.

paramecium in pond water ▶

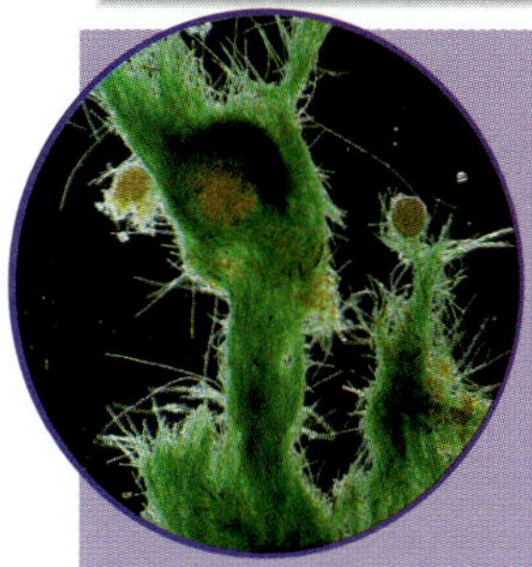

▲ blue-green bacteria

MONERAN KINGDOM Bacteria belong to the moneran (mə nir′ən) kingdom. Unlike other monerans, blue-green bacteria make their own food. All monerans are made up of one cell.

bacteria cells that form a chain ▶

Internet Field Trip

Visit **www.eduplace.com** to learn more about how living things are classified.

C11

Making Comparisons

- **In which kingdoms do some of the organisms have structures for moving from place to place?** Animal, fungi, protist, moneran
- **In which kingdoms are some organisms one-celled?** Fungi, protist, moneran
- **In which kingdoms do some organisms make their own food?** Plant, protist, moneran
- **In which kingdoms do some organisms use other organisms for food?** Animal, fungi, protist, moneran

Meeting Individual Needs

Students Acquiring English Divide the class into cooperative groups of four students. Using the chart and pictures from pp. C9–C12, have each group member construct three sets of index cards to use to play a three-level concentration game. Each student should be assigned five organisms (one from each kingdom). The student should write each kingdom on a different card, draw or paste a picture of each organism on a different card, and write the traits of each organism on a different card, creating 15 cards in all. Then all 60 cards from the group can be mixed together to play concentration.

3. Assess Understanding

Students can work in groups of three or four to play a game based on the five kingdoms. They should first make a set of cards, writing each characteristic in the chart on p. C9 on a separate index card. They can also draw pictures of organisms on cardboard disks to use for scoring. The pack of cards should be shuffled before the game begins. To take a turn, a player selects a card from the pack, names a kingdom in which the characteristic on the card is found, and gives an example of an organism in that kingdom. Students can help each other assess which answers are correct. To keep score, students can earn a disk for each correct answer. The player with the most disks wins.

Reading Focus Answer

Organisms can be classified into large groups called kingdoms. Students should be able to name the following kingdoms—animal, plant, fungus, protist, moneran—and give a brief description of each kingdom.

Internet Field Trip

From **www.eduplace.com** students can link to a Web site about how living things are classified. A trip log will guide their visit to the site.

Science & Social Studies

NATIVE AMERICAN STUDIES

What to Do Ask students to research the relationship that the Native Americans had with the animal and plant kingdoms.

What's the Result? Each student can do a brief presentation for the class about the importance of a particular plant or animal to a specific Native American group. For example, a student may share how the Plains Indians used each part of a buffalo for their survival.

Multi-Age Classroom Provide research materials that are geared towards various levels of reading difficulty.

RESOURCE

Classifying Past and Present

Reading Focus Point out that students will need to ***draw conclusions*** as they read to answer the Reading Focus question.

1. Get Ready

Background

- *Spider* is the common name for an animal species called arthropods, animals with eight legs. We know about 34,000 species of arthropods. Spiders are usually less than one centimeter long, although the largest has a body length of about nine centimeters. Some spiders catch their prey by spinning silky, sticky webs to catch unsuspecting insects. Other spiders hunt for their food, or pounce on their prey as they come near, such as the Jumping Spider and the African Wolf Spider. With all of the different types of spiders on the earth, it's not surprising that scientists have difficulties classifying living things!

Discussion Starter

- **How is the way a person might sort a baseball card collection or a seashell collection like a classification system?** For a collection, you have many different items to put into groups, and you can sort them in a variety of ways. Living things can be sorted and grouped the same way. Students might give examples of ways they have sorted collections and how they chose the basis for sorting.
- **Which kingdom do you think is the most difficult for scientists to work with, and why?** Students may say that protists and monerans are difficult for scientists to work with because they are often microscopic in size, so they are difficult to find and examine. They are often found within other organisms or in water.

RESOURCE

Classifying— Past and Present

Reading Focus How has the way people classify living things changed since ancient times?

TIME Capsule

For over 3,000 years, scientists have looked for traits that would relate living things to one another. From about 350 B.C. to the mid-1900s, most scientists were content to classify organisms into just two groups—plants and animals.

But as science has advanced over the years, so have ideas about classifying organisms. The time line tells about a few of the people throughout history who have invented classification systems. Scientists continue to change classification systems as they learn more about living things.

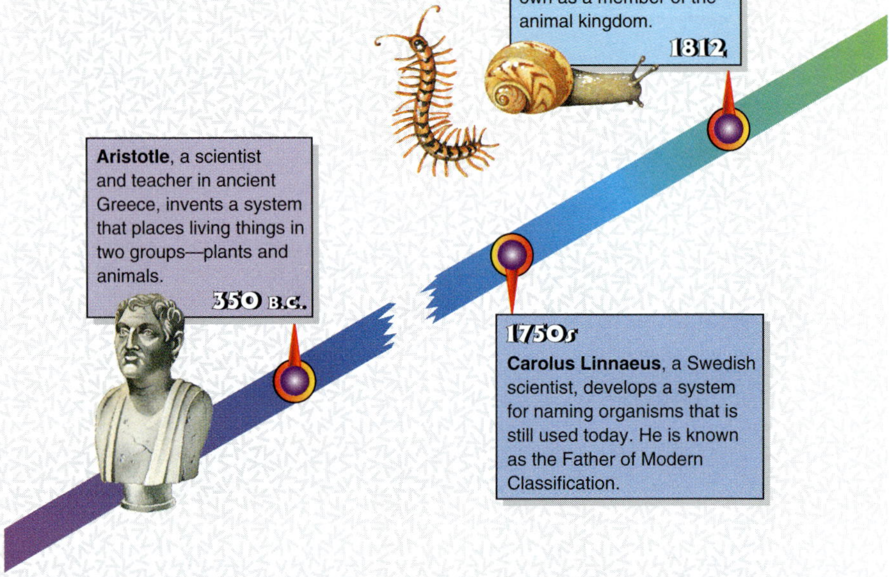

Georges Cuvier classifies everything that can move from place to place on its own as a member of the animal kingdom. 1812

Aristotle, a scientist and teacher in ancient Greece, invents a system that places living things in two groups—plants and animals. 350 B.C.

1750s **Carolus Linnaeus**, a Swedish scientist, develops a system for naming organisms that is still used today. He is known as the Father of Modern Classification.

C12

Science & Math

TIME LINES

What to Do Have student groups make a time line. They should include the dates and events listed on pp. C12–C13, and position the events at intervals to show how much time passed between events. Tell students to find the total number of years the time line represents (about 2,340 years). Then have them calculate the number of years per 2.5 cm (1 in.) on a time line that is 91 cm (3 ft) long (about 65 years per in.). Have them mark 100-year intervals and write the dates when classification systems were invented.

What's the Result? How does this time line look different from the one in the book? This time line shows how much time passed between Aristotle and Linnaeus.

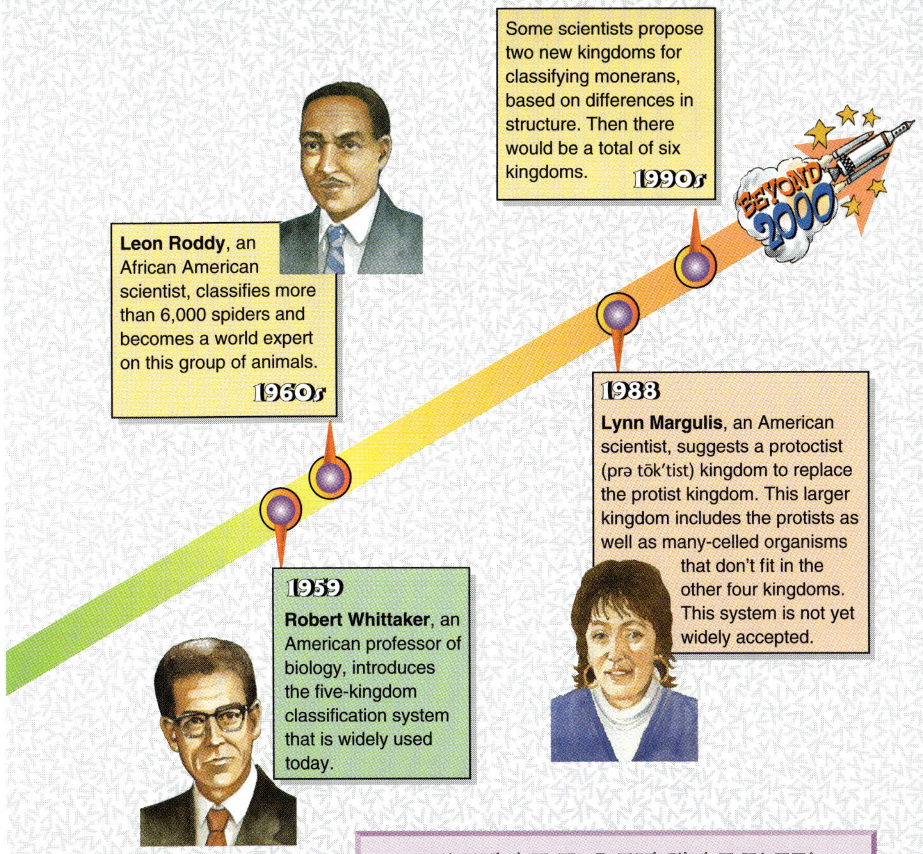

UNIT PROJECT LINK

For this Unit Project you will make a field guide to local plants or animals. With your group, choose the plants or animals to include. Find out information about each one. You might contact your state's Department of Natural Resources for help. Then put the information you gather in your field guide.

TechnologyLink

For more help with your Unit Project, go to **www.eduplace.com**.

C13

UNIT PROJECT LINK

Encourage students to make their final lists on *Science Notebook,* TRB p. 31. Then distribute copies of Unit Project Master 1 (TRB p. 16) and have students record information on each plant or animal they choose. Use Unit Project Masters 2 and 3 (TRB pp. 17–18) if students have trouble doing research. Tell students that every organism has a scientific name. Using library materials, have students label the plants and animals with both their common and scientific names.

TechnologyLink

Have students visit **www.eduplace.com** to link to content-related sites and obtain Unit Project Masters, including a scoring rubric to assess students' progress

2. Guide the Discussion

Choose from the following strategies to facilitate discussion.

Connecting to the Activities

- ***Animals Are Different, p. C6***
- Remind students that they studied three animals on the basis of how they were alike and different. Ask: **How does what you did in the activity compare to how a scientist classifies living things?** Scientists also find similarities and differences to help them classify organisms.

Drawing Conclusions

- **Based on what you know about classification systems, how might the study of living things today be different if scientists had never developed such systems?** Students may respond that classification systems help scientists look for and find similarities among living things. Without seeing similarities, scientists would not be able to relate living things to one another. Scientists also would not be able to concentrate their study on a particular group.

Meeting Individual Needs

Gifted and Talented Ask students to use the library to do research on an organism of their choice. Students should find information about how the organism was discovered and how it can be classified. Students can report their findings to the class through a presentation or a written report.

Science Processor Have students use the CD-ROM data table to make charts to accompany their presentations or reports.

3. Assess Understanding

Arrange students into six groups, and assign each a scientist from the time line on pp. C12–C13. Groups should make a sign naming their scientist and the date that the scientist's system was developed. Then students should form a "living" time line across the classroom, with each group in its proper position. Have each group explain how living things should be classified according to the group's scientist.

Reading Focus Answer

In ancient times, living things were classified into only two groups, plants and animals. Today, living things are classified into five or more groups.

RESOURCE

Classification of Animals

Reading Focus Encourage students to use what they know about ***comparing and contrasting*** to answer the Reading Focus question.

1. Get Ready

Vocabulary

Science Terms vertebra, vertebrates, invertebrates, exoskeleton

Support Terms microscope, classified, backbones

Background

- Since soft body parts don't fossilize as easily as hard substances, such as bones, the history of invertebrates is not as well known as that of vertebrates.

2. Guide the Discussion

Connecting to the Activities

- ***Animals Are Different, p. C6***
- **How would the life of an earthworm change if it suddenly had a backbone?** It would move differently. **How would the life of a bird change if it did not have a backbone?** It would not be able to fly.

3. Assess Understanding

Ask students in groups, to list traits of vertebrates and invertebrates, and give examples of each.

Reading Focus Answer

Animals are classified as vertebrates or invertebrates. Vertebrates and invertebrates are alike because they both move on their own, can be seen without a microscope, get their own food, and produce young. They are different because vertebrates have backbones and invertebrates do not.

RESOURCE

Classification of Animals

Reading Focus Into what two groups are all animals classified, and how are the groups alike and different?

▲ Examples of vertebrates

Each organism in the animal kingdom moves on its own, is large enough to be seen without a microscope, gets its own food, and produces young. These few traits are common to all animals. The activity on pages C6 and C7 shows that different kinds of animals can have different traits. For this reason, scientists have further classified animals into smaller groups within the animal kingdom.

Who Has a Backbone?

Animals that have backbones make up one group. You can feel the knobs of your backbone down the center of your back. Each knob is part of a separate bone. Each bone that makes up the backbone is called a **vertebra**. Animals that have backbones are called **vertebrates** (vʉr'tə brits).

Vertebrates include many different kinds of animals. They can be found just about anywhere—in oceans, rivers, forests, mountains, and deserts. Horses, hippos, cats, birds, snakes, lizards, frogs, and fish are all vertebrates. All vertebrates have one thing in common—a backbone.

C14

Science & Social Studies

DIFFERENT FEET

What You Need books about mammals

What to Do Share with students that some cultures long ago developed dietary rules that classified which animals people could or could not eat. For example, in the Orthodox Jewish religion, animals that both chew cud and have cloven hooves were considered suitable to eat. Thus, cattle and sheep were considered suitable, but horses, donkeys, camels, and pigs were not. Encourage pairs of students to research information about animals' feet in books about mammals. Have students develop a classification system based on the similarities and differences they found.

What's the Result? Invite partners to explain their classification system and name examples of animals in each category.

Life Without a Backbone

The members of many different animal groups don't have backbones. Animals that don't have backbones are called **invertebrates**. In fact, 97 percent of the animal kingdom is made up of invertebrates! They include some of the smallest animals, such as spiders, mites, and insects. Some invertebrates can be found in ponds, oceans, and other water environments where they can move about easily. Others have no trouble moving about on land or in the air.

Insects and some other invertebrates have exoskeletons (eks ō-skel′ə tənz). An **exoskeleton** is a hard outer covering that protects an animal's body and gives it support.

The animals within each of the major groups of the animal kingdom have many different traits. These major animal groups, then, are classified into even smaller groups. These groups are based on traits that the animals within the groups share. ■

Examples of invertebrates ▼

INVESTIGATION 1 WRAP-UP

REVIEW

1. Name three kingdoms of living things. Name one organism that belongs to each kingdom.

2. Which group makes up most of the animal kingdom, vertebrates or invertebrates?

CRITICAL THINKING

3. An organism has no structures for moving from place to place. It makes its own food, and it reproduces by seeds. In what kingdom would you place this organism? Explain your answer.

4. As you pet a dog, you feel hard knobs along its back. What are these knobs? Based on this feature, into what group of animals would you classify the dog? Explain your answer.

C15

Assessment

Performance

Debate Have students debate whether an exoskeleton or a backbone is more beneficial for an animal. Encourage students to mention the traits of specific animals to support their positions.

Investigation Review ▶

Use Investigation Review p. 93 in the *Teacher Resource Book*.

Investigation Review

Label the drawing of each animal below as a vertebrate or an invertebrate.

1. vertebrate
2. vertebrate
3. invertebrate
4. invertebrate
5. vertebrate
6. invertebrate

Draw a line to match each living thing with its kingdom.

7. bacteria	Animal
8. paramecium	Plant
9. mushroom	Fungus
10. maple tree	Moneran
11. horse	Protist

Process Skills
Classifying

You observe a many-celled organism. It does not have a structure for moving from place to place. It absorbs food from other organisms. It is not a protist. In which kingdom would you classify the organism and why?

The organism is a fungus. It is not a moneran because it is many-celled. It does not move from place to place, so it is not an animal. It does not make its own food, so it is not a plant.

Close the Investigation

INVESTIGATION WRAP-UP

REVIEW

1. Students should be able to name at least three of the kingdoms (animal, plant, fungus, protist, moneran). They should be able to give at least one example of each.

2. Invertebrates make up most of the animal kingdom.

CRITICAL THINKING

3. Students should infer that this organism belongs to the plant kingdom because it makes its own food and produces seeds. ***(Analyzing, Synthesizing, Applying)***

4. Each hard knob under the dog's skin is a vertebra, so the dog should be classified as a vertebrate. ***(Analyzing, Synthesizing, Applying, Expressing Ideas)***

CHALLENGE

Tell students that although most of the smallest animals are invertebrates, some invertebrates are very large. Assign students to small groups, and have them look in books to find out about very large invertebrates that live in the ocean. Students can then report their findings to the class. (Among the largest invertebrates are the giant squid and the spider crab.)

FOLLOWING UP

Baseline Assessment Return to the class drawings that each student completed of their own backbones. Ask the students to draw another picture of their backbone, labeling the vertebra. If they think their original drawing was inaccurate, they should make changes in this second drawing.

Reteaching Discuss the investigation subconcept with students. Ask students to work in groups to list the physical traits and behaviors that members of each kingdom share with others in the same kingdom.

Use *Science Notebook*, TRB p. 32.

Start the Investigation

How Do Vertebrates Differ?

pages C16–C23

Planner

Subconcept Animals with backbones are called vertebrates. Vertebrate groups are distinguished by how they maintain their body temperatures, how they breathe, and their body coverings.

Objectives

- **Observe** and **infer** how temperature affects breathing.
- **Differentiate** among kinds of vertebrates.

Pacing 4 class periods

Science Terms fish, gills, amphibian, reptile, birds, mammals

Activate Prior Knowledge

Baseline Assessment Ask students to identify a characteristic that makes one vertebrate, such as a dog, different from other vertebrates, such as birds. Save students' responses for use in Following Up.

Investigation 2: How Do Vertebrates Differ?

A backbone, two eyes, and one mouth are some traits shared by a snake, a cat, and a human. But you probably can name many more ways in which snakes, cats, and people are different. In Investigation 2 you'll explore ways that vertebrates differ.

Activity

Cold Fish

How is the way a fish breathes different from the way you breathe? Find out what change might make a fish breathe faster or slower.

MATERIALS
- goldfish in large plastic jar
- thermometer
- timer
- ice cubes
- *Science Notebook*

SAFETY
Be careful when handling a glass thermometer.

Procedure

1. In your *Science Notebook*, **make a chart** like the one shown.

	Water Temperature	Breathing Rate
First reading		
Two minutes after ice cubes were added		

2. Your teacher will give your group a plastic jar with a goldfish in it. Use a thermometer to **measure** the temperature of the water. **Record** the temperature in your chart.

C16

Activity: Cold Fish

Preview *Students find that a cooler temperature leads to a slower breathing rate in fish.*

Advance Preparation *See p. C4b*

1. Get Ready

GROUPS OF 4–6 | 30 MINUTES

Key Science Process Skills observe, measure, collect, record, and interpret data

Collaborative Strategy Groups can assign a data recorder, thermometer reader, ice cube manager, breath counter, and a timer.

Meeting Individual Needs

STUDENTS ACQUIRING ENGLISH

Carefully go over the steps of the procedure. Model each of the steps. Use your hands to represent the gill flaps opening and closing. Count out loud as you move your hands back and forth, simulating the breathing of the fish. Compare the opening and closing of the gill cover with your own breathing as you inhale and exhale. Help students verbalize a prediction of the fish's breathing rate in colder water. Students might say, "I think the fish will breathe faster in colder water," or they might say, "I think the fish will breathe slower in colder water." Help them understand the difference between their choice of "faster" or "slower."

VISUAL/SPATIAL

3. **Observe** two flaps behind the fish's eyes. Under the flaps are **gills**, which help the fish "breathe." The flaps open and close once with each breath. **Count** and **record** the number of breaths the fish takes in one minute. Repeat your counting several times. Then find the average of your results.

See **SCIENCE and MATH TOOLBOX** *page H5 if you need to review* ***Finding an Average.***

4. **Predict** how the number of times the flaps open and close in one minute will change if ice cubes are added to the water. **Record** your prediction. Gently place two or three ice cubes in the water in the jar.

5. Wait two minutes. Then **measure** the temperature of the water again. **Count** the number of times the flaps open and close in one minute. **Record** your observations. Repeat your counting several times and find the average. Remove the ice.

Step 5

Analyze and Conclude

1. How does the temperature of the water affect how the fish breathes? **Compare** your results with your prediction.

2. Think about what happens when you go outside in very cold weather. Does your breathing rate change when you go from warm air into cold air? **Draw a conclusion** about how you are different from a fish, in terms of breathing.

Technology Link CD-ROM

INVESTIGATE FURTHER!

Use the **Science Processor CD-ROM**, *Animals* (Investigation 2, Skin and Bones) to explore how the skeletons of fish, mammals, birds, reptiles, and amphibians are alike. Watch a video about how a backbone is useful. Learn about the body temperatures of different groups of animals.

C17

Technology Link CD-ROM

INVESTIGATE FURTHER!

Students can use the **Science Processor CD-ROM** *Animals,* Investigation 2, "Skin and Bones" to investigate more about how the skeletons of different creatures are alike. Students learn about which animals have backbones and which do not. They use the Vertebrates Data Pack to explore vertebrate characteristics and record their findings in a chart. They use what they have learned to sort and classify the creatures that appear on the screen. Students also can take the temperatures of animals and record the temperatures in a chart. To extend this investigation, students can study a Data Pack or play a vertebrate trivia game.

Safety Review safety precautions with students. Be careful when handling a glass thermometer.

2. Guide the Procedure

- Have students count out loud each time the gill cover opens. The recorder can make a dot or a slash mark for each count.
- **On what did you base your predictions for the fish's breathing rate after the ice cubes were added?** Being cold would slow down the fish.

Have students record their predictions, observations, and measurements, and answer questions on *Science Notebook,* TRB, pp. 33–34.

Science Processor You may wish to have students use the CD-ROM Spreadsheet to organize and display their data.

3. Assess Performance

Process Skills Checklist

- Did students **observe** the movement of the gill covers? Did they measure the time interval between gill openings?
- Did students **predict** how the fish's respiration rate would change?
- Did students accurately **record** their predictions and data about the fish's respiration rate?
- Did students carefully **measure** the temperature of the fish's water?

Analyze and Conclude

1. Students may conclude that decreasing the temperature slows the breathing of the fish. Accept students' predictions whether or not they were correct.
2. Students may respond that people do not breathe more slowly when the weather is colder. They may infer that they are different from fish in this respect and that, whereas fish use gills for breathing, humans use lungs for breathing.

RESOURCE

Swim, Leap, and Slither

Reading Focus Have students ***use a graphic***. Have them make a 3-column chart in which they can list and ***compare/contrast*** traits of fish, amphibians, and reptiles. The chart helps answer the Reading Focus question.

1. Get Ready

Vocabulary

Science Terms fish, gills, amphibian, reptile

Support Terms steer, balance, scales

Background

- Fish, amphibians, and reptiles cannot regulate their body temperature internally. Instead, they depend on the heat in their environment to warm them. However, these animals can control their temperatures to some extent through their behavior. They bask in the sun to warm up, and slow down in the cold to save energy. Although they are called cold-blooded, their temperature can be warm or cool, depending on their surroundings.
- Mammals are called warm-blooded animals because they conserve body heat. They maintain a relatively constant body temperature. As a result, they can live in both cold and warm climates.

Discussion Starter

- Write the title of this resource section on the chalkboard. Ask: **To which animals do you think the title *Swim, Leap, and Slither* applies?** Students may infer that "swim" applies to fish, "leap" to frogs, and "slither" to snakes. Encourage them to suggest other animals to which each action word might apply.
- **How are these animals alike?** Students may respond that they all have a backbone. They may add that they all have two eyes, a mouth, and a brain. **How are they different?** Students may mention that fish have fins and gills, frogs have moist skin, and snakes and fish have scales. Fish live in water, frogs live in water and on land, and most snakes live on land.

RESOURCE

Swim, Leap, and Slither

Reading Focus What traits are used to classify a vertebrate as a fish, an amphibian, or a reptile?

Has anyone ever told you that you're one in a million? Actually, as a vertebrate, you're one in several thousand. Vertebrates can be sorted into smaller groups, classified by traits that they have in common. Fish, amphibians (am fib′ē ənz), and reptiles are three of these groups.

Fish Tales

Did you know that fish are the largest group of vertebrates? There are more than 30,000 different kinds of fish in all. They come in many sizes and shapes, from the tiny minnow to the great white shark.

Many vertebrates that live in water are classified as **fish**. Most fish have body temperatures that vary with the temperature of the environment.

Most fish also have fins that help them steer and balance in the water. The feathery parts on the side of a fish's head are called **gills**. Water flows over the gills and allows the fish to "breathe" underwater. Many fish are covered with scales. Scales, which are hard, help protect fish.

Fish are vertebrates that live in water. ►

C18

Science & Math

VERTEBRATE PIE GRAPH

What to Do Have students make a pie graph to show the relative numbers of species for each group of vertebrates. Provide students with this list of approximate number of species for each group: fish—30,000, amphibians—4,000, reptiles—5,000, birds—9,000, and mammals—4,500. Students can first convert each figure to a percentage by dividing each figure by the total number of vertebrate species (52,500) and then multiplying by 100. Then they can draw a large circle and measure off a section that is the approximate size for each group.

Science Processor Have students use the CD-ROM Grapher to make their graphs.

What's the Result? Suggest students check each other's graphs.

Slippery Amphibians

There are almost 4,000 varieties of frogs, toads, salamanders, and other amphibians. An **amphibian** is a vertebrate that usually lives in water after hatching from an egg, but as an adult can live on land. The body temperature of an amphibian varies with the temperature of its surroundings. On land, amphibians live in wet environments. Some amphibians have smooth, moist skin, which makes them look and feel slippery.

Amphibians hatch from jelly-coated eggs. Their young usually do not look anything like the parents. Young amphibians start life with gills and breathe like fish. They even have tails that help them swim.

As they get older, amphibians grow legs and lose their gills. Adult amphibians breathe air with lungs. Frogs and toads lose their tails as adults, but salamanders keep theirs.

Using Math *A wood frog develops from a tadpole in about 77 days. How many weeks is that?*

2. Guide the Discussion

Choose from the following strategies to facilitate discussion.

Connecting to the Activities

- ***Cold Fish, pp. C16–C17***
- **What characteristics did you notice that make fish different from other vertebrates?** Students might mention that they noticed that the fish has fins, a streamlined body shape, and scaly skin. It has gills and swims in water. Note that some other vertebrates might have one or more of these traits, but that only fish have all these traits.
- **If you could measure the fish's body temperature after you added ice cubes to the water, how do you think it would change?** Students might suggest that the body temperature would be lower because a fish's body temperature varies with its environment.

Using Math *To find the number of weeks, students need to divide the number of days by the number of days in a week (77 by 7). The result is 11 weeks.*

Making Comparisons

- **How do fish, amphibians, and reptiles differ in the way they breathe?** Fish breathe under water using gills. Amphibians start life with gills and breathe like fish. Adult amphibians live on land and breathe air using lungs. Reptiles breathe air using lungs.
- **A salamander is an amphibian, and a lizard is a reptile. How do their outer coverings differ?** The salamander has smooth, moist skin, and the lizard has dry, scaly skin.

Drawing Conclusions

- **If you found eggs in leathery shells near the water, would you conclude that the eggs belong to a fish, an amphibian, or a reptile?** Only a reptile lays eggs with a leathery shell. Also, a fish or an amphibian would lay their eggs in the water, not on dry land near the water.
- **If someone told you that she has a pet that has scales and no legs, what kind of animal would you conclude it is?** The animal could be either a fish or a snake.

Science & Social Studies

DINOSAUR TREASURE MAP

What You Need reference books or Internet access about dinosaurs, reference map of the United States, outline map of the United States.

What to Do Point out that the fossilized remains of vertebrates help us learn about the past. Suggest students work in groups to search periodicals or the Internet to learn where in North America fossilized bones of dinosaurs have been found. Students can mark their maps to show dinosaur finds.

What's the Result? Have students share their maps. **Which states have many dinosaur finds?** Utah, Colorado, Wyoming, Montana, South Dakota, Kansas, and Texas **Where was Sue, the most complete T. Rex skeleton, found?** South Dakota

Thinking Critically

- **How is it beneficial that reptiles lay eggs with leathery shells and that fish and amphibians lay their eggs in water?** Students may respond that reptiles lay their eggs on land and that the leathery shells keep their eggs from drying out. But fish and amphibians lay their eggs in water because the young live in water when they hatch.

Meeting Individual Needs

For Extra Help Have students make a drawing of a fish, an amphibian, and a reptile. Ask them to show in their drawings what the outer covering of each animal is like, how it moves from place to place, where the animal lives, and where it lays its eggs. Students may share their drawings with the class.

Science Processor Have students use the CD-ROM Painter to make their drawings.

3. Assess Understanding

Students can work in groups of three or four. Have them plan a chart in which they can compare fish, amphibians, and reptiles. They may select headings such as Breathing, Moving About, Temperature, and Body Covering. Students should share their charts with other groups and use the charts to make up questions about these three kinds of vertebrates. Questions can be saved and used as review for the chapter assessment.

Science Processor Have students use the CD-ROM Spreadsheet to make their charts.

Reading Focus Answer

A fish lives in water and breathes with gills. An amphibian hatches from an egg, breathes with gills when young and with lungs as an adult, and lives on land as an adult. A reptile has dry, scaly skin, lays eggs that have a leathery shell, and breathes air.

Variety Is the Spice of Reptile Life

Reptiles have some features that differ from those of amphibians and fish. A **reptile** is a vertebrate that has dry, scaly skin and lays eggs that have a leathery shell. All reptiles lay their eggs on land, and all breathe air. Like fish and amphibians, reptiles have body temperatures that vary with the temperature of the environment.

Reptiles include animals as large as the Nile crocodile, 5.5 m (18 ft) long. They also include animals as small as the bog turtle, 10 cm (4 in.) long. Reptiles live in hot, dry deserts and in warm, wet tropical rain forests.

These animals vary in other ways as well. They may move as quickly as a rattlesnake or as slowly as a tortoise. Snakes are reptiles that slither. Some turtles swim underwater. Reptiles may or may not have tails or even legs. Lizards and snakes are able to shed their skins, and chameleons can change colors!

Fish, amphibians, and reptiles have some very different features. But these vertebrates all have one thing in common—a backbone! ■

▲ Jackson's chameleon

A crocodile is a reptile. ▼

Integrating the Sciences

EARTH SCIENCE

What You Need recent publications on ocean-floor exploration, Internet access

What to Do Tell students that although people have discovered millions of species of living things, more are yet to be discovered. Some parts of the earth, such as ocean floors, have not been fully explored. Invite students to investigate methods of exploring along ocean trenches and vents using periodicals and selected Internet web sites.

What's the Result? Hold a class discussion in which students can share their research and ideas, and explain their thinking. Students may suggest that new species are likely to be discovered in parts of the unexplored ocean.

RESOURCE

Fly, Dive, and Gallop

Reading Focus What traits are used to classify a vertebrate as a bird or a mammal?

Besides fish, amphibians, and reptiles, there are two other groups of vertebrates with some very different traits. These are the birds and the mammals.

No matter their size, their color, or where they live, all birds have feathers covering their bodies. No other group of animals has this feature.

A scarlet macaw ▼

▲ A close-up view of a macaw's feathers

To Fly Like a Bird

There are about 9,000 types of birds in the world. **Birds** are vertebrates that have wings and are covered with feathers. These vertebrates lay hard-shelled eggs, which hatch in their nests. Birds range in size from the very small hummingbird, no bigger than your finger, to the large ostrich, taller than an adult human.

A bird's skeleton is very light in weight. Its bones are hollow. Having hollow bones helps to make the bird light enough to fly through the air. The fastest of all birds is the white-throated spinetail swift. This little bird can fly over 160 km/h (100 mph)!

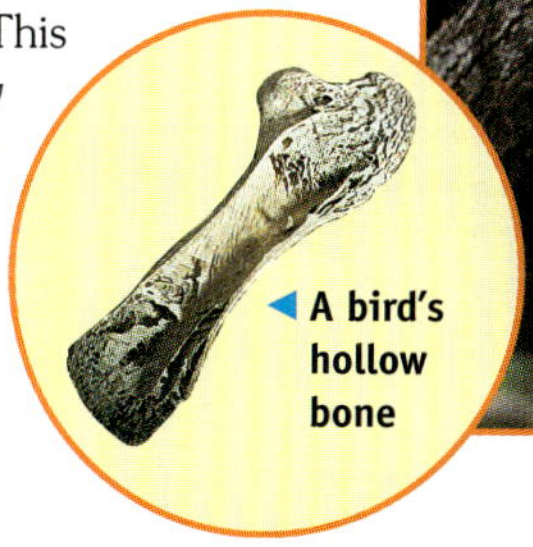

◀ A bird's hollow bone

C21

Science & the Arts

ANIMAL WALTZ

What to Do Invite small groups of students to choose one animal they have studied. Challenge groups to figure out a way to use their bodies to demonstrate how a particular animal moves. Each student in the group should take part in the demonstration. For example, to demonstrate the movement of a snake, students can form a connected line on the floor with one person being the head, and another the tail of the snake.

What's the Result? Each group should perform their animal's movements for the rest of the class. The audience should guess what animal is being depicted.

RESOURCE

Fly, Dive, and Gallop

Reading Focus Have students ***use a graphic.*** Have them make a 2-column chart in which they can list and ***compare/contrast*** traits of birds and mammals. The chart will help answer the Reading Focus question.

1. Get Ready

Vocabulary

Science Terms birds, mammals

Support Term skeleton

Background

- The general layout of a vertebrate's body is similar to that of all other vertebrates. For example, the arm bones have the same basic structure; one upper arm bone is connected to two lower arm bones, which are connected to hand bones. The bones may differ in size and shape, but the overall structure is the same in a person's arm, a dog's front leg, a bat's wing, or a whale's flipper.

Discussion Starter

- **How are birds different from the other vertebrates you have studied?** Birds have feathers and wings.

2. Guide the Discussion

Choose from the following strategies to facilitate discussion.

Connecting to the Activities

- ***Cold Fish, pp. C16–C17***
- Remind students how changes in temperature affected the fish in the activity. Note that a fish's body temperature decreases as its environment gets colder.
- **How do cold temperatures affect your body?** Students might mention that they feel colder, they shiver, or their teeth chatter. Guide them to see that, unlike fish, their bodies conserve heat even if the surroundings are cold. Point out that shivering is one way that the body stays warm.

Making Inferences

- **How would you classify a sheep, a bat, and a penguin? Explain your answers.** A sheep and a bat are mammals, while the penguin is a bird. Students should support their answers by mentioning traits of each group, such as having fur and producing milk (for mammals) and having feathers and wings and laying eggs (for birds).

Drawing Conclusions

- Tell students that whales do not have a coat of fur on their bodies. **Because fur helps keep most mammals warm, what can you conclude about the way that whales keep warm?** Students may conclude that whales have another way to keep warm. They may know that a whale's body has a layer of blubber that helps insulate it.

Using Math *Students should be able to divide to determine that a baby whale drinks about 2 L ($2\frac{2}{5}$ qt) in one minute.*

Meeting Individual Needs

For Early Finishers Students can make bar graphs to compare various traits of mammals or birds. Direct students to find information about birds' or mammals' lengths or heights, masses, speeds, or life spans. Encourage students to use their graphs. For example, you might ask a student, "Which animal would win a running race, a rabbit or a house cat?" You may want students to use the Activity Support Master "Graph Paper" (TRB p. 8).

Science Processor Have students use the CD-ROM Grapher to assist them.

3. Assess Understanding

Have students make a chart entitled "Traits of Birds and Mammals." The chart should list the characteristics that distinguish birds and mammals from each other and from other animals.

Reading Focus Answer

Birds are vertebrates that have wings and feathers. Mammals are vertebrates that feed milk to their young and have hair or fur.

Using Math *A baby whale can drink 11 L (3 gal) of milk in less than five minutes. About how much milk is that in one minute?*

Our Group, the Mammals

Do you remember your first meal? It was milk, and it probably made you stop crying. Vertebrates that feed milk to their young and have hair or fur are called **mammals**. The young of most mammals grow inside the mother. When they have developed enough, the young are born live. But the young of the duckbill platypus, also a mammal, are not born live. Instead, they hatch from eggs.

You may not have realized that mammals include a wide range of animals. Apes, lions, hippos, dogs, elephants, kangaroos, squirrels, cats, pigs, bats, horses, rabbits, and even whales are all mammals. They're mammals because they all have hair or fur and feed milk to their young.

◀ **A squirrel is a mammal that can live in a city.**

Science & Writing

ANIMAL STORIES

What You Need index cards with a name of a different vertebrate written on each card

What to Do Have students draw, from a pile of index cards, a card with the name of a vertebrate on it. Invite students to write a story about a day in the life of that vertebrate. The story should include what the animal would eat, what its surroundings would be like, and a physical description of the animal.

What's the Result? Stories can be displayed in the classroom for all students to read.

Science Processor Students can use the CD-ROM Painter to create illustrations of the vertebrate they wrote about and include them with their story.

Most mammals have furry coats. Hair or fur traps a layer of air near the body, which helps the mammal stay warm. Humans don't have as much hair as other mammals. So wearing clothes helps people stay warm.

There are many different kinds of mammals in the world around you. The next time you watch a squirrel scramble up a tree or find a raccoon in your trash, remember that they're mammals, just as you are! ■

▲ The timber wolf pup will get a thicker coat of fur as it grows.

INVESTIGATION 2 WRAP-UP

REVIEW

1. What are the five groups of vertebrates? Name one animal that belongs to each group.

2. Give the traits of any two groups of vertebrates.

CRITICAL THINKING

3. Animal *A*, at a zoo where you work, comes from a rain forest. Animal *B* comes from a desert. Both lay eggs that do not have hard shells. Their body temperature varies with the temperature of the environment. To what vertebrate section of the zoo should you assign each animal?

4. Compare a salmon, a penguin, and a whale.

Close the Investigation

INVESTIGATION WRAP-UP

REVIEW

1. Fish, reptiles, amphibians, birds, and mammals. Students should list one animal per group.

2. Fish: live in water; most have body temperatures that vary with the temperature of the environment; most have fins, have gills; and many have scales. Amphibians: usually hatch from an egg in water and live on land as adults; cold-blooded; smooth, moist skin. Reptiles: have dry, scaly skin; eggs have a leathery shell; have body temperatures that vary with the temperature of the environment; breathe air; Birds: have wings; covered with feathers; lay eggs. Mammals: feed milk to their young and have hair or fur.

CRITICAL THINKING SKILLS

3. Animal *A* should be assigned to the amphibian section. Animal *B* should be assigned to the reptile section. ***(Analyzing, Synthesizing, Applying)***

4. Accept all reasonable responses. Responses might include that all are vertebrates, live in or near a body of water, and survive by eating other organisms, but that a salmon is a fish, a penguin a bird, and a whale a mammal. ***(Analyzing, Synthesizing)***

CHALLENGE

Have groups make posters using a picture from each vertebrate group—fish, amphibian, reptile, bird, and mammal—and arrange the pictures in a concept map, with words telling how the animals are alike and different.

FOLLOWING UP

Baseline Assessment Return to the class list of how one vertebrate differs from other vertebrates that was generated at the beginning of this investigation. Invite students to classify the animals into the five groups of vertebrates.

Reteaching Use the materials that students have produced to review the five vertebrate groups and their traits. Have students classify the animals into the five groups of vertebrates.

Use *Science Notebook*, TRB p. 35.

Assessment

Portfolio

Diagram Encourage students to make a drawing of an imaginary vertebrate. This animal should have at least one trait of each of the five groups of vertebrates. Students should be able to describe their animals. For example, a student might say that his imaginary animal has fur like a mammal, wings like a bird, and so on.

Investigation Review ▸

Use Investigation Review p.94 in the *Teacher Resource Book*.

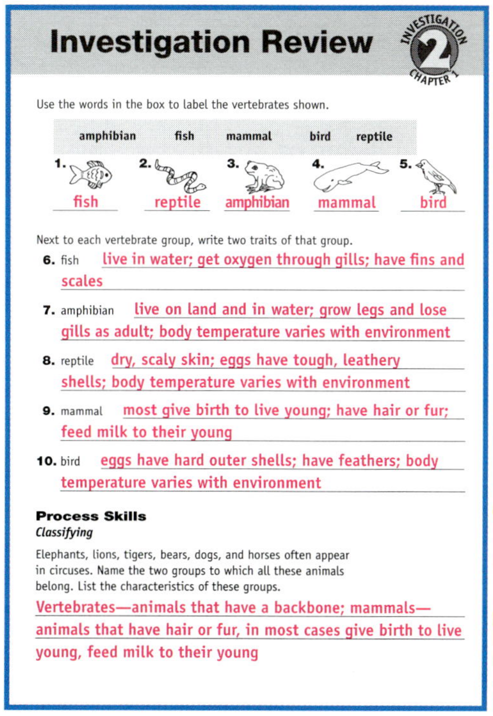

Investigation Review

Use the words in the box to label the vertebrates shown.

amphibian	fish	mammal	bird	reptile

1. fish 2. reptile 3. amphibian 4. mammal 5. bird

Next to each vertebrate group, write two traits of that group.

6. fish live in water; get oxygen through gills; have fins and scales

7. amphibian live on land and in water; grow legs and lose gills as adult; body temperature varies with environment

8. reptile dry, scaly skin; eggs have tough, leathery shells; body temperature varies with environment

9. mammal most give birth to live young; have hair or fur; feed milk to their young

10. bird eggs have hard outer shells; have feathers; body temperature varies with environment

Process Skills
Classifying

Elephants, lions, tigers, bears, dogs, and horses often appear in circuses. Name the two groups to which all these animals belong. List the characteristics of these groups.

Vertebrates—animals that have a backbone; mammals—animals that have hair or fur, in most cases give birth to live young, feed milk to their young

Start the Investigation

How Do the Groups of Invertebrates Differer?

pages C24–C31

Planner

Subconcept Animals without backbones are called invertebrates. Different groups of invertebrates are classified by body structures, feeding behaviors, and methods of locomotion.

Objectives

- **Predict** which environment the earthworm will move toward.
- **Identify** characteristics that distinguish invertebrate groups.
- **Describe** the possible medical uses of leeches.

Pacing 3 class periods

Science Term molts

Activate Prior Knowledge

Baseline Assessment Ask: **How do vertebrates and invertebrates differ?** Record students' responses for Following Up.

How Do the Groups of Invertebrates Differ?

You learned that many animals don't have a backbone supporting their body. How are these animals without backbones grouped? Find out in this investigation.

Activity

Worming Their Way Home

Earthworms have no backbone and no eyes. How do you think these animals find their way around? How do they know when they are in their "home" environment? After doing this activity, you'll know how.

MATERIALS

- goggles
- cardboard box
- dry soil
- damp soil
- sand
- dry leaves or shredded newspaper
- hand lens
- earthworm
- timer
- *Science Notebook*

SAFETY

Wear goggles. Wash your hands when you have finished.

Procedure

1. Mark off four sections inside a cardboard box. Label the sections 1 through 4, as shown.
2. Place each material in a different section of the box, as shown in the diagram.
3. Remove the earthworm from its container and gently place it in section 1 of the box. With your group, **predict** which numbered section the worm will move toward. **Record** your prediction in your *Science Notebook*.

Step 1

1 newspaper	2 dry soil
3 damp soil	4 sand

C24

Activity Worming Their Way Home

Preview *Students discover that an earthworm prefers a damp soil environment.*

Advance Preparation *See p. C4b*

1. Get Ready

GROUPS OF 4–6 **30 MINUTES**

Key Science Process Skills predict, observe, describe

Meeting Individual Needs

STUDENTS ACQUIRING ENGLISH

Before beginning the activity, have students create two word webs. The first word web should consist of words associated with soil and dirt, such as *rough*, *smooth*, *dry*, *wet*, and *damp*. The second word web should consist of words about earthworms, such as *wet*, *slimy*, *soft*, *squishy*, and *wiggly*. Encourage students to include words about how earthworms move. Leave the word webs on the chalkboard so that students can use them as they record their observations during the activity.

LOGICAL/ANALYTICAL

4. Using a hand lens, **observe** the location of the worm each minute for ten minutes. Also **observe** how it uses its body parts to move. **Record** your observations. When you finish observing the worm, gently place it back in its container.

See **SCIENCE and MATH TOOLBOX** *page H2 if you need to review* ***Using a Hand Lens.***

Analyze and Conclude

1. Into which sections did the worm move during the ten minutes? Which materials are in those sections? Where did the worm spend the most time? the least time?

2. **Describe** how the worm used its body parts to move.

3. **Compare** your results with your predictions. **Infer** the kind of environment earthworms like best.

INVESTIGATE FURTHER!

RESEARCH

Some people are using earthworms to recycle trash. Find out how worms are able to turn trash like paper into a useful material called compost.

C25

INVESTIGATE FURTHER!

RESEARCH

Students may find that a compost pile consists of alternate layers of plant matter and soil. Some people add newspapers to compost in addition to plant matter. Then they add earthworms, which burrow through the soil, breaking up the plant matter and moist paper. The burrowing permits air to penetrate into the soil. As the earthworms burrow, they take in soil and other compost materials. The worms grind these materials in their gizzards. Even though the earthworm does not completely digest the paper and plant matter, it gets these materials ready to be further broken down by microorganisms in the soil. Remind students to record their findings on *Science Notebook,* TRB p. 37.

Materials Hints A shirt–size cardboard gift box would make a suitable container. Earthworms can be obtained at a bait shop, by ordering from a garden supply or science catalog, or by digging in soil.

Safety Review safety precautions with students. To protect the worms, distribute them in covered containers. Worms should not be allowed to dry out. Students should wash their hands after the activity.

2. Guide the Procedure

- Periodically moisten the worms with water from spray bottles to keep them from drying out. Those handling worms should moisten their hands. Keep worms in about 58 cm of moist soil and at a temperature range of 5–15°C. Make sure students return the worms to the container after the 10-minute observation period.
- **Which section of the box is most like the worm's natural environment?** Students may suggest that the moist soil or newspaper is like the worm's natural environment.
- **What do you think earthworms in the wild would do if their soil became too wet or dry?** They might suggest that the worms would move to a new area, just as the worms in the box did.

Have students record their predictions and observations and answer questions on *Science Notebook,* TRB, pp. 36–37.

Science Processor Students can use the CD-ROM Writer to record observations.

3. Assess Performance

Process Skills Checklist

- Did students **predict** which section the earthworm would move toward? Did they take into account both darkness and wetness?
- Did students **observe** the movement of the earthworm and **record** their observations?
- Did students **infer** the kind of environment preferred by earthworms?

Analyze and Conclude

1. Accept answers based on careful observations.
2. The worm moves by stretching its front half, pushing itself forward, and pulling the rest of its body.
3. Earthworms prefer a moist environment.

RESOURCE

Lifesaving Leeches

Reading Focus Have students ***summarize*** the resource to help them answer the Reading Focus question.

1. Get Ready

Background

- A leech has a sucker at each end, but the sucker at the back end is just for holding onto surfaces and moving. To move, the mouth sucker attaches to a surface. The back sucker releases its grip and moves to the mouth sucker. Then, the mouth sucker lets go of the surface and moves forward again.

Discussion Starter

- **Suppose scientists had never studied leeches. How might that affect the field of medicine?** Students might respond that without this study, doctors and researchers would not know that leeches can play a role in preventing blood clots and in helping scientists learn about nerves in humans.

2. Guide the Discussion

Connecting to the Activities

- ***Worming Their Way Home, pp. C24–C25***
- **How is a leech like and unlike the earthworm in the activity?** Leech and earthworm bodies are both divided into segments, but an earthworm lacks a suction-cup mouth and does not suck blood.

3. Assess Understanding

Have groups of three or four students prepare a report on possible medical benefits and problems of using leeches in the future.

Reading Focus Answer

Leeches were once used to suck a patient's blood. Today they are used to help prevent blood clots and in learning more about nerves in humans.

RESOURCE

Lifesaving Leeches

Reading Focus How were leeches once used, and how are they used today?

HOW IT Works

It may be brown, black, or covered with colored spots and stripes. It has 32 body segments and can grow as long as 45 cm (18 in.). What is it? It's an invertebrate called a leech. It feeds on the blood of other animals.

Doctors of the 1800s often used leeches to treat sick people. They believed that removing blood from a patient would help cure the patient's disease.

Today leeches have a different kind of role. Scientists have found that chemicals in the saliva of a leech can prevent blood clots. Blood clots can cause a heart attack or a stroke. Scientists hope that the use of leeches will help prevent these life-threatening events.

Scientists have also found that damaged nerves in a leech can regrow. By studying leeches, scientists may increase their understanding of nerves in humans.

In the past, people used leeches to cure almost any illness. ▼

C26

▲ **Leeches have suction-cuplike mouths. They use their pointed teeth to attach themselves to another animal. Then they feed on its blood.**

Science & Social Studies

PET THERAPY

What to Do Encourage students to describe any pets they have. Explain to students that animals can help people with physical ailments and emotional problems in many ways. For example, doctors have found that stroking or petting a dog or cat can often lower a person's blood pressure.

What's the Result? Why do you think petting an animal has a calming effect? Students may say that the repetitious action might be calming. They might also mention that spending time with a pet can make a person happy, which can calm the person.

RESOURCE

Nothing Much in Common

Reading Focus What are the traits of some groups of invertebrates?

Some tumble along the ocean floor. Others glide through the water. Some burrow into the soil. Others fly through the air. The groups of animals without backbones are very different from one another. From spikes and soft bodies to claws and hard shells, you'll see how different some of these groups are.

Sponges

In the ocean you might mistake some animals for plants. Sponges are one group of invertebrates that look like plants. That's because they stay fixed in one place—on a rock, for example. Sponges are animals that have bodies full of holes and skeletons made of spiky fibers.

If a sponge can't move around, how does it catch a meal? Water flows through the holes of a sponge. Small pieces of food in the moving water become trapped in the sponge.

These animals, called sponges, ▶ look like plants. The holes in a sponge (*inset*) trap food for the animal.

C27

Integrating the Sciences

EARTH SCIENCE

What to Do Have students use specimens (if available) and reference books to determine how coral reefs and limestone are related. Suggest they make a list or cause-and-effect chart of the relationship. Students should find that coral reefs are made out of limestone. The coral animals take in calcium from the ocean water. They use the calcium and produce calcium carbonate (limestone), from which their skeletons are made.

What's the Result? How do you think a limestone skeleton helps the coral animals? Students might speculate that the hard skeleton supports the colony of animals and protects them from being eaten by predators.

RESOURCE

Nothing Much in Common

Reading Focus Tell students to ***preview*** by looking at the headings to list the names of invertebrate groups. As they read, students should ***take notes*** about traits. The finished list will answer the Reading Focus question.

1. Get Ready

Vocabulary

Science Term molts

Support Terms sponges, invertebrates, fibers, tentacles, anemones, arthropods

Background

- If you pressed a natural sponge through a cheesecloth, it would separate into many cells. These cells can live independently, but if the individual cells are put in contact with each other again, they will stick together and collect to form a large sponge again. Also, pieces of sponge that break off a large sponge can regenerate, forming a whole new sponge.

Discussion Starter

- **If you saw a sign at the zoo that was marked *Invertebrates*, what animals would you expect to see?** Students may mention octopuses, sea urchins, starfish, and lobsters, among others.
- **What invertebrates do you think might make good pets?** A common invertebrate pet is the hermit crab.

2. Guide the Discussion

Choose from the following strategies to facilitate discussion.

Connecting to the Activities

- ***Worming Their Way Home, pp. C24–C25***
- **How do you think the worm knew what kind of environment it was in?** Students may infer that the worm was able to feel where it was.
- **Which other invertebrates live in environments where they do not need to see?** Students might mention animals that live in dark ocean depths, worms that live inside other animals' bodies, or insects that live underground.

Making Judgments

- **Do you think that jellyfish or corals would be good choices to include in a home aquarium? Why or why not?** Students may think that these animals would be interesting to keep in a home aquarium, but that they might be hard to feed. A large jellyfish might also eat other animals in the tank, such as pet fish, or sting people who reached into the tank.

Drawing Conclusions

- Some protists that can make their own food live inside reef-building corals. The corals depend on these protists for much of their food. **What benefit do you think the protists get from living in the corals?** Students might suggest that the corals, with their limestone structure, provide a safe habitat for the protists.

Meeting Individual Needs

Inclusion If possible, show students a natural sponge and let them feel its texture. Explain that this is the skeleton of the sponge. The living part of the sponge has dried up. Ask: **How does the sponge's skeleton differ from your skeleton?** Students may respond that the sponge's skeleton is like a mesh that makes up the whole body of the sponge. They may say that their own skeleton is made of separate bones and has soft parts around it.

Corals, Hydras, and Jellyfish

Corals may also look like plants, but they belong to another group of invertebrates. The animals in this group have soft, tubelike bodies with a single opening surrounded by armlike parts called tentacles. At night, corals feed by catching tiny animals in their tentacles.

Sea anemones (ə nem′ə nēz) and hydras also belong to this group. Sea anemones have tentacles that may look like the petals of a flower. But unlike flowers, sea anemones can move from place to place, gliding or tumbling along the ocean floor. Hydras are much smaller animals, with lengths of about 1 cm (0.4 in.). Like the larger animals in their group, hydras use their tentacles to trap food.

Jellyfish are part of the group that includes corals, sea anemones, and hydras. If you've ever gone to the seashore, you may have seen jellyfish floating in the water or washed up on the sand. As a jellyfish drifts through the ocean, it catches shrimp, fish, and other animals in its tentacles.

▲ Featherworm, a segmented worm that lives in the ocean

Worms of Different Shapes

Worms are tube-shaped invertebrates. They can be found in both land and water environments. Worms are classified into groups by their body designs.

Although they may not look as if they belong, corals are members of the animal kingdom. ▼

Jellyfish shoot tiny poison darts from their tentacles to paralyze or kill their prey. ▼

C28

Science & Writing

FEEDING THE STARS

What to Do Discuss with students how a starfish feeds on a clam. To open the tightly closed shell, the starfish attaches its tube feet to the two sides of the shell and begins to pull. The clam closes its shell even tighter. The starfish uses its tube feet in relays, and is able to outlast the clam. When the clam's muscles grow tired, it relaxes a little, opening its shell. The starfish then turns part of its own stomach inside out and pushes it through the narrow opening in the clamshell. Digestive juices start to digest the clam tissue. Have students write stories about a squeamish starfish who doesn't like to eat clams and has to find other food to eat.

What's the Result? Encourage students to share their stories.

▲ Flatworm

▲ Roundworms

Flatworms are a group of worms that have heads and tails, and flattened bodies. A tapeworm is a flatworm that can live inside the body of other animals—even humans!

Roundworms are another group of worms. As you might guess, these worms have rounded bodies. They live in damp places and can also live inside humans and other animals. Both flatworms and roundworms can make people and other animals sick.

Another worm group, called the segmented worms, includes leeches and earthworms. The observation of the earthworm in the activity on pages C24 and C25 shows that an earthworm's body is divided into segments, or sections. All earthworms and other worms in this group have bodies made up of segments.

The earthworm activity also shows that the earthworm prefers burrowing through moist soil. In such a dark, damp environment, the earthworm can move easily and can keep from drying out.

Starfish and Sea Urchins

A starfish is an odd-looking underwater animal. It belongs to a group of invertebrates that have many tiny tube feet. Animals in this group have body parts arranged around a central area. The starfish shown has five arms and no head! It's hard spiny covering helps to give the animal protection.

The sea urchin belongs to the same group as the starfish. A sea urchin's body is covered with long spines. Like a starfish, it moves around on tiny tube feet.

Using Math *A starfish, such as the one shown here, can move over the sea floor at a rate of 10 cm (4 in.) per second. How far is that in one minute?*

C29

Science, Technology & Society

STS

SOAK IT UP

What to Do Most sponges used in homes are synthetic, but some people use natural sponges. Natural sponges hold more water and last longer than synthetic sponges. However, a natural sponge may cost thirty dollars, while a synthetic sponge may cost thirty cents. To harvest natural sponges, divers cut them from the ocean floor. The sponges are hung to dry out and decay. Then the skeletons are cleaned and are ready to use.

What's the Result? Why do you think it's a good idea to invent and use synthetic materials to replace natural ones? Advantages for synthetic sponges: natural sponges would not have to be killed; synthetic sponges are cheaper. The disadvantages are that synthetic sponges don't work as well or last as long; and are not biodegradable.

Making Inferences

- Tell students that the beef tapeworm can be taken into the body when someone eats infected meat that is raw or rare. The tapeworm hooks itself inside the intestine and takes in the digested food that is there. A person with a tapeworm may eat well but soon become undernourished because much of the food goes to the tapeworm.
- **How could someone avoid being infected with a beef tapeworm?** Students may infer that a person can avoid being infected by not eating raw or rare meat.
- **How well do you think a starfish's skeleton protects it in the water?** Students may determine that the skeleton offers good protection because it seems rigid and would be difficult for a predator to feed on. Note that it also protects the organs that are inside the skeleton.

Thinking Critically

- **What are some ways that you could classify the worms described on these pages?** Students might suggest classifying the worms by their shape (flat, round, or segmented), or by where they live (in land, water, or animals' bodies).

Making Comparisons

- Explain to students that living tissue covers the hard skeleton of a live starfish. **Is this skeleton more like your skeleton or like an exoskeleton?** Students may think the starfish skeleton is like an exoskeleton because it consists of a large surface that protects internal organs. They may also think it is like a bony skeleton, because it is covered with soft tissue.
- **How is the body shape of a starfish like that of a sea anemone?** Students may say that both animals have a roundish body with parts radiating out.
- **Do any vertebrates have this type of starburst arrangement?** Guide students to see that the bodies of vertebrates are arranged with right and left halves, rather than a circular arrangement.

Math Hint *If a starfish can move 10 cm (4 in.) per second, it can move 10 cm/sec × 60 sec = 600 cm (150 in.) in one minute.*

Making Inferences

- **How do you think water pollution would affect sponges?** Students might suggest that water pollution would be a serious problem for sponges, since they take in their food from the water that flows through the holes in their bodies. Pollution could clog up the holes in the sponge or kill off the food in the water.

Making Comparisons

- **How are the shells of a clam, a snail, and a squid different?** The snail has a single coiled shell, the clam has two hinged shells, and the squid has a small, internal shell.
- **Although clams have a muscular "foot" that they can use to move from place to place, they do not go in search of food. Instead, they wait for food to come to them. A clam draws water into its shell and strains out food particles from the water. What other animals wait for food to come to them?** Students might mention sponges, corals, spiders, or roundworms.

Thinking Critically

- **How is a knight without his armor like an arthropod that has just molted?** Both have lost their protective covering. They would be in danger of being hurt until they are covered again.

Transparency 16: Visual/Spatial Activity
Use "Traits of Arthropods" to help students learn the characteristics of arthropods.

3. Assess Understanding

Students can work in groups of three or four. Have students pretend that they are in charge of setting up an exhibit of invertebrate animals. Part of their exhibit will be a terrarium for land animals, and the other part will be for animals that live in water. Have them draw a map of the exhibit, including labels for the animals they will include in each part. After each animal's name, they should also note what kind of environment the animal will live in.

Reading Focus Answer

Responses should include traits of any of the groups of invertebrates included in the resources—sponges; corals, sea anemones, hydras, and jellyfish; worms; starfish and sea urchins; mollusks; and arthropods.

Shells Outside or Inside

The mollusks make up another group of invertebrates. A mollusk has a soft body, a hard shell, a rough tongue, and a muscular foot. A snail is a mollusk with a single hard shell protecting its soft body. A clam has two shells joined together by a hinge.

Squids and octopuses also belong to this group. But their hard shells are small and *inside* their bodies.

Lobsters to Butterflies

Arthropods are a group of invertebrates with jointed legs and hard exoskeletons that protect the animals. There are nearly 1 million known kinds of arthropods!

As an arthropod grows, it **molts**, or sheds its old exoskeleton. Then the animal grows a new, larger exoskeleton that allows its body to continue growing. A lobster is an arthropod with a thick exoskeleton.

Insects make up the largest subgroup in the arthropod group and include the only invertebrates that can fly. Insects, such as ladybugs, have bodies divided into three parts, and six legs arranged in three pairs. Most insects have two pairs of wings.

Like other arthropods, spiders have jointed legs. But spiders are *not* insects. Spiders have eight legs—two more legs than insects. They also have jaws and fangs!

◀ An octopus is a mollusk.

C30

UNIT PROJECT LINK

Students might organize their plants according to where they grow, whether they have flowers or cones, or what kinds of leaves they have. They might organize their animals according to where they live, how they breathe, how they reproduce, or what kind of body covering they have. Encourage students to record information about their plants or animals on *Science Notebook,* TRB p. 38. Then have students use Unit Project Masters 4 and 5 (TRB p. 19–20) to develop their own systems of classification.

Technology Link
Have students visit **www.eduplace.com** to find names and addresses of agencies that can provide help with the Unit Project.

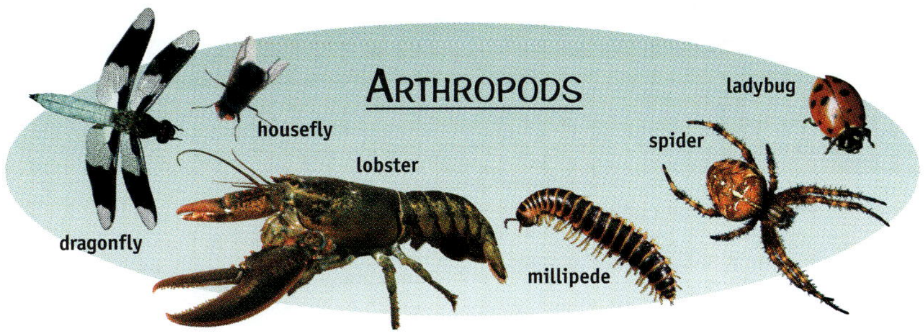

Centipedes and millipedes are also arthropods. But they are not insects either. Centipedes can have up to 175 pairs of legs. They can use their many legs to run from enemies.

Millipedes can have up to 240 pairs of legs! But unlike centipedes, they don't use their legs to run from enemies. Instead, millipedes roll up their bodies when they sense danger approaching.

As you can now see, some of the groups of invertebrates are very different indeed. A sponge is very different from an arthropod. And a worm is very different from a jellyfish. But there is one way in which they are all alike—they have no backbone. ■

▲ Arthropods can look very different from each other.

UNIT PROJECT LINK

Make a drawing (or use a camera to take photos) of plants or animals for your field guide. Think about ways you can classify the plants or animals. How might you organize the descriptions and pictures in your guide?

Technology Link
For more help with your Unit Project, go to **www.eduplace.com**.

INVESTIGATION 3 WRAP-UP

THINK IT WRITE IT

REVIEW

1. What are eight of the groups of invertebrates? Name one animal that belongs to each group.

2. Give the traits of two groups of invertebrates.

CRITICAL THINKING

3. How could you use a mirror on this page to show that a spider has symmetry—that one half matches the other?

4. Normally, clotting stops bleeding. Suppose you have cut your finger badly. Might leeches play a role in helping stop the bleeding? Explain your answer.

INVESTIGATION 3 Close the Investigation

THINK IT WRITE IT

INVESTIGATION WRAP-UP

REVIEW

1. The invertebrate groups include sponges, corals, sea anemones, hydras, jellyfish, flatworms, roundworms, segmented worms (leeches), starfish, sea urchins, mollusks (snails), and arthropods (insects and spiders).

2. Sponges—bodies full of holes and skeletons of spiky fibers; corals—soft bodies and tentacles; sea anemones—tentacles that look like flower petals; hydras—tentacles that trap food; flatworms—heads, tails, and flattened bodies; roundworms—round bodies, live in damp places; segmented worms—bodies divided into segments; starfish—tube feet and body parts around a central area; mollusks—soft bodies, hard shells, muscular foot; arthropods—jointed legs and hard exoskeletons

CRITICAL THINKING

3. Put the edge of a mirror on the photo of the spider so that the mirror reflects half of the spider's body and gives the illusion of a whole spider. ***(Evaluating, Solving Problems)***

4. No, leeches would not help to stop bleeding. When you have a cut, your blood will clot to prevent excessive bleeding. Chemicals in the saliva of leeches can prevent blood clots from forming. ***(Analyzing, Synthesizing, Evaluating, Solving Problems)***

CHALLENGE

Order a preserved invertebrate from a scientific supply company for students to examine. Encourage students to investigate external features to help classify the animal. Then let students examine its internal organs.

FOLLOWING UP

Baseline Assessment Review the list of students' responses from the beginning of the investigation, and allow them to change and add to it.

Reteaching With students, create a chart of the principal groups of invertebrates and their defining characteristics.

Science Processor Have students use the CD-ROM Spreadsheet to make their charts.

Use *Science Notebook,* TRB p. 39.

Assessment

Portfolio

Diagram Encourage students to work in groups to prepare a display of the invertebrates they have learned about. They could label each specimen with its name and its defining characteristics.

Investigation Review ▶
Use Investigation Review p. 95 in the *Teacher Resource Book.*

Investigation Review

INVESTIGATION 3 CHAPTER 1

Circle the word or words that complete each sentence.

1. (Sponges, Corals) look like plants but are actually animals with soft, tubelike bodies.

2. As an arthropod grows, it molts or sheds its (exoskeleton, wings).

3. A jellyfish catches food with its (muscular foot, tentacles).

4. Complete the diagram about the traits of arthropods by listing some defining characteristics of each subgroup.

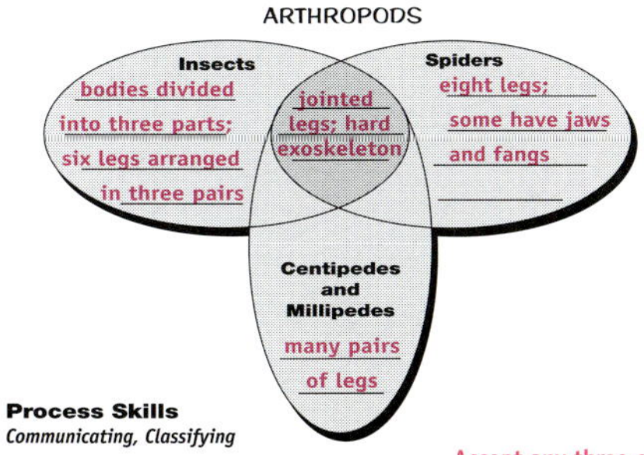

Process Skills
Communicating, Classifying

Name three different groups of invertebrates. List one trait that only that group has. Accept any three of the following groups—sponges, the coral and jellyfish group, worms, the starfish and sea urchins group, mollusks, or arthropods. Students should list an accurate characteristic for each invertebrate group chosen.

Start the Investigation

INVESTIGATION 4: How Are Plants Classified?

pages C32–C38

Planner

Subconcept Plants can be classified by whether or not they reproduce through seeds. Seed plants are classified further by whether they produce flowers or cones.

Objectives

- **Collect, record,** and **interpret** data about a variety of plants.
- **Identify** distinguishing characteristics of plants.

Pacing 3 class periods

Science Terms nonseed plants, seed plants, mosses, liverworts, ferns, horsetails, conifers, monocot, dicot

Activate Prior Knowledge

Baseline Assessment Students can draw pictures of plants they see and label them with any information they know. Save the drawings for Following Up.

INVESTIGATION 4: How Are Plants Classified?

From an airplane high in the sky, a forest looks like just a sea of green. But up close, you can see that the forest is made up of many different plants. How are all these different plants classified?

Activity
Looking at Leaves

What traits can you use to classify plants? In this activity you'll classify plants according to their leaves.

MATERIALS
- gloves
- 5 sheets of paper
- pencil
- 5 sealable plastic bags
- "Leaf Characteristics and Classification" table
- *Science Notebook*

SAFETY
Wear plastic gloves and clothing that covers your arms and legs.

Procedure

1. With your teacher's permission, go outdoors with a partner to observe the variety of plants.
2. Look at the trees, shrubs, flowering plants, and nonflowering plants. Choose five very different plants to examine closely. Observe the whole plant.
3. On a separate sheet of paper, draw each plant and one of its leaves. Place the drawings for each plant in a separate plastic bag. Label the bags 1–5.

C32

Activity: Looking at Leaves

Preview *Students will examine different types of leaves in order to classify a variety of plants.*

Advance Preparation *See p. C4b.*

1. Get Ready

GROUPS OF 2–3 | **45 MINUTES**

Key Science Process Skills observe, describe, classify, infer, collect and interpret data

Meeting Individual Needs

EARLY FINISHERS

Invite students to make leaf rubbings. Have them place individual leaves on a flat surface, and cover each leaf with white paper. Demonstrate how to rub a crayon or pastel stick over the paper. Leaf rubbings should be dark enough for students to see the direction that the veins run on the leaves. Have students identify and label the different parts of each leaf and classify them according to their plant type.

KINESTHETIC

4. Carefully remove a small sample of leaves from each plant. Place each sample in the bag with its drawings. Seal each bag. Take your samples back to class.

5. **Observe** the leaves on the plants you chose. Are the leaves needlelike or are they broad leaves that drop in autumn? Are their veins branched or do they run side by side down the length of the leaf? In your *Science Notebook*, make a chart like the one shown. **Record** your observations in the chart. Write each plant's name if you know it.

Classifying Leaves		
Bag	Leaf Characteristics	Group Name
1		

See SCIENCE and MATH TOOLBOX page H10 if you need to review **Making a Chart to Organize Data**.

Analyze and Conclude

1. Look at the information in the "Leaf Characteristics and Classification" table. Use the table to **classify** each plant you chose as one of the major plant groups. **Record** your classification in your chart.

2. **Compare** your conclusions with those of other groups. **Discuss** any differences in the way the plants were classified.

3. Which plant group is most common? Are there any plant groups you did not find examples of? If so, **infer** why.

INVESTIGATE FURTHER!

RESEARCH

Use field guides to plants that are written for your region of the country. Try to identify the names of the plants you classified in the activity.

C33

INVESTIGATE FURTHER!

RESEARCH

Obtain field guides to plants for your region from the school or local library. Help students learn how to use field guides as they identify the leaves they have collected. When students locate their plants in the field guides and identify their names, they can draw pictures of and write descriptions about each plant. These pictures and descriptions can be compiled to create a class field guide for your region. Students can write their descriptions and draw their pictures on *Science Notebook*, TRB, p. 41.

Collaborative Strategy If possible, have different groups of students examine plants in different areas of the school grounds or neighborhood. Groups can share their information.

Materials Hints Use Activity Support Masters C1 and C2 (TRB pp. 14–15).

Safety Be aware of any student allergies to plants. Be certain to obtain permission for gathering leaves on private property.

2. Guide the Procedure

- Try to have students finish the activity on the same day as they collect their leaves, so the leaves can be classified before they dry out.
- **Which leaves would provide the best shade on a hot summer day? Explain your answer.** The broad leaves would provide the best shade, because when several of them are bunched together they form an "umbrella" that protects people from the sun.

Have students record their observations and answer questions on *Science Notebook,* TRB, pp. 40–41.

Science Processor You may wish to have students use the CD-ROM Spreadsheet to record their observations.

3. Assess Performance

Process Skills Checklist

- Were students able to **infer** why they could not find examples of some types of plants? Were they specific in describing the plants they did not find?
- Did students **collect** and **record data** correctly?
- Were students able to **classify** their leaves?

Analyze and Conclude

1. Students should be able to find a classification category for each leaf. Answers will vary with the leaves a group collects.
2. When comparing conclusions with the other groups, each student should be able to provide reasons for their classification of each leaf.
3. The most common plant group will depend upon the climate of the region in which you are located. Your climate may be too warm for some plants to survive, or too cool for others. Some plants thrive with a lot of rain, while others need very little. Accept other reasonable answers.

RESOURCE

Plants to the Rescue

Reading Focus Have students ***use the graphic*** (chart and pictures) to answer the Reading Focus question.

1. Get Ready

Background

- One of the earliest recorded uses of plants for medicine is by ancient Greek physician Diodcorides. In the first century A.D. he produced a book of herbal treatments for a variety of illnesses. Herbal treatments were the only source of drugs available until the 1800s.

Discussion Starter

- **What are some uses that humans have for plants?** Food, clothing, shelter, and medicines.
- **If you found a plant that could cure any illness, what illness would you want to cure, and why?** Encourage students to give reasons for their responses. **What would you do to ensure there was always a supply of the plant?** Responses might refer to setting up nature preserves in areas where the plant grows.

2. Guide the Discussion

Making Inferences

- **How do you think pollution will affect our ability to find new plants to treat illnesses?** Many species of plants may die because of air pollution and water pollution. If these plants die, we will never be able to use them in treating illnesses.

3. Assess Understanding

Have students ask their parents if there are any plants that they use (including vegetables) to improve their health. Students can then discuss these plants as a class.

Reading Focus Answer

Many medical illnesses are treated using plants, such as ginkgo for Alzheimer's, digitalis for heart disease, and Pacific yew for cancer.

RESOURCE

Plants to the Rescue

Reading Focus What are some ways that plants can be useful in the field of medicine?

STS SCIENCE TECHNOLOGY & SOCIETY

Who usually answers a call for help? It might be a fire department or police department. It might be a paramedic or lifeguard. Would you ever expect it to be a plant?

You probably already know some ways that plants are used to help people. For example, plants are used to make clothing and shelter. And without plants, there would be no food. But did you know that plants are the source of most medicine?

Today, scientists search the world over for more plants used as medicine. The discovery of new medicines from plants is a costly business. But the business of healing is very important.

PLANTS USED FOR HEALING

GINKGO The leaves of the ginkgo tree are thought to help in treating Alzheimer's (ôlts′hī mərz) disease. This disease affects the way brain cells function. Ginkgo leaves are also believed to help relieve hearing loss, headaches, and asthma.

GINGER The root of this plant was used as long ago as the 16th century to settle upset stomachs. It has also been used for colds and flu.

PACIFIC YEW In the 1960s, scientists found a cancer-killing drug in the bark of the Pacific yew tree.

CHILIES Scientists have found that these peppers send signals to the brain to kill pain. Today a cream made from chilies is used to "rub out" pain.

GARLIC Garlic is used to help keep the heart and the blood vessels working properly. Except for medicines prescribed by doctors, garlic has become one of Europe's fastest-selling "medicines" for this purpose.

FOXGLOVE The medicine digitalis, from the foxglove plant, is used to stimulate the heart.

C34

Science & Writing

LEAF PICTIONARY

What You Need a variety of leaves, paper, colored pencils

What to Do Ask students to examine the leaves, taking note of their size (small, large), shape (oval, round, long and thin), and their edges (wavy, smooth, toothed). Ask students to identify at least four characteristics of each leaf. Then they can make a picture dictionary that explains each of the terms they used to describe the leaves.

What's the Result? Students will have a selection of adjectives they can use to describe plants. Encourage students to share their pictionaries and add entries to their own based on what they see on other's pictionaries.

RESOURCE

All Kinds of Plants

Reading Focus What traits are used to classify the members of the plant kingdom?

All plants are members of the plant kingdom. The family tree of the plant kingdom on this page shows that all plants are related. But in the activity on pages C32 and C33, different types of plants are shown to have different traits. Scientists use such differences to classify plants. For example, they divide the plant kingdom into two major groups: nonseed plants and seed plants. **Nonseed plants** do not reproduce with seeds. This group includes mosses and ferns. **Seed plants** do reproduce with seeds. This group includes plants that have flowers or cones.

Mosses and Liverworts

If you walk through a forest, you may notice a spongy carpet underfoot. This carpet is formed of mosses. **Mosses** are small nonseed plants that lack true roots, stems, and leaves.

Like other nonseed plants, mosses can reproduce by means of spores. Spores are one-celled structures that grow into new plants. Mosses also have male and female parts used in reproducing.

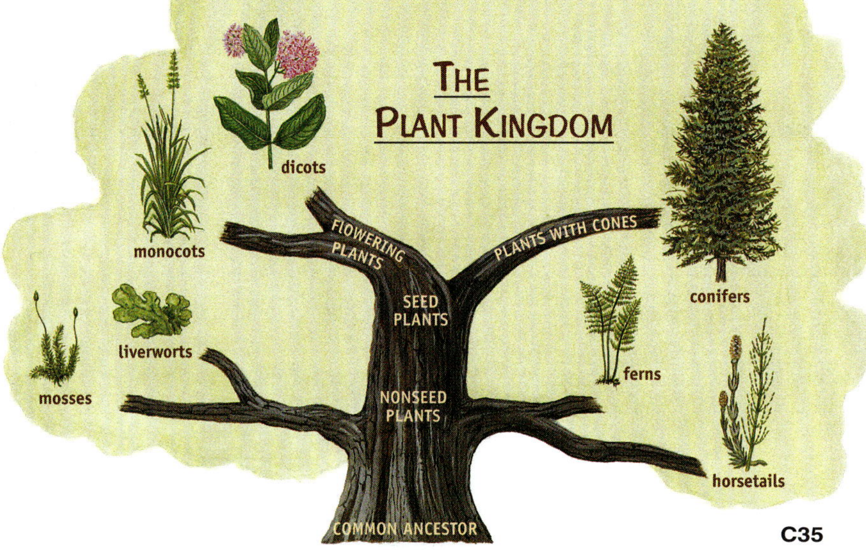

C35

Integrating the Sciences

EARTH SCIENCE

What You Need research materials about climate and the plant life suited to particular climates

What to Do Ask students to do research on one of the major climate regions of the Earth (tropical humid, dry, subtropical, temperate, boreal, polar, and highland). For the climate they choose, students should study one or two plants suited to live in that climate, focusing on the adaptations the plant has made to survive.

What's the Result? Students can present a two-minute "Plant and Climate" segment for a nature television show.

RESOURCE

All Kinds of Plants

Reading Focus Tell students they can answer the Reading Focus question if they read the first paragraph, noting the main idea and important terms, and ***study the graphic*** on page C35.

1. Get Ready

Vocabulary

Science Terms nonseed plants, seed plants, mosses, liverworts, ferns, horsetails, conifers, monocot, dicot

Support Terms traits, classify, spores, reproduce, fronds, cones, parallel

Background

- Why do some leaves change color in the fall? Leaves get their green appearance from a chemical called chlorophyll. Chlorophyll inside a plant absorbs red, blue, and violet light, and reflects green light. In the fall, the chlorophyll gets less sunlight, so the other pigments within the plant become dominant.

Discussion Starter

- Imagine you are walking through a dense forest. **How do you think that forest, containing many different types of plants, formed?** Students may respond that the forest began with just a few of each type of plant, but the plants reproduced enough over hundreds of years to form the forest.

2. Guide the Discussion

Choose from the following strategies to facilitate discussion.

Connecting to the Activities

- ***Looking at Leaves, pp. C32–C33***
- **In *Looking at Leaves*, you classified different types of leaves based on their physical characteristics. Can you tell which of those leaves come from seed plants? Which come from nonseed plants?** Answers will vary depending upon the climate of your region. Generally speaking, students probably examined both seed and nonseed plants.

Making Comparisons

- **How are ferns and horsetails alike? How are they different?** They are alike because they are both spore-forming plants that have underground stems. They are different because ferns have leaves called fronds, and horsetails do not have leaves.

Making Inferences

- **Where do you think ferns will grow the best? Explain your answer.** Ferns grow the best in a temperate climate that is very moist. A climate that is too hot will prevent ferns from getting enough water. Since ferns have tubes that carry water from the roots to the other parts of the plant, a climate that is too cool might cause the tubes to freeze.

Identifying and Solving Problems

- **If you had a conifer growing in one area of your yard at home, and you wanted another conifer to grow somewhere else in the yard, what would you do to make this happen?** Students may respond that they would pick up some of the cones when they fell off of the plant, and move them to the area in which they wanted the new plant to grow.

Meeting Individual Needs

For Extra Help Have each student create a word web that shows the different types of plants (mosses, ferns, horsetails, liverworts, conifers, monocots, and dicots) and provides a description for each one.

▲ Mosses produce spores at the tips of tall leafless stalks.

▲ The liverwort *Marchantia* produces spores on stalks with umbrella-shaped tops.

Mosses don't have special structures for carrying water. Because mosses lack such structures, water must move from cell to cell throughout the plant. This explains why mosses are small plants that are found growing only in moist places.

Liverworts are nonseed plants that lack true roots, stems, and leaves. Liverworts grow in moist places, such as along the banks of streams.

Ferns and Horsetails

Ferns are spore-forming plants that have roots, stems, and leaves. Before the dinosaurs lived, giant ferns covered much of Earth. Today, there are still many kinds of ferns. But they are not so common. They grow in very moist places that are not too hot or cold.

Like mosses, ferns reproduce by spores. They also have male and female parts used in reproducing.

Unlike mosses, ferns have special tubes that carry water from the roots to other parts of the plant. The roots of ferns anchor the plant in soil and carry water to scaly underground stems.

The most obvious parts of ferns are their leaves, called fronds. Some fern fronds appear to be made of many smaller leaves attached to a central stem. Actually, all of these smaller leaflike parts form one large fern frond. Spore cases are often produced on the undersides of the fronds. Spore cases contain spores.

Horsetails look more like paintbrushes than the tails of horses. About 30 species of horsetails live in marshes and swamps around the world. Like ferns, horsetails reproduce by spores and have underground stems.

Horsetails, nonseed plants ▶

Each spot on the underside of a fern frond is a cluster of spore cases. ▶

C36

Science Around the World

MAKING A MAP

What to Do Suggest students use the Internet and encyclopedias to research the origins of several common foods. They may research yams, corn (maize), peanuts, rice, tapioca, tomatoes, or a food of their choosing. Challenge them to find out where the food originated and how it traveled from that location to others around the world.

What's the Result? Students can plot their information on a world map and use the map to identify trade routes. Have them use the information to create "packing lists" for ships trading in the seventeenth and eighteenth centuries.

Using Math

Suppose this ponderosa pine cone has 76 scales. Each pine cone can release 2 seeds per scale. About how many seeds could be released from this cone?

Conifers

Many plants, such as firs, produce seeds in cones. Cone-bearing plants are called **conifers** (kän′ə fərz). Like ferns, conifers have roots, stems, and leaves. However, conifers differ from ferns in the way they reproduce. Conifers reproduce by forming seeds. The seeds are located between the scales of protective cones.

Conifers may be small shrubs or tall trees. Huge forests of conifers cover much of the northern part of the world. Unlike other kinds of trees, most conifers keep their leaves in autumn. Many conifers, such as pines, spruces, and firs, have needlelike leaves. Others, such as cedar trees, have leaves that look like overlapping scales.

Science in Literature

Eyewitness Living Earth
by Miranda Smith
DK Publishing, 1996

Leaf Talk

"Leaves are so varied that botanists had to invent a whole new language to describe their shapes. . . . A plant living on the gloomy floor of a rain forest may need large leaves to catch enough sunlight. However, a plant growing on a mountaintop has plenty of light, but is battered by winds, and needs small, strong leaves to survive."

These words come from *Eyewitness Living Earth* by Miranda Smith. This book will amaze you with facts about all kinds of living things.

C37

Science & the Arts

MAKING A MODEL

What You Need green clay, construction paper, tools for working with clay.

What to Do Students can work in groups to create a model of a type of plant they studied. Each group should choose a different type of plant to model. Students should attempt to make their models as true-to-life as possible.

What's the Result? A written description should accompany each model. Each group can give a brief presentation explaining their model to the rest of the class and comparing their model plant to the real plant.

Making Inferences

- **How do you know when a flowering plant is a monocot or a dicot?** It is a monocot if it has leaves with parallel veins. A dicot has netted veins that form a branching pattern.
- **In what ways are flowering plants important to people?** People eat fruits and vegetables from flowering plants, and use them for medicine and for shelter.

Using Math

Assist students in calculating the total number of seeds released from the cone (2 × 76 = 152 seeds).

Meeting Individual Needs

Students Acquiring English Students can work in pairs. While one student keeps his or her eyes closed, a second student examines some cones and tries to find the seeds that are protected by the scales of the cone. The second student describes for the first student what he or she learns by examining the cones.

Science in Literature

Eyewitness Living Earth
by Miranda Smith

Provide time for students to examine the illustrations of plants and animals in *Eyewitness Living Earth*. Then have them share their observations about structures in these living things that enable them to survive in their environment.

3. Assess Understanding

Ask students to work with a partner to create a poster showing an example of each different type of plant. Each plant should be correctly labeled. Partners can share their posters with their classmates.

Reading Focus Answer

Responses might include that plants are classified by how they reproduce; whether or not they have true roots, stems, and leaves; whether they have flowers or cones; and by their leaves.

Investigation 4 Close the Investigation

INVESTIGATION WRAP-UP

REVIEW

1. Seed plants and nonseed plants are the two main groups of plants.

2. The two main groups of seed plants are flowering plants (lima beans) and conifers (pine trees).

CRITICAL THINKING

3. Monocots and dicots are alike because they are both flowering plants. They have roots, stems, and leaves. They reproduce through seeds that are protected by a fruit. They are different in that monocot seeds are in one piece, and dicot seeds are in two pieces. The leaves of monocots have parallel veins, and the leaves of dicots have netted veins. ***(Analyzing, Synthesizing, Evaluating, Applying, Solving Problems)***

4. This shrub would be a conifer. A conifer does not lose its needlelike leaves. ***(Analyzing, Synthesizing, Evaluating, Applying, Solving Problems)***

CHALLENGE

Bring in a variety of leaves, without telling students where they came from. Have students work in small groups to classify all of the leaves according to their type of plant.

FOLLOWING UP

Baseline Assessment Return to the drawings students made of the plants they find in their neighborhoods. Ask them to use a different color ink from their original to label each plant correctly, based on their new knowledge of plants.

Reteaching Ask students to make flash cards about each type of plant. One side should state the type of plant, and the other side of the card should state some of its general characteristics. Students can use these flash cards to quiz each other.

Use *Science Notebook*, TRB p. 42.

▲ The leaf of a hosta plant, a monocot, has parallel veins.

▲ The leaf of a cyclamen plant, a dicot, has netted veins.

Flowering Plants

Most of the plants familiar to you are flowering plants. Flowering plants are plants that have roots, stems, and leaves. These plants reproduce by seeds formed in flowers. As the seeds are formed, a fruit develops to cover and protect them.

A flowering plant may be classified as a monocot (män′ō kät) or as a dicot (dī′ kät). A **monocot** is a flowering plant that produces seeds that are in one piece. The seed stores food for the developing plant. Corn plants are examples of monocots. Each kernel is a seed. A **dicot** is a flowering plant that produces seeds that have two sections. A lima bean plant is an example of a dicot.

One way to tell if a plant is a monocot or a dicot is to look at its leaves. The leaf of a mature monocot has veins that are parallel (par′ə lel). Parallel veins run side by side down the length of the leaf. The leaf of a mature dicot has netted veins. Netted veins form a branching pattern. You can see the two kinds of vein patterns in the pictures on this page.

Flowering plants are important. If you eat an orange or a carrot, you've eaten part of a flowering plant. On a summer day, you might cool off in the shade of a flowering plant, such as a maple tree. You might sit on a chair made of cherry wood. When you're sick, you might even take medicine made from flowering plants! ■

INVESTIGATION 4 WRAP-UP

REVIEW

1. What are the two main groups of plants?

2. Name the two main groups of seed plants. Give one example from each group.

CRITICAL THINKING

3. How are monocots and dicots alike and different?

4. In late autumn, you find a shrub that has no flowers. Its leaves are needlelike and green. How would you classify this plant? Explain your answer.

C38

Assessment

Investigation Review

Use the words in the box to complete each sentence.

mosses conifers ferns dicot

1. Small nonseed plants that lack true roots, stems, and leaves are called mosses.

2. Before the dinosaurs lived, giant ferns covered much of Earth.

3. Huge forests of conifers cover much of the northern part of the world today.

4. A lima bean plant is an example of a dicot.

Draw a line to match each of the plants with its trait.

5. conifer — dicot
6. fern — nonseed plants
7. corn — monocot
8. lima bean — plants with cones

Processing Skills
Communicating, Classifying

List three traits of mosses. List one way in which mosses differ from ferns.

Three traits are as follows: mosses are nonseed plants; mosses lack true roots, stems, and leaves; mosses grow only in moist places. Mosses differ from ferns in that they do not have roots, stems, or leaves.

Performance

Newscast Ask students to imagine a situation where several acres of land have been destroyed by a forest fire. Small groups should act out a television newscast in which a botanist is interviewed to describe the types of plants that were lost in the fire.

◀ Investigation Review

Use Investigation Review p. 96 in the *Teacher Resource Book.*

Coming Up

Dog trainer Ellen Torop's student learns to take a telephone to a disabled person.

C41

Chapter Road Map

INVESTIGATION 1 What Are the Basic Needs of Living Things?

Activities
- * Needs in Common

Resources
- * The ABCs of Survival
- The African Savanna

INVESTIGATION 2 How Do Living Things Meet Their Needs?

Activities
- * Feather Feats
- * Tap, Tap, Tap

Resources
- * The Survival Game
- * Is It Ever Too Late?

* Pressed for Time?

If you are pressed for time, focus on the Activities and Resources identified by this clock.

Home-School Connection

Distribute the Explore at Home Activity "Animal Detectives" (Teacher Resource Book, page 4) to students after they have completed the chapter.

Technology Link

CD-ROM

Science Processor ***Animals***

To enhance or replace Investigations 1 and 2, use **It's Alive** and **Feed Me!**

It's Alive sends students on a wildlife expedition to a South American rain forest. They examine and write about differences between plants and animals, using the Plants and Animals Data Packs for more information.

In **Feed Me!** students become entomologists in Florida. They click on insects to see how their body parts are used to eat. Finally students view a video about mammals and how they obtain their food.

Correlation to AIMS

If you use AIMS Activities, you may wish to use the activity Fishing for Clues on pages 26–31 in the *Field Detectives* book to further explore the basic needs of living things.

Investigation 1 Start the Investigation

What Are the Basic Needs of Living Things?

pages C42–C49

Planner

Subconcept All animals share the need for food, water, and shelter, as well as the need to maintain body temperature within certain ranges.

Objectives

- **Identify** the needs of animals.
- **Describe** how some animals meet their needs.

Pacing 2–3 class periods

Science Terms environment, savanna

Activate Prior Knowledge

Baseline Assessment Ask: **What are some animals that live nearby and what are their needs?** Students may identify many kinds of animals, including insects, fish, reptiles, amphibians, birds, and mammals. Save students' responses for use in Following Up.

Investigation 1 What Are the Basic Needs of Living Things?

Have you ever seen a duck put its head and neck underwater? The duck is looking for food. Food is one thing that all animals need. Find out in Investigation 1 about some other needs animals have in common.

Activity Needs in Common

MATERIALS
- *Science Notebook*

Scientists are trained to make careful observations. In this activity, see what you can find out about the needs of animals through careful observation.

Procedure

1. In your *Science Notebook*, **make a chart** like the one shown. **Identify** the animals pictured on pages C42 and C43. In your chart, **record** the names of the animals.

Animal	Need

See SCIENCE and MATH TOOLBOX *page H10 if you need to review* ***Making a Chart to Organize Data.***

C42

Activity Needs in Common

Preview *Students focus on the needs of animals and identify those needs.*

1. Get Ready

GROUPS OF 4–5 **30 MINUTES**

Key Science Process Skills collect and record data, infer, predict

Multi-Age Strategy Encourage students to use experiences with pets to infer and discuss the animals' needs from the photos.

Meeting Individual Needs

STUDENTS ACQUIRING ENGLISH

Ask students to describe what they see in the pictures. Elicit key words, such as *food*, *water*, and *shelter*, that relate to the needs of the animals shown. On the chalkboard, record in English the names of the animals shown in one list and the key words in another. Then help students use the words to complete the charts they made.

LINGUISTIC

2. **Infer** what need each animal is trying to meet. Then **record** your inference in your chart.

Analyze and Conclude

1. How many different needs did you identify? Do some needs seem more important than others? Explain your answer.
2. Do all animals seem to share the same basic needs? **Predict** how the other basic needs of each animal shown might be met.
3. **Compare** your predictions with those of other group members. Explain each prediction you made.

C43

Meeting Individual Needs

EARLY FINISHERS

Have students look at the photos shown. Ask them how people might meet those same needs. Have students make drawings of how people meet the same needs, and then have them label the needs being met.

VISUAL/SPATIAL

2. Guide the Procedure

- Students can expand on the activity by bringing in photos of pets, animals at zoos, or other animals. Add these photos to the ones in the text for use in the activity.
- If you can see any animals from your classroom windows, encourage students to observe their behavior. **How are these animals meeting their needs? Are any birds looking for food or building shelters? Are squirrels gathering food?**

Have students make and complete their charts on *Science Notebook,* TRB, pp. 47–48.

Science Processor You may wish to have students use the CD-ROM Spreadsheet to organize and display their data.

3. Assess Performance

Process Skills Checklist

- Did students **observe** pictures of animals and infer the needs that the animals are trying to meet? Did students list things that the animals truly need to survive?
- Did students **communicate** the needs of the animals in the form of a chart? Were students' charts complete and well organized?
- Did students **predict** how or where each animal meets its needs? Were their predictions reasonable?

Analyze and Conclude

1. Students should infer from the pictures that animals need food, water, and shelter. Students should conclude that all needs are equally important because an animal could not live without any of them.
2. Students' predictions will vary but should show an understanding of the basic needs all animals share. For example, students might suggest that the lions in the photo get food by eating other animals and seek shelter under trees or in caves.
3. Students' responses will depend upon their predictions. Accept all reasonable comparisons.

RESOURCE

The ABCs of Survival

Reading Focus Tell students as they read to look for a paragraph that ***summarizes*** the information in the resource and also answers the Reading Focus question. Recall that summaries are usually at the end of a discussion.

1. Get Ready

Vocabulary

Science Term environment

Support Terms survive, energy

Background

- A basic need of animals is to maintain a body temperature within a certain range. The body temperature of most animals (insects, fish, reptiles, and amphibians) is determined by the temperature of the environment in which they live.
- Endotherms are animals that maintain a constant body temperature. This group is made up of birds and mammals, including people. Most endotherms depend on their body fat to conserve heat. For instance, aquatic mammals, such as seals, porpoises, and whales, have a thick layer of blubber. Fur and feathers are important for insulation, too. In cold weather, birds fluff up their feathers to trap body heat, keeping it against their bodies.

Discussion Starter

- **What wild animals have you seen recently? What were the animals doing? Were they meeting their needs? What were those needs?** Encourage students to think of occasions when they have seen wild animals such as insects, fish, amphibians (toads, frogs, and salamanders), reptiles (snakes and turtles), mammals (mice, squirrels, deer), and birds (sparrows, pigeons, gulls, hawks). Discussion should center on the animals' needs for food, water, shelter, and a suitable environment in which to live.

Caption Answer: Hippopotamuses eat plants.

RESOURCE

The ABCs of Survival

Reading Focus What basic needs of living things can the environment provide?

If you had to take care of a pet dog, cat, and bird, how would you remember what each one needs? It wouldn't be very difficult. All three animals share a basic need for food and water.

Animals in the wild need food and water, too. What other basic needs do animals share? The activity found on pages C42 and C43 shows how some animals' needs are being met. Besides food and water, animals also need shelter to survive.

All animals need a suitable environment (en vī′rən mənt). An animal's **environment** is everything, both living and nonliving, that surrounds and affects the animal. To survive in its environment, an animal needs to keep

A hippopotamus spends much of its time in water. What does a hippopotamus eat? ▼

C44

Science Around the World

ARCTIC LIFE

What to Do Despite the harsh conditions, several cultures have adapted to living in the Arctic. Encourage students to work in groups to find out about some of these cultures, such as the Canadian Inuits. What skills and practices have these peoples developed for meeting their needs for food, water, warmth, and shelter?

What's the Result? Suggest that students work together to describe the ways that traditional Arctic peoples used plant and animal materials to construct dwellings and make clothing and weapons.

Multi-Age Classroom Students who enjoy conducting research, or who are knowledgeable in using a variety of reference books, might help other students to find out about Arctic cultures.

▲ The food of a killer whale includes penguins, walruses, and fish such as salmon, cod, and herring.

▲ A leopard takes its meal high up into a tree, where other animals cannot easily get at its food.

its body temperature within a certain range. This range varies, depending on the type of animal. In an environment that is suitable for an animal, that animal can meet all of its basic needs.

First, Some Food

All animals need food to grow, stay healthy, and survive. A mole dies after only a few hours without food! Other animals can wait an entire day for their next meal. Some animals, like snakes, can go for weeks without a meal.

Different animals eat different kinds of food. In the spring and summer, a rabbit feasts on plants such as dandelions and chickweed. But in the winter it settles for bark, roots, and dry leaves. A hippopotamus wanders out of the water to enjoy a meal of grass. A killer whale fills its stomach with fish, squid, sea birds, and even seals. Look at the photo caption to find out more about the foods a killer whale eats. A leopard hunts and kills other animals and then eats them while high up in the trees.

▼ A mole eats mainly worms and insects.

Integrating the Sciences

PHYSICAL SCIENCE

What to Do Students can work in groups to find out how fur and fat help prevent an animal from losing body heat. Students should half-fill three small cans with warm water and place them in each of three larger cans. In one set of cans, fill the space between the small and large cans with cotton to represent fur. In the second set of cans, fill the space with vegetable oil to represent body fat. Leave the space in the third set of cans empty. Cover the three setups of cans with foil and place a thermometer in each small can through the foil cover. Record the temperature of each setup at regular intervals.

What's the Result? The cans with the cotton and oil should keep the heat in longer than the can without any insulation.

- **What kinds of needs do pets have? Are they the same as those of wild animals?** Lead students to recognize that pets have needs similar to those of wild animals, although the amounts and characteristics of those needs may vary.

2. Guide the Discussion

Choose from the following strategies to facilitate discussion.

Connecting to the Activities

- ***Needs in Common, pp. C42–C43***
- **Think about the chart you made in the activity. How do the needs of animals you listed compare to those shown in the pictures?** Students should conclude that the needs of all animals are basically the same.

Drawing Conclusions

- **How do you take care of a pet?** Lead students to conclude that they help their pets meet their basic needs by providing them with food, water, and shelter. For example, students keep pets inside on cold days to help them maintain an appropriate body temperature.

Making Judgments

- **What is a suitable environment for a polar bear? A monkey?** Students should recognize that a monkey and a polar bear require different environments in which to meet their needs. For example, a polar bear requires a cold environment near the ocean, whereas most monkeys need a warm, forest environment.

Making Comparisons

- **What do people need to survive?** Students should realize that people have the same basic needs as animals.
- **How do people in different parts of the world meet these needs?** The way people meet their needs depends on many factors, such as traditions and local factors of weather, climate, geography, and available materials. Discuss the differences in foods, sources of water, and types of shelter. Encourage students to relate personal experiences regarding ethnic foods and other cultural differences that make each culture interesting and unique. Bring the discussion back to the common needs. Use the Activity Support Master "Venn Diagram" (TRB p. 10).

Making Inferences

- **What happens to animals when their needs are not met?** Animals react in a variety of ways. If food or water is scarce, animals continue to look for it. Availability of food and water can affect an animal's ability to survive in its environment. Animals that do not satisfy their needs may become sick or die, often because they are so weakened that predators can successfully attack.
- **A koala doesn't drink. Does this mean it does not need water?** No. Students should infer that some animals get the water they need by eating certain foods. The foods contain enough water for the koala to survive.

Meeting Individual Needs

Students Acquiring English Use the discussion described under Making Comparisons above to promote an environment for students to relate personal experiences describing how people in different cultures meet their needs. Compare cultures to find similarities.

Using Math *Remind students that a year has 365 days. A koala eats about 1 kg/day × 365 day = 365 kg (2.2 lb/day × 365 day = 803 lb) of leaves in a year.*

Some Water, Please

Plants and animals need more than just food to survive. They also need water. Many animals drink water every day from water holes, ponds, lakes, rivers, and streams. A budgerigar (buj'ər i gär), an Australian parakeet, can go a long time without taking a drink. But when it's time for that drink, the bird will probably flock together with tens of thousands of other budgerigars at one water hole.

A few animals hardly ever, or even never, drink! A kangaroo rat rarely drinks. It gets its water from the seeds and cactus pulp that it eats. An Australian koala never needs to drink. It gets the water it needs by eating eucalyptus (yo͞o kə lip'təs) leaves.

Using Math *This koala is eating leaves. A koala eats about 1 kg (2.2 lb) of leaves each day. Estimate how much it eats in one year.*

▲ A flock of budgerigars visit a water hole to drink.

▲ Plants, such as these mangroves, need water to survive.

C46

Science, Technology & Society

A ZOO HABITAT

What to Do Zoos and aquariums show animals in their natural habitats. Scientists work with technicians to design and develop exhibits that meet an animal's needs. Students can use reference books to find out about a zoo animal's needs and then design and construct a habitat that meets those needs.

What's the Result? Invite students to prepare oral presentations in which they explain and show their habitats to the class. Have students compare their model design to that of a real zoo habitat.

Multi-Age Classroom Have students work together to arrange their habitats into a zoo. Suggest that they draw a map showing the location of each habitat in the zoo.

Step 3

2. Work with group members to **identify** the central shaft and the barbs on your feather. Use the picture on page C50 for help. Gently pull some of the barbs apart. **Record** your observations.

3. Pull the feather through your fingers as shown. **Observe** and **record** what happens.

4. Repeat steps 1 and 3, but this time examine a down feather.

5. Wave the tail or wing feather through the air. Then do the same with the down feather. **Observe** how the two types of feathers push the air around them. **Record** your observations.

Analyze and Conclude

1. **Compare** the two types of feathers. In what ways are they alike? What differences did you observe?

2. **Infer** which type of feather would help a bird fly. **Infer** which type of feather would help a bird keep warm. Discuss your inferences with other members of your group. Explain your thinking.

▲ Down feather

INVESTIGATE FURTHER!

EXPERIMENT

Make a plan to find out about body coverings other than feathers. With your teacher's help, collect samples of different body coverings. Then use a microscope to examine them. Make a drawing of each type of body covering. List questions about what you observe under the microscope.

C51

INVESTIGATE FURTHER!

EXPERIMENT

Students should find that body coverings other than feathers include fur, hair, moist smooth skin, scales, and spines. Some animals have soft bodies that are covered with shells or outer skeletons. Body coverings serve as protection from the physical environment and potential predators. Encourage students to record their findings on *Science Notebook,* TRB, p. 52 and share their reports with classmates.

Note: The U.S. Fish and Wildlife Service regulates the collection, possession, sale, or barter of feathers, eggs, or nests of migratory birds. Possession or collection without a permit is illegal.

Safety Review safety precautions with students.

2. Guide the Procedure

- **Have you ever seen feathers lying on the ground? What did they look like? Were they wing, tail, or down feathers?** Students may have seen both kinds of feathers, but perhaps never thought of them as coming from the same bird.
- **Based on your observations, which type of feather do you think is stronger?** Students should conclude that wing and tail feathers are stronger than down feathers because they keep their shape when they are waved through the air.

Have students record their observations and answers on *Science Notebook,* TRB, pp. 51–52.

Science Processor You may wish to have students use the CD-ROM Painter to draw diagrams of the feathers.

3. Assess Performance

Process Skills Checklist

- Did students **observe** differences between the two types of feathers?
- Did students **collect and record data**? Did they **make drawings** of the two types of feathers?
- Did students **infer** the functions of the two types of feathers based on their observations?

Analyze and Conclude

1. Both types of feathers are made from the same material and have barbs attached to a shaft. However, down feathers are fluffy, whereas tail and wing feathers are smooth. The barbs of a down feather are not held together as they are in a tail or wing feather. Also, down feathers spread apart when they are waved through the air, whereas wing and tail feathers keep their shape.
2. The strong wing and tail feathers are used for flying. The fluffy down feathers help keep a bird warm.

Activity Tap, Tap, Tap

Preview *By training a goldfish to associate a tapping sound with the arrival of a meal, students draw conclusions about how a goldfish may use hearing to find food.*

Advance Preparation *See p. C40b.*

1. Get Ready

GROUPS OF 4–6 | **30 MINUTES**

Then 5 minutes each day for two weeks

Key Science Process Skills **collect and record data, predict, experiment, observe, hypothesize**

Multi-Age Strategy Students of all ages and abilities should be able to alternate roles daily as they switch between observing goldfish, tapping on the glass, feeding the fish, and recording data.

Materials Hints Be sure the fish tank is equipped with a filter and aerator. Check with the pet shop owner as to how many fish you can have in the tank and how to care for the fish.

Safety Make sure students tap lightly on the tank to avoid breaking the glass and harming the fish.

2. Guide the Procedure

- Be sure students treat the fish properly. Students should not put their hands in the tank or try to pick up the fish. Also, they should tap the tank only for the activity. Loud tapping may harm the fish.
- Note that fish do not "hear" in the same way humans do. Instead, they have a group of specialized cells that detect vibrations in the water.

Activity

Tap, Tap, Tap

In this activity you'll test whether you can change the behavior of goldfish as they learn that food is on the way.

MATERIALS
- fish tank with water and goldfish
- fish food
- pencil
- *Science Notebook*

Procedure

1. In your *Science Notebook*, **make a chart** like the one shown. With your group, **observe** how goldfish move in their tank. In your chart, **record** the movement you observe.

Day	Conditions	Observations
1	Without tapping or food (step 1)	
	With tapping but no food (step 3)	
1–10	With tapping and with food (step 5)	Day 1 ____ Day 2 ____ Day 3 ____ Day 4 ____ Day 5 ____
10	With tapping but no food, at the end of two weeks (step 6)	

See **SCIENCE and MATH TOOLBOX** *page H10 if you need to review* ***Making a Chart to Organize Data.***

2. **Talk with your group** and **predict** how the behavior of the goldfish might change if you try to attract them by making a sound. **Record** your prediction.

Step 1

C52

Meeting Individual Needs

EARLY FINISHERS

Students could repeat the activity while using a stopwatch or other timer to record the movements of the goldfish. Challenge students to time how long the goldfish perform certain reactions. For example, they could record how long the goldfish are distracted by tapping and how long they swim aimlessly before noticing food is available. Have students compile their timing data into a chart.

LOGICAL/MATHEMATICAL

Science Processor Students can use the CD-ROM Spreadsheet to record their data.

3. Test your prediction. Use a pencil to tap gently ten times on one wall of the fish tank. **Record** what you observe. Look for any changes in the behavior of the fish.

4. Sprinkle some fish food on the surface of the water at one end of the fish tank. At the same time, have another student tap the wall of the fish tank near where the food is sprinkled. **Record** the behavior of the fish.

5. Repeat step 4 each school day for two weeks. **Record** what you observe.

Step 4

Math Hint *"Each school day for two weeks" means you will do this 10 times.*

6. At the end of two weeks, tap on the wall of the fish tank ten times, but do *not* put any food in the water. **Observe** and **record** the behavior of the goldfish.

Analyze and Conclude

1. With your group, **compare** what you observed during step 3 with what you observed in step 6. How did the behavior of the goldfish change?

2. **Hypothesize** about how a sense of hearing might help fish survive. **Compare** your hypothesis with hypotheses of other group members. Explain why you came up with the hypothesis you did.

UNIT PROJECT LINK

Create a plan to publish your field guide to local plants or animals. Think of different ways to present your facts, such as in a booklet, in a bulletin-board display, or on audiotape.

Technology Link

For more help with your Unit Project, go to **www.eduplace.com**.

C53

UNIT PROJECT LINK

Have students begin by brainstorming on various formats for their field guides. Formats include sets of fact cards, posters, charts, bulletin boards, booklets, and sound recorders. Help students determine what materials and supplies they will need to carry out their plan. Encourage students to seek feedback from other class members. They can record their ideas on *Science Notebook,* TRB, p. 55.

Technology Link

Visit **www.eduplace.com** for a scoring rubric to assess students' progress and to share students' results on-line.

- If the fish move toward the tapping sounds at the end of the two-week period, ask: **How might you explain the movement of the fish?** The fish have become used to finding food when the wall of the tank is tapped.

Math Hint *Remind students that a school week consists of 5 days and that multiplying 5 by 2 gives the number of school days in two weeks.*

Have students record their observations and answer questions on *Science Notebook,* TRB, pp. 53–54.

Science Processor You may wish to have students use the CD-ROM Spreadsheet to organize and display their data.

3. Assess Performance

Process Skills Checklist

- Did students **predict** how the goldfish's behavior would change when they tapped on the tank? Were their predictions based on a knowledge of how fish behave?
- Did students **observe** the goldfish as they tapped on the tank and sprinkled food for the fish? Did they note changes in the goldfish's behavior?
- How carefully did students **collect data**? Did they notice and record details of the fishes' behavior?
- Did students **hypothesize** how a sense of hearing might help fish survive by guiding them toward prey and away from predators? Were their hypotheses based on their observations?

Analyze and Conclude

1. Initially, goldfish are frightened by tapping, but gradually lose their fear. Eventually they become attracted to the tapping as a signal that food is present.
2. Hearing can help fish detect the movement of prey (food), and predators. Accept all reasonable explanations.

RESOURCE

The Survival Game

Reading Focus Have students ***summarize*** the resource. Help them ***evaluate*** their summaries by comparing them to: *Body parts and behaviors help living things meet their basic needs, and therefore, survive.*

1. Get Ready

Vocabulary

Science Terms adaptations, behaviors, instinctive behaviors, learned behaviors

Support Terms prey, flexible, inherit

Background

- The bodies and behavior of meat-eating animals, such as lions, make them skillful hunters. A lion's keen sense of smell and eyesight help it locate prey, while its sharp claws and teeth, its speed, and its powerful jaws and forelegs help it bring down large animals. Lion cubs learn complex hunting behaviors, such as stalking, remaining hidden from view, and learning to stay downwind from game, by first observing the adults. They practice these skills and improve their coordination by playing with other cubs. They may stalk, chase, pounce on, and wrestle with other cubs. Eventually a young lion becomes an adept hunter and is able to catch large prey, which it shares with other lions.

Discussion Starter

- **Where have you seen animals use a combination of senses and behaviors to find food and water? What senses did they use? How did they behave?** Encourage students to share their past experiences in the outdoors where they witnessed animals using their senses of sight, hearing, or smell and behaviors such as grazing, hunting, and digging to find food and water.
- **Suppose you have a dog that loves to go out for walks. As the dog sees you approaching with a leash, what might you expect the dog to do? Why?** Students might expect the dog to bark, wag its tail, or show some other sign of becoming excited. This behavior shows that the dog has come to expect to go out for a walk when it sees the leash because of its past experiences.

RESOURCE

The Survival Game

Reading Focus How do body parts and behaviors help living things survive?

Have you ever wondered how penguins, birds that can't fly, use their wings? Animals have different parts, or adaptations (ad əp tā′shənz), that help them meet their needs. **Adaptations** are body parts or behaviors of living things that help them survive in a certain environment.

Wings, Trunks, and Teeth

What are some body parts that help an animal get food? A penguin's strong wings are terrific for paddling underwater. A penguin can chase after fish and squid at speeds up to 32 km/h (20 mph).

An alligator snapping turtle swims with its mouth open. At the end of its tongue is a pink flap that looks like a worm. When a fish swimming by tries to eat the "worm," the turtle eats the fish.

Animals also have parts that are adaptations for getting water. An elephant can use its tusks for drilling to underground water. Then it uses its trunk to lift the water to its mouth. Dogs use their long tongues to scoop up water into their mouths.

Animals get some water from their food. A vampire bat's food is the blood of another animal. The blood

▲ An alligator snapping turtle waits underwater for food.

▲ An elephant can use its tusks and trunk to get water.

C54

Integrating the Sciences

PHYSICAL SCIENCE

What You Need cotton balls or small squares of paper, petroleum jelly, tub of water

What to Do Invite students to demonstrate how oil in the feathers of water birds such as penguins and ducks helps to keep the birds dry and buoyant. Students should coat a cotton ball or piece of paper thoroughly with petroleum jelly. Have them place the ball or paper in a tub of water. Direct them to put an uncoated cotton ball or paper in the water.

What's the Result? What happened to the cotton balls? Students should see that the uncoated balls become wet and sink while the coated balls float and even bob up again if pushed under the water.

▲ The ears of a fennec, a kind of fox, help keep the animal cool.

▲ An armadillo's covering is its shelter.

contains water. To get the blood, the bat sticks its sharp teeth into the skin of its prey.

Claws, Feathers, and Ears

Some animals have parts that serve as shelters or help them make shelters. Snails and armadillos have hard outer coverings. Pocket gophers have large front teeth, sharp claws, and flexible bodies. These adaptations help the gophers dig tunnels that shelter them.

Animals have parts that help provide a proper temperature for them. The fluffy down feathers used in the activity on pages C50 and C51 help keep a bird warm. The large ears of an animal such as an elephant or a fennec help keep it cool. Blood passing through the animal's ears gives off heat, cooling the entire animal.

Behaviors for Survival

Suppose you go to a park and see a dog and its owner playing with a ball. When you walk over to pet the dog, the owner tells the dog to sit. The dog sits. Then the owner tells the dog to lie down. But just as the dog is beginning to lie down, a squirrel scampers past. The dog leaps up and runs after the squirrel. You have just observed some interesting **behaviors**, or ways living things act or respond to their environment.

Technology Link **CD-ROM**

INVESTIGATE FURTHER!

Use the **Science Processor CD-ROM**, *Animals* (Investigation 1, Feed Me!) to discover how different animals use their body structures to get food. Watch a video about how mammals use their bodies to meet their needs.

C55

Technology Link **CD-ROM**

INVESTIGATE FURTHER!

Students can use the **Science Processor CD-ROM** *Animals*, Investigation 1, "Feed Me!" to investigate more about how different animals use their body structures to get food. Students can click on insects to watch them eat and hear information about each insect's adaptations. Students predict what kinds of food the insects eat and then test their predictions. Students then explore the adaptations that enable certain mammals to eat. They compare adaptations of insects and mammals and write about their findings.

2. Guide the Discussion

Choose from the following strategies to facilitate discussion.

Connecting to the Activities

- ***Feather Feats, pp. C50–C51***
- **Which kind of feather that you observed in the activity is most like a polar bear's fur?** Down feather; Both down feathers and fur help keep the animal warm.
- ***Tap, Tap, Tap, pp. C52–C53***
- **What kind of behavior did the goldfish show in the activity?** The goldfish showed learned behavior as they were trained to expect food at the sound of tapping on the wall of the tank.

Drawing Conclusions

- **What would happen if a bear suddenly lost one of its adaptations for getting food, such as its sharp claws?** Students should conclude that the bear would be hampered in its ability to capture, hang onto, and kill prey. The bear would still have hunting capabilities, but it would probably not be able to eat as often and might die sooner. Encourage students to speculate what learned behaviors might help a bear survive despite such a loss.

Making Inferences

- **Suppose you could add an adaptation to each animal shown in this resource. What might you add? How would the adaptation help the animal get food or water? Might it be harmful to the animal in any way?** Students might suggest wider wings, larger claws, bigger feet, or a whole new body part for attracting prey or finding water. Lead students to realize, however, that animals survive because they are well suited to their environment. If the environment doesn't change, then any sudden change in the animal might do more harm than good. For example, larger tusks on a boar might help it dig deeper, but they may catch on bushes and trees when the boar is trying to escape a predator.

Meeting Individual Needs

For Extra Help Display as many pictures of animals as you can. Then describe an adaptation that applies to at least one of the animals pictured. Let students point to the picture of the animal to which the adaptation applies and describe how that adaptation helps the animal survive in its environment.

Making Inferences

- **Do you think an animal that has been raised in a zoo could survive very long if it were suddenly released into the wild?** Students should understand that the animal probably has not had the advantage of learning all the behaviors that would allow it to survive in the wild. For example, it probably would not be a very effective hunter or know how to elude predators. Point out that the animal would always have its instinctive behaviors because they are inherited traits.

Making Comparisons

- **How do you adapt to the environment from winter to summer?** Depending on your part of the country, students may say they dress differently, eat more or less, are more active, and so on. Make it clear that the word *adapt* is used loosely here. People are adapted to living in a variety of environments under a variety of climatic conditions.
- **What adaptations do some animals have that allow them to change from one season to another?** Some animals change color from season to season. For example, the Arctic fox and Arctic hare grow white coats in winter and brown coats in summer. Some Arctic birds grow double layers of feathers in winter. Behavioral adaptations include migration and hibernation.

Meeting Individual Needs

Students Acquiring English Students should choose an animal they have read about. Help them create a list of words that describe what that animal needs to survive. Ask students to describe verbally how the animal behaves in order to meet that need.

Internet Field Trip

From **www.eduplace.com** students can link to a Web site about animal behavior. A trip log will guide their visit to the site.

▲ A mother crocodile cradles baby crocodiles in her mouth.

Animals sometimes respond in ways that are instinctive. **Instinctive behaviors** are behaviors that living things inherit from their parents. Other behaviors, called **learned behaviors**, develop after birth. When the dog in the park sits on command, it is performing a learned behavior. The owner taught the dog to sit when told. But the dog's owner didn't teach it to chase squirrels! Running after a squirrel is an instinctive behavior of dogs.

Internet Field Trip

Visit **www.eduplace.com** to learn more about animal behavior.

Chasing and Cradling

Both kinds of behavior—learned and instinctive—help animals survive. A young wolf is born with deer-chasing behavior but must learn how to catch the deer for food. As a pup, a wolf learns this behavior by chasing and jumping on other wolf pups and its parents. It also learns by watching other wolves catch deer.

Animals have behaviors that help them protect themselves or their young. When there is danger, a mother crocodile instinctively keeps her young safe by cradling them in her mouth and throat. When the danger is past, the crocodile spits out her young!

Unlike a crocodile, a newborn rattlesnake doesn't need help from a parent. It can defend itself. A young rattlesnake instinctively coils and strikes at danger, just as its parent does.

Spinning and Shivering

Different kinds of animals have different behaviors for getting food. Some spiders have the instinctive

◀ Wolf pups pounce on and playfully bite each other.

C56

Science & Writing

WRITE STORIES

What to Do Encourage students to write a story about an animal character in which that animal's behavioral adaptations become important in the story. The stories can be funny, fanciful, scary, or adventurous. Students can include a picture that shows the adaptation.

What's the Result? Encourage students to share their stories with the class. Other students can first look at the illustration to guess how the special adaptation would be useful.

Multi-Age Classroom Have students who are proficient writers help others who may be having difficulty thinking of a story idea or writing their stories.

◀ A spider spins a web that catches prey.

behavior of spinning a silk web that catches prey. When an unlucky bee gets stuck in a spider's web, the spider bites the bee to paralyze it. The spider then wraps the bee in silk, preventing the bee from escaping.

Animals also have behaviors for keeping their temperatures within a certain range. Turtles and lizards bask in the sun to warm up. When their body temperatures get too high, they move to cooler shady places. Birds and many other animals shiver when they're cold. This behavior warms up their bodies. ■

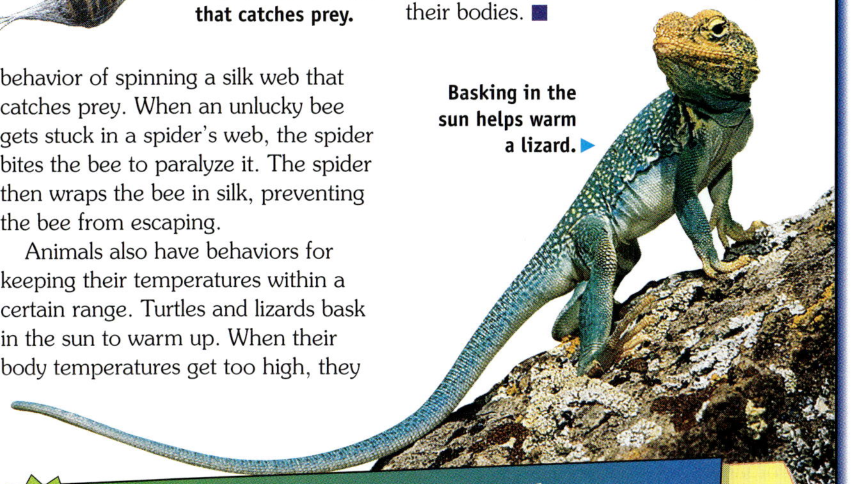

Basking in the sun helps warm a lizard. ▶

Science in Literature

Snakes and Other Reptiles
by Mary Elting
Illustrated by Christopher Santoro
Simon & Schuster, 1987

BEWARE OF SNAKES!

"When an animal—perhaps a wild pig—comes to the stream for a drink, the snake moves suddenly. It grabs the pig's leg in its mouth. Then with swift looping motions it wraps itself in coils around the animal's body. The pig cannot move. Little by little the snake squeezes its coils tighter and tighter till the pig cannot breathe and in a short while is dead."

This description of an anaconda is from the book *Snakes and Other Reptiles* by Mary Elting. Read this book for more exciting tales of reptile survival.

C57

Science & the Arts

COLLAGE MAKING

What to Do Have students search through magazines for photos that depict animal behaviors. Examples include fleeing, hunting, running, and eating. Working in small groups, have students divide their posterboard into two sections—one for instinctive behaviors and one for learned behaviors. Have students glue their cut-out photos onto their posterboard to make collages according to the behaviors shown in the photos.

What's the Result? Have students share their collages with other groups. Suggest that they tell why they classified an illustrated behavior as instinctive or learned. Examples of instinctive behaviors might include animals hunting or building shelter. Learned behaviors may include animals doing tricks or dogs acting as guides.

Identifying and Solving Problems

- **Suppose some people are thinking of moving into a harsh environment, such as the Arctic. What might they want to learn about the Arctic before moving there?** Responses might include the weather conditions and the animals that inhabit the area.
- **How might observing the animals in the Arctic help the people who live there?** The people who live in the Arctic could see how animals have adapted to that environment. They could observe ways the animals get food and stay warm. People could also observe the animals' shelters and try to mimic them when they build their own homes.

Science in Literature

Snakes and Other Reptiles
by Mary Elting

Have students compile lists of "Did You Know?" items gathered from their reading in *Snakes and Other Reptiles.* Have them share the information from their lists by creating informational posters to display on a bulletin board.

3. Assess Understanding

Students can work in small groups of three or four. Have group members work together to think of pantomimes that show an animal using an adaptation or a behavior, or both, to meet its needs. Students can choose from among many examples, including a hummingbird probing and sucking nectar from flowers, an African elephant flapping its ears to remain cool, and a woodpecker chiseling a cavity nest in a tree. Have groups of students perform their pantomimes for other groups, challenging the onlookers to guess what actions the "animal" actors are portraying.

Reading Focus Answer

Body parts and behaviors—learned and instinctive—help animals meet their needs for food, water, and shelter.

RESOURCE

Is It Ever Too Late?

Reading Focus Call on students to use their ***prior knowledge*** and the graphics on pages C59 and C60 to answer the Reading Focus question.

1. Get Ready

Vocabulary

Science Term extinct

Support Terms species, endangered

Background

- Be sure to explain to students that recorded history is a written account of events that occur. One of the most dramatic extinctions in history occurred about 65 million years ago, when dinosaurs and other large reptiles died out. Many researchers believe this extinction is related to an asteroid collision with Earth. According to this theory, the impact of the asteroid set off huge fires throughout the world. Vast clouds of dust and ash blocked out the sun and lowered temperatures. The cool weather killed those dinosaurs adapted to warm weather. Worldwide darkness also destroyed much of the vegetation. Plant-eating dinosaurs starved. As a result, the meat-eating dinosaurs that preyed on them also starved. Birds and mammals were better adapted to withstand the harsh conditions. Their feathers and fur kept them warm. In addition, they may have survived by eating decaying plant material as well as seeds and nuts, which would have survived the fires, darkness, and cold.

Discussion Starter

- **Imagine that one or more animals that are familiar to you suddenly became extinct. How might it affect your life?** Students may name domestic or wild animals. They may note that harmful pests might not be controlled if certain predators became extinct. Students may observe that they would feel emotions such as sadness, if companion animals or beautiful wild animals were to disappear.
- **To what living species do the extinct species shown in the picture on p. C59 compare?** Accept all reasonable responses. Encourage students to give reasons for their comparisons.

RESOURCE

Is It Ever Too Late?

Reading Focus What can happen if the needs of living things are not met?

A species, or group of living things that produce living things of the same kind, has many members. Some members may die out because their needs can't be met. Other members have characteristics that help them to survive. If the needs of *all* members of a species can't be met, that species becomes **extinct** (ek stiŋkt′), or dies out.

Organisms are produced, grow and mature, produce young, and then eventually die. But as long as an organism has produced young, its species will continue to exist.

To survive, an organism must be able to meet its needs in the environment where it lives. But environments differ. A polar bear cannot survive in a desert. It would die from the heat. But camels, who can live in desert heat with little water, can survive there. A camel cannot survive in the Arctic. It would die from the cold. But polar bears have a layer of fat that helps them survive the cold.

When Environments Change

Naturally caused forest fires, earthquakes, and long periods of drought or rainfall may change an environment. Then living things in that environment may die.

But not all living things die because of natural forces. Sometimes people change environments. Then the needs of plants and animals in that environment may no longer be met. When trees are cut down, many animals lose both their food and their shelter. Oil spills can ruin water environments. For example, crabs soaked with oil die. Then the animals that rely on the crabs as food also die.

▲ Florida's 1998 forest fires destroyed the environment of many living things.

C58

Integrating the Sciences

EARTH SCIENCE

What You Need roasting pan, newspapers, 4 to 5 cups of dry clay, water, several rocks in various shapes and sizes

What to Do Invite students to demonstrate the craters that result when an asteroid or comet, such as the one that may have killed the dinosaurs, strikes Earth. Have them mix the clay with water in the pan until it is soft but not runny. Direct the students to drop the rocks into the clay from various heights. To make the rocks strike from different angles, tip the pan.

What's the Result? What happened to the clay? Students should see that the dropped rocks created "craters" of various shapes and depths, much as large asteroids or comets do.

When It's Too Late

There are fewer than 50,000 Asian elephants left in the world. But because these animals do exist, it isn't too late for that species to survive. It is too late, however, for species that are already extinct. Some of these are shown on this page.

One species of extinct animal is the woolly mammoth. As you can see in the picture above, it looked very much like an elephant. Elephants exist today. But for 10,000 years, there have been no woolly mammoths.

Among extinct animals that lived before recorded history, dinosaurs are the most famous. Dinosaurs lived more than 50 million years ago. According to some scientists, today's birds are very similar to dinosaurs. Those scientists think that birds should be considered living dinosaurs. Dinosaurs were very large reptiles. Even though there are no more dinosaurs, other reptiles, such as alligators and crocodiles, exist today.

When It's Not Too Late

Sometimes plants and animals become endangered, or scarce, because they are killed for use in products. Because snow leopards have been killed for their skins, these animals have become endangered. By law, endangered animals can no longer be hunted and killed.

On the island of Guam, brown snakes ate albatross young and their eggs until none were left on the island. On other islands in the Pacific, the albatross was hunted for its feathers. After a period of time, the species was declared extinct. Then a few remaining birds were discovered, so the albatross is not extinct after all.

C59

Science & Writing

REPORT WRITING

What to Do Ask students to read one or more magazine articles that feature animals, their environments, and possible threats to these animals. Good sources for articles include *Ranger Rick, National Geographic World, National Wildlife, International Wildlife,* and *Audubon Magazine.* Have students write a report on whether their chosen animals are endangered or not and what has been done to protect the animals, or what needs to be done to help those that are endangered.

What's the Result? Invite students to share the information they learned with the class.

Multi-Age Classroom Have pairs of students work together to locate and read a suitable article.

2. Guide the Discussion

Connecting to the Activities

- ***Feather Feats, pp. C50–C51***
- **What do you think would happen to a bird whose feathers became coated with oil from a spill?** Students will observe that oil-coated wing feathers might weigh the bird down and make it unable to fly. They may also mention that down feathers would lose their ability to keep a bird warm if they are soaked in oil. They may conclude that a bird in this predicament would probably die.

Identifying and Solving Problems

- **One of the chief threats to endangered animals is habitat loss caused by people's activities. What are some of the activities that lead to habitat loss?** Students may observe that people build on land, cut down trees for farmland, dig mines, and spoil land by pollution and through such accidents as oil spills and fires.
- **What are some ways that people prevent habitat loss?** Students may mention that countries protect land and the plants and animals on it by setting up national parks and captive breeding programs. They also pass laws to reduce pollution.

Meeting Individual Needs

Students Acquiring English Direct students to look at the pictures of extinct animals on p. C59 and endangered species on p. C60. Have them copy the names of the species and help them identify each one as a plant, a mammal, or a bird. Encourage them to pick a species mentioned in the text and express a fact about it.

3. Assess Understanding

Have students work in groups of three or four to write a letter to a conservation group, such as Greenpeace, the National Audubon Society, the National Wildlife Federation, the Sierra Club, or the World Wildlife Fund. These organizations can supply information on endangered species and offer suggestions on ways to help save them. Encourage the groups to come up with conservation plans based on the information they receive and share them with the class.

Reading Focus Answer

If the needs of a living thing are not met, it will die.

INVESTIGATION 2 Close the Investigation

INVESTIGATION WRAP-UP

REVIEW

1. Instinctive behavior is behavior that animals inherit from their parents. Students might describe a dog chasing a squirrel, a spider spinning a web, or a lizard sunning itself to stay warm.

2. Students might describe animals discussed in the investigation. Behaviors that help an animal meet its needs include chasing other animals, spinning a web, shivering, and basking in the sun.

CRITICAL THINKING

3. Among the many circus animals students may choose are a lion, elephant, zebra, chimpanzee, horse, and seal. Instinctive behaviors include running and walking, vocalizing, climbing, wagging tails, and eating. Learned behaviors include jumping through hoops, balancing on balls, riding tricycles, and standing on hind legs. ***(Applying, Generating Ideas)***

4. An Asian elephant can use its tusks to drill into the ground to find water. Then it can use its trunk to bring the water up to its mouth. The elephant can use its large ears to keep itself cool in the heat of Asia. ***(Analyzing, Synthesizing)***

CHALLENGE

To determine students' understanding of the relationships among needs, adaptations, and survival, have them make a list of seven living animals. Then ask them to describe the adaptations that help each animal get food and water. Ask them to make a similar list for three extinct animals. Students can consider the possible reasons that the extinct animals died out.

FOLLOWING UP

Baseline Assessment Return to students' drawings and responses about adaptations. Ask students if there is anything they would like to change according to what they now know about adaptations.

Reteaching Discuss the Investigation subconcept with students. Together create a word web based on the different ways animals behave while meeting their needs. Use Activity Support Master "Web" on TRB p. 12.

Use *Science Notebook*, TRB p. 56.

As long as some individuals of a species exist, it's not too late to save the species. People can help endangered species recover. It's not too late, then, for the snow leopard. It's also not too late for the fewer than 50,000 Asian elephants left in the world. For the albatross, it was almost too late.

A change in environment, whether natural or caused by people, affects living things. Living things in the environment can become endangered or even extinct. For extinct species, it's too late. But it's never too late for people to rebuild environments. And it's never too late for people to protect environments. ■

INVESTIGATION 2 WRAP-UP

REVIEW

1. What is instinctive behavior? Describe an example of it.

2. Name two animals. Describe one behavior that helps each animal meet a basic need.

CRITICAL THINKING

3. Choose a circus animal. Describe one instinctive behavior and one learned behavior.

4. Think about the adaptations of animals that help them to survive. What traits might help some Asian elephants to survive?

C60

Assessment

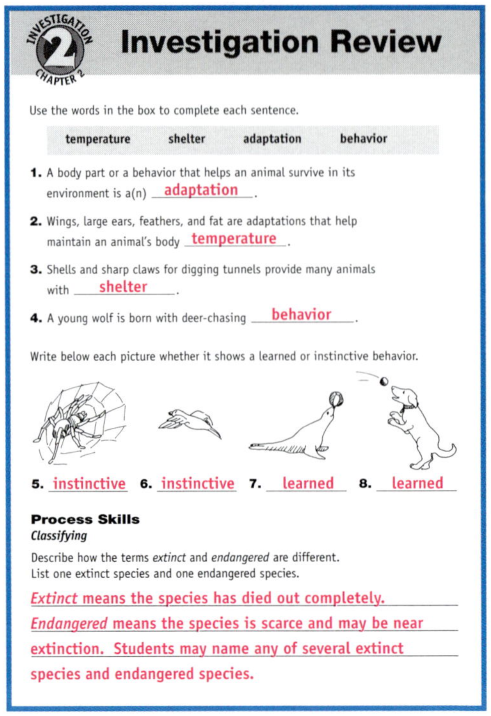
Investigation 2 Chapter 2 — **Investigation Review**

Use the words in the box to complete each sentence.

temperature	shelter	adaptation	behavior

1. A body part or a behavior that helps an animal survive in its environment is a(n) adaptation.

2. Wings, large ears, feathers, and fat are adaptations that help maintain an animal's body temperature.

3. Shells and sharp claws for digging tunnels provide many animals with shelter.

4. A young wolf is born with deer-chasing behavior.

Write below each picture whether it shows a learned or instinctive behavior.

5. instinctive **6.** instinctive **7.** learned **8.** learned

Process Skills
Classifying

Describe how the terms *extinct* and *endangered* are different. List one extinct species and one endangered species.

Extinct means the species has died out completely. *Endangered* means the species is scarce and may be near extinction. Students may name any of several extinct species and endangered species.

Performance

Models To help broaden their understanding of animals and adaptations, students can choose a favorite animal and make a model of it. Students might use clay, salt clay, or modeling compound for their animals. Provide index cards and toothpicks and ask students to place signs on the model explaining the animal's various adaptations and its potential for survival.

◀ Investigation Review

Use Investigation Review p. 101 in the *Teacher Resource Book*.

Chapter 2 Review — Reflect & Evaluate

Word Power

Write the letter of the term that best completes each sentence. *Not all terms will be used.*

1. Behaviors that living things inherit are called ___.
2. Everything, both living and nonliving, that surrounds and affects an animal is its ___.
3. To die out is to become ___.
4. Behaviors that develop after birth are ___.
5. A grassland found in tropical climates is a ___.

a. adaptations
b. environment
c. instinctive behaviors
d. learned behaviors
e. savanna
f. extinct

Check What You Know

Write the term in each pair that best completes each sentence.

1. The basic needs of animals include food, water, proper temperature, and (learned behaviors, shelter).
2. An example of an extinct animal is the (elephant, dinosaur).
3. Body parts or behaviors that help living things survive in a certain environment are called (adaptations, instinctive behaviors).
4. Endangered animals are animals that have become (extinct, scarce).

Problem Solving

1. Suppose you take an imaginary trip to an African savanna. You see many different kinds of animals. Identify some of the things the animals of the savanna use for food.
2. On a cold day you see a bird sitting with its feathers fluffed out. It's shivering. What need is the bird meeting? What adaptations does the bird have to help meet that need?

Build Your Portfolio

Study the photograph. Make a list of the armadillo's basic needs. Describe how the animal is meeting one of its basic needs.

C61

Assessment

Chapter Test (Chapter 2)

Check What You Know Each item is worth 10 points.

For questions 1–4, circle the letter of the correct answer.

1. Which of these statements can be said about the pine tree pictured?
   - **a.** It is a conifer.
   - **b.** It is a nonseed plant.
   - **c.** It is a flowering plant.
   - **d.** It is a dicot.

2. The body parts of the elephant that enable it to dig to underground water are its ___.
   a. ears **b.** eyes **c.** tusks **d.** feet
3. What kind of behavior is a parrot showing when it says its own name?
   a. instinctive **b.** learned **c.** basic **d.** suitable
4. Doris has a pet hamster. She just received a pet salamander for her birthday. Which of the following needs will she have to provide for both the hamster and the salamander?
   - **a.** food, water, shelter, and the proper temperature
   - **b.** food, water, and shelter only
   - **c.** food and water only
   - **d.** food and shelter only

Chapter Test

Problem Solving Each item is worth 20 points.

5. List the four basic needs of living things and describe one way a bird might meet each of these needs. Possible answers are shown.
   - **a.** Getting food—catching insects or worms, finding seeds
   - **b.** Getting water—drinking rain as it falls, drinking from puddles or ponds
   - **c.** Finding shelter—building nests, perching in trees or bushes
   - **d.** Maintaining body temperature—fluffing feathers to keep in body heat, bathing to cool off
6. The crab spider can change colors to blend in with its surroundings. How might this adaptation help it survive?
   It protects the crab spider from its enemies because they may have trouble seeing it.

Word Power Each item is worth 5 points.

Write the letter of the term that best completes the sentence.

7. A savanna is a type of ___.
8. An elephant's tusk is a(n) ___.
9. A shivering cat is showing ___.
10. A circus dog doing tricks is showing ___.

a. learned behavior
b. environment
c. adaptation
d. instinctive behavior

Chapter 2 Review — Reflect & Evaluate

Word Power

1. c **2.** b **3.** f **4.** d **5.** e

Check What You Know

1. shelter **2.** dinosaur **3.** adaptations **4.** scarce

Problem Solving

1. Foods include plants, insects, and other animals.

2. A fluffy layer of feathers traps air and helps reduce the amount of body heat a bird loses to the air. As the bird shivers, its body burns energy for warmth.

Build Your Portfolio

Remind students to consider elements of the environment such as weather and predators. The armadillo's hard outer shell provides shelter and protects it from predators.

Assess Performance

Student Task

To determine how well students understand the relationships among adaptations, behaviors, and survival, have them observe goldfish in a tank. Direct them to identify the basic needs of the goldfish, noting the body parts and behaviors that help the goldfish meet those needs.

Scoring Rubric

Points	What to Look For
3	Student identifies a goldfish's basic needs, makes relevant observations on its adaptations and behavior, and clearly expresses how these characteristics help the fish meet its needs.
2	Student may understand the goldfish's basic needs, but has incomplete understanding of how adaptations and behaviors fulfill these needs.
1	Student does not understand the goldfish's needs or how it is equipped to meet these needs.

◀ Chapter Test

Use pp. 102–103 in the *Teacher Resource Book*.

Using READING SKILLS

Compare and Contrast

Review Reading Strategies

Have students turn to *Reading to Learn* on pp. S12–S13 to review the reading strategies.

Reinforce the Reading Skill

Ask a volunteer to read the Reading Skills title on page C62 (*Compare and Contrast*). Reinforce that **compare** means "to show likeness" and **contrast** means "to show difference." Then have students take turns reading aloud the introductory paragraph and the tips in the notepad ("Look for these signal words . . ."). Explain that some signal words show likeness and other signal words show difference.

Model these strategies for comparing and contrasting.

- **Before Reading** Have students read the titles and the first sentence in each paragraph. Ask students: **What two things are being compared?** (Animals with backbones are being compared to animals that don't have backbones.)
- **While Reading** Point out the science terms in boldface. Explain that students should read the words around each highlighted word to help them figure out the meaning of the science terms. **What is a vertebra?** (It is a bone in the backbone.) **What are vertebrates?** (They are animals with backbones.) **What are invertebrates?** (They are animals that don't have backbones.) Tell students to look for likenesses and differences. Ask: **How are vertebrates like or different from invertebrates?** (They are both animals; vertebrates have backbones and invertebrates don't have backbones.)
- **After Reading** Students should complete the exercise. (1. vertebrates and invertebrates; 2. d) If they are having trouble, encourage students to look back at the titles and highlighted words.

Apply the Reading Skill

Suggest that students can use these strategies for comparing and contrasting in Unit Resources.

Using READING SKILLS

Compare and Contrast

Making comparisons when you read helps you understand what a writer is saying. As you read, ask if two things or ideas are alike or different from each other.

Read the passages below. Then complete the exercises that follow.

Look for these signal words to help you compare and contrast.
- To show similar things: *like, the same as, in common*
- To show different things: *different from, by contrast*

Who Has a Backbone?

Animals that have backbones make up one group. You can feel the knobs of your backbone down the center of your back. Each knob is part of a separate bone. Each bone that makes up the backbone is called a **vertebra**. Animals that have backbones are called **vertebrates**.

Vertebrates include many different kinds of animals. Horses, hippos, cats, birds, snakes, lizards, frogs, and fish are all vertebrates. All vertebrates have one thing in common—a backbone.

Life Without a Backbone

The members of many different animal groups don't have backbones. Animals that don't have backbones are called **invertebrates**. In fact, 97 percent of the animal kingdom is made up of invertebrates! They include some of the smallest animals, such as spiders, mites, and insects. Some invertebrates can be found in ponds, oceans, and other water environments where they can move about easily. Others have no trouble moving about on land or in the air.

1. What two things are being compared?

2. What is the main difference between the two things that are being compared? Write the letter of the answer.

   a. Where they live
   b. How they move
   c. How big they are
   d. Whether they have a backbone

C62

Meeting Individual Needs

STUDENTS ACQUIRING ENGLISH

To help students compare and contrast, use word wheels to expand their understanding of the signal words. Label one word wheel *compare,* and write *same* in the hub of the wheel. Have students brainstorm to list other words that mean "same." Write them as spokes around the hub of the word wheel. Label another wheel *contrast,* and write *different* in the hub of that wheel. Have students list words to write in the spokes of that wheel. Keep the word wheels where students can refer to them as they read.

VISUAL/SPATIAL

Using Math Skills

Using Math: Analyze Data

The average lengths in meters of various dolphins and whales are shown in this table.

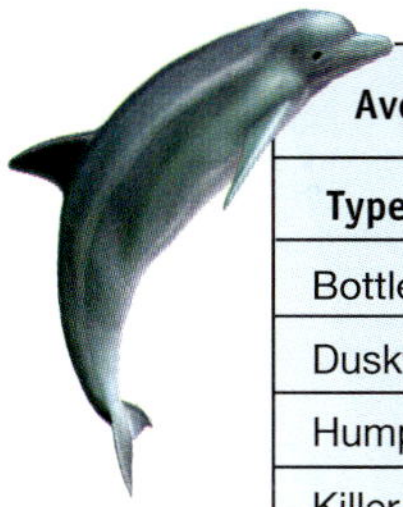

Average Lengths of Dolphins and Whales

Type of Dolphin or Whale	Length (m)
Bottlenosed dolphin	3.9
Dusky dolphin	1.6
Humpback dolphin	2.4
Killer whale	8.0
Long-finned pilot whale	7.0
Melon-headed whale	2.6

Use the information in the table to complete the exercises that follow.

1. Which animal has the greatest length? the shortest length?
2. Which two types of animals, lined up nose to tail, would have a length of exactly 5 m?
3. Which animal is as long as five dusky dolphins lined up nose to tail?
4. About how many times longer is a killer whale than a bottlenosed dolphin?
5. The range of a set of data is found by subtracting the smallest number from the largest number in the set of data. What is the range of data in the table?
6. Estimate how many of your arm spans would equal the length of the killer whale.

Unit C: Using Math Skills

Using Math: Analyze Data

Reinforce the Math Skill

Be sure that students realize that a table is a useful way to organize data. Have students look at the table on the pupil page. Point out the title of the table as well as the titles at the top of each column.

Apply the Math Skill

Explain to students that to find a particular dolphin or whale's length, they should find the correct row and then read across. Once you are certain that students understand how to read the table, have them complete the pupil page.

Answers

1. Killer whale; dusky dolphin
2. Humpback dolphin and melon-headed whale
3. Killer whale
4. About twice as long
5. 6.4 meters
6. Answers will vary. A student who is approximately 1.3 meters tall might estimate that it would take 6 arm spans to equal the length of a killer whale.

Science & Math

ANIMAL TABLES

What to Do Have students research some of their favorite animals to find out the animals' average lengths or weights. Suggest resources such as library books, the Internet, and nature magazines such as *Ranger Rick* and *My Big Backyard.*

What's the Result? Have students compile their information into a table similar to the one shown on this page.

UNIT C WRAP-UP!

THINK LIKE A SCIENTIST

Before students begin with this page, you may want to have them review the steps in the scientific process. Refer students to pages S2–S11 and have them briefly summarize how they would apply the process as they complete the page. They can refer to their summaries as they proceed with the steps of the Unit Wrap-up.

WRITING IN SCIENCE

Students can work together to identify the main ideas and supporting details in "The ABCs of Survival." Have students draft their summaries individually. They may work with a partner to revise and proofread their summaries.

Use these questions to evaluate student performance.

- Does the summary include the main ideas and important supporting details of the selection?
- Does the summary include a statement that sums up the content?

UNIT PROJECT WRAP-UP

You may wish to have your students plan a Safari Day to wrap up their projects. Students can invite classmates, other classes, families, and friends to use the students' field guides to identify local plants and animals. Students could make maps of routes for people to follow. If students made audiotapes for their field guides, have portable cassette players on hand for visitors to use. Suggest that students make lists of plants and animals included in the field guides. Visitors can use copies of these lists to check off what they see along the route.

- For more information on how to wrap up the Unit Project, see pages C1o and C1p.
- For suggestions on how to assess the Unit Project, see Unit Project Scoring Rubric Master 6 (Teacher Resource Book p. 21).

UNIT C WRAP-UP!

On your own, use scientific methods to investigate a question about living things.

THINK LIKE A SCIENTIST

Ask a Question

Pose a question about living things that you would like to investigate. For example, ask, "How can an animal's color help it survive?"

Make a Hypothesis

Suggest a hypothesis that is a possible answer to the question. One hypothesis is that an animal's color helps it blend into its environment so that predators cannot find it.

Plan and Do a Test

Plan a controlled experiment to find out if an animal's color helps it hide from predators. You could start with a large brown cloth, pipe cleaners in assorted colors (including brown), and a timer. Develop a procedure that uses these materials to test the hypothesis. With permission, carry out your experiment. Follow the safety guidelines on pages S14–S15.

Record and Analyze

Observe carefully and record your data accurately. Make repeated observations.

Draw Conclusions

Look for evidence to support the hypothesis or to show that it is false. Draw conclusions about the hypothesis. Repeat the experiment to verify the results.

WRITING IN SCIENCE

Summary

Write a summary of "The ABCs of Survival," pages C44-C47. Use these guidelines to write your summary.

- State the main ideas of the resource.
- Briefly list the main supporting details.
- Write a concluding statement that sums up the content.

C64

Home-School Connection

The Closing Letter at the end of this unit suggests additional activities about plants' and animals' needs that family members can do at home as well as books students and their families can read together. Distribute the Closing Letter (TRB p. 5) to students at the end of this unit.

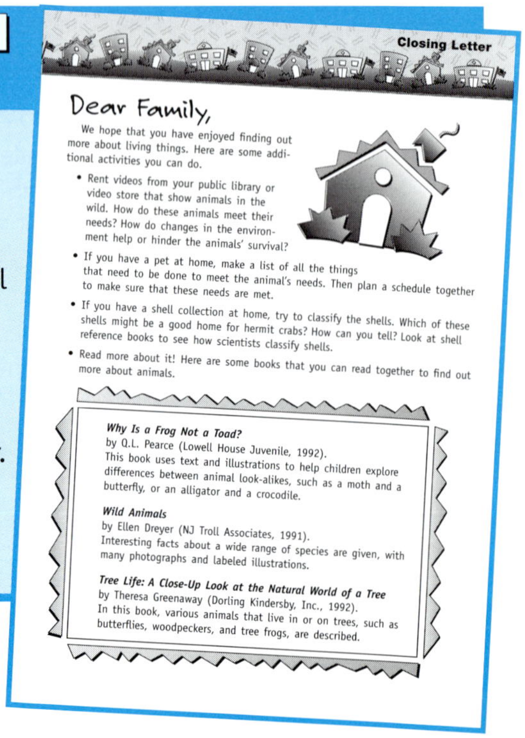

Closing Letter

Dear Family,

We hope that you have enjoyed finding out more about living things. Here are some additional activities you can do.

- Rent videos from your public library or video store that show animals in the wild. How do these animals meet their needs? How do changes in the environment help or hinder the animals' survival?
- If you have a pet at home, make a list of all the things that need to be done to meet the animal's needs. Then plan a schedule together to make sure that these needs are met.
- If you have a shell collection at home, try to classify the shells. Which of these shells might be a good home for hermit crabs? How can you tell? Look at shell reference books to see how scientists classify shells.
- Read more about it! Here are some books that you can read together to find out more about animals.

Why Is a Frog Not a Toad?
by Q.L. Pearce (Lowell House Juvenile, 1992).
This book uses text and illustrations to help children explore differences between animal look-alikes, such as a moth and a butterfly, or an alligator and a crocodile.

Wild Animals
by Ellen Dreyer (NJ Troll Associates, 1991).
Interesting facts about a wide range of species are given, with many photographs and labeled illustrations.

Tree Life: A Close-Up Look at the Natural World of a Tree
by Theresa Greenaway (Dorling Kindersby, Inc., 1992).
In this book, various animals that live in or on trees, such as butterflies, woodpeckers, and tree frogs, are described.

Teacher Notes

Teacher Notes

Teacher Notes

Teacher Notes

Teacher Notes

Teacher Notes

Teacher Notes

CREDITS

Student Edition

ILLUSTRATORS

Cover Genine Smith.

Think Like a Scientist 14: Laurie Hamilton. *Border* Genine Smith.

Unit C 8–9: Lee Steadman. 12–13: Susan Melrath. 13: Linda Warner. 13: Eldon Doty. 14–15: Dave Barber. 18–20: Jim Deal. 30: Barbara Hoopes Ambler. 35: Wendy Smith-Griswold. 40–41: Phil Wilson. 44: Jackie Urbanovic. 44–47: Julie Tsuchya. 48–49: Linda Howard. 54–57: Richard Cowdrey. 59–60: Randy Hamblin.

Science and Math Toolbox *Logos* Nancy Tobin. 14–15: Andrew Shiff. *Borders* Genine Smith.

Glossary 17: *t.r.* Dan McGowan. *m.l.* Richard Cowdrey. *b.r.* Dale Gustafson. 18: Mike Quon. 19: Dale Gustafson. 20: Dan McGowan. 21,22: Dale Gustafson. 23: Robert Roper. 24: A.J. Miller. 26–27: Patrick Gnan. 28: Hans & Cassady Inc. 29: Dan McGowan. 30: Hans & Cassady Inc. 32: David Barber. 33: Patrick Gnan.

PHOTOGRAPHS

All photographs by Houghton Mifflin Company (HMCo.) unless otherwise noted.

Cover *t.* Superstock; *m.l.* Bill Brooks/Masterfile Corporation; *m.r.* Tim Flach/Tony Stone Images; *b.l.* Barbara Leslie/FPG International; *b.r.* Greg Ryan & Sally Beyer/Tony Stone Images.

Table of Contents iv: *l.* Harold Sund/The Image Bank; *r.* Cromosohm/Sohm/The Stock Market. viii: Stan Osolinski/The Stock Market. xiii: *t.r.* Brian Parker/Tom Stack & Associates; *b.l.* Tony Freeman/PhotoEdit; *b.m.* Buff Corsi/Tom Stack & Associates; *b.r.* Gary Withey/Bruce Coleman Incorporated. xiv: © 2000 Juha Jormanainen/Woodfin Camp & Associates. xv: *l.* NOAA; *r.* NOAA/NESDIS/NCDC/SDSD.

Think Like a Scientist 2: *t. bkgd.* PhotoDisc, Inc. 3: *t.* PhotoDisc, Inc. 4–5: *bkgd.* Chip Henderson Photography.

Unit C 1: Stuart Westmorland/Tony Stone Images. 2–3: Stuart Westmorland/Tony Stone Images. 4–5: *bkgd.* Inga Spence/Tom Stack & Associates; *inset* Frans Lanting/Minden Pictures. 7: Richard Hutchings for HMCo. 10: *t.l.* © Tom McHugh/Photo Researchers, Inc.; *t.r.* Jane Burton/Bruce Coleman Incorporated; *b.* © Hermann Eisenbeiss/Photo Researchers, Inc. 11: *t.* Dwight R. Kuhn; *m.l.* © Michael Abbey/Photo Researchers, Inc.; *m.r.* © Gary Reterford/Science Source/Photo Researchers, Inc.; *b.l.* Kim Taylor/Bruce Coleman Incorporated; *b.r.* © Biophoto Associates/Science Source/Photo Researchers, Inc. 19: *t.* to *b.* Dwight R. Kuhn; Donald Specker/Animals Animals/Earth Scenes; E.R. Degginger/Color-Pic, Inc.; Zig Leszczynski/Animals Animals/Earth Scenes; Dwight R. Kuhn. 20: Art Wolfe/Tony Stone Images. 21: *bkgd.* David Sailors/The Stock Market; *l.* G.I. Bernard/Oxford Scientific Films/Animals Animals/Earth Scenes; *inset* Al Hamdan/The Image Bank. 22: *t.* Doug Perrine/DRK Photo; *b.* S. Nielsen/Imagery. 23: © Tom & Pat Leeson/Photo Researchers, Inc. 25: Richard Hutchings for HMCo. 26: *t.* Dwight R. Kuhn; *b.l.* The Granger Collection, New York; *b.r.* B.W. Payton. 27: *bkgd.* Larry Lipsky/Bruce Coleman Incorporated; *inset* M.C. Chamberlain/DRK Photo. 28: *t.* M.C. Chamberlain/DRK Photo; *b.l.* Mike Severns/Tom Stack & Associates; *b.r.* Brian Parker/Tom Stack & Associates. 29: *t.l.* Carl Roessler/Bruce Coleman Incorporated; *t.r.* Carol L. Geake/Animals Animals/Earth Scenes; *b.* Stephen Frink/Corbis Media. 31: *l.* to *r.* E.R. Degginger/Color-Pic, Inc.; James Cotier/Tony Stone Images; Andrew J. Martinez/Stock Boston; E.R. Degginger/Color-Pic, Inc.; Charles Sleicher/Tony Stone Images; Rosemary Calvert/Tony Stone Images. 32: *l.* © Rod Planck/Photo Researchers, Inc.; *r.* Phil Degginger/Color-Pic, Inc. 34: *t.l.* E.R. Degginger/Color-Pic, Inc.; *t.r.* © Alan & Linda Detrick/Photo Researchers, Inc.; *m.r.* Maximillian Stock/Stock Food America; *b.l.* Ray Pfortner/Peter Arnold, Inc.; *b.r.* E.R. Degginger/Color-Pic, Inc.; *l. inset* Tom & Pat Leeson/DRK Photo; *r. inset* E.R. Degginger/Color-Pic, Inc. 36: *t.l.* Runk/Schoenberger/Grant Heilman Photography, Inc.; *t.r.* © Alvin E. Staffan/Photo Researchers, Inc.; *b.l.* K.G. Preston Mafham/Animals Animals/Earth Scenes; *b.r.* Carl Wolinsky/Stock Boston. 37: *t.l.* © Dan Suzio/Photo Researchers, Inc.; *t.r.* © Dan Suzio/Photo Researchers, Inc. 38: *l.* E.R. Degginger/Color-Pic, Inc. 39: © Tom McHugh/Photo Researchers, Inc. 42: Stan Osolinski/The Stock Market. 43: *t.l.* © Renate & Gerd Wustig/Okapia/Photo Researchers, Inc.; *t.r.* Gary W. Griffen/Animals Animals/Earth Scenes; *b.l.* Robert A. Ross/Color-Pic, Inc.; *b.r.* Fred Bruemmer/DRK Photo. 44: *bkgd.* Spencer Swanger/Tom Stack & Associates; *inset* E.R. Degginger/Color-Pic, Inc. 45: *t.l.* Fred Fellerman/Tony Stone Images; *t.r.* Peter Drowne/Color-Pic, Inc.; *b.* Robert Maier/Animals Animals/Earth Scenes. 46: *t.* John Cancalosi/Tom Stack & Associates; *b.l.* R.J.B. Goodale/Animals Animals/Earth Scenes; *b.r.* M.C. Chamberlin/DRK Photo. 47: © Craig K. Lorenz/Photo Researchers, Inc. 54: *l.* © Cosmos Blank/National Audubon Society/Photo Researchers, Inc. 55: *l.* M. Austerman/Animals Animals/Earth Scenes; *r.* C.C. Lockwood/Animals Animals/Earth Scenes. 56: *t.* © M. Reardon/Photo Researchers, Inc.; *b.* Charlie Palek/Animals Animals/Earth Scenes. 57: *t.* Rod Planck/Tony Stone Images. 59: CNP/Archive Photos. 61: C.C. Lockwood/Animals Animals/Earth Scenes.

Glossary 19: Buff Corsi/Tom Stack & Associates. 25: E.R. Degginger/Color-Pic, Inc. 31: Gary Withey/Bruce Coleman Incorporated.

Teaching Guide

ILLUSTRATORS

Cover Genine Smith.

Contributing Artists Barbara Hoopes Ambler, Garry Colby, Genine Smith, Nancy Tobin.

PHOTOGRAPHS

All photographs by Houghton Mifflin Company (HMCo.) unless otherwise noted.

T2–T3: Dan Levinski/Masterfile Corporation. T3: J. Carmichael/The Image Bank. 1: Stuart Westmorland/Tony Stone Images. 1e: Hans Pletschinger/Peter Arnold, Inc. 1f: *t.l.* Courtesy, Jean Harris; *t.r.* Courtesy, Roy Boyle; *b.* Courtesy, Morris Chestang. 1q: © Disney. 1r: *bkgd.* PhotoDisc, Inc.

Science and Math Toolbox

Using a Hand Lens

A hand lens is a tool that magnifies objects, or makes objects appear larger. This makes it possible for you to see details of an object that would be hard to see without the hand lens.

Look at a Coin or a Stamp

▲ Place the lens above the object.

▲ Move the lens slowly toward you.

1. Place an object such as a coin or a stamp on a table or other flat surface.

2. Hold the hand lens just above the object. As you look through the lens, slowly move the lens away from the object. Notice that the object appears to get larger.

3. Keep moving the lens until the object begins to look a little blurry. Then move the hand lens a little closer to the object until the object is once again in sharp focus.

If the object starts to look blurry, move the lens toward the object. ▶

Making a Bar Graph

A bar graph helps you organize and compare data.

Make a Bar Graph of Animal Heights

Animals come in all different shapes and sizes. You can use the information in the table to make a bar graph of animal heights.

Heights of Animals

Animal	Height (cm)
Bear	240
Elephant	315
Cow	150
Giraffe	570
Camel	210
Horse	165

1. Draw the side and the bottom of the graph. Label the side of the graph as shown. The numbers will show the height of the animals in centimeters.

2. Label the bottom of the graph. Write the names of the animals at the bottom so that there is room to draw the bars.

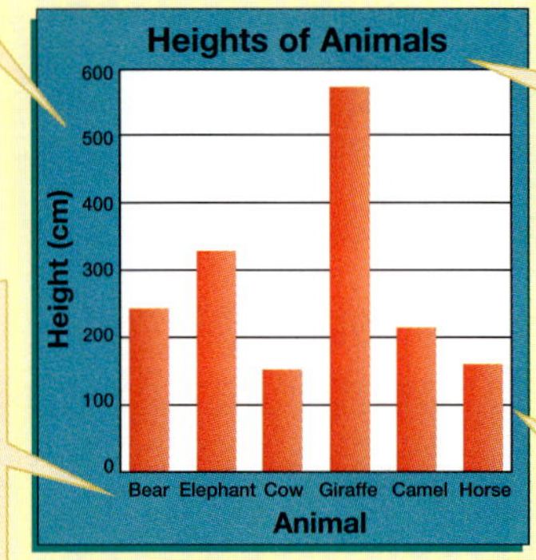

3. Choose a title for your graph. Your title should describe the subject of the graph.

4. Draw bars to show the height of each animal. Some heights are between two numbers.

Using a Hand Lens

Helpful Hints Hand lenses are listed as 3X, 6X, 8X, etc. This means that the usual maximum magnification is, in the case of the 3X, 3 times the size of the object. In order to attain the greatest magnification, the lens must be held away from the eye.

Try It Out

- Have your students inspect a sheet of graph paper with a hand lens. When the squares are as large as possible, how many squares do they see? How many squares can they see when the lens is held near the eye?
- Placing one lens directly on top of an identical lens doubles the magnification. Have your students try it. Can they find Lincoln's statue in the Lincoln Memorial on a penny? Can they find the designer's initials under Lincoln's shoulder on the face of the penny?

Making a Bar Graph

Helpful Hints A good bar graph always has a title and horizontal and vertical axes that are labeled to show what they represent. The label at the base of each bar may be a word or a symbol. If it is a symbol, the graph should include a Key or Legend that tells what each symbol means. If the axis parallel to the bars shows relative numbers, it should be scaled from zero at its base. If it shows measurements, the unit of measure (e.g., cm) should appear in parentheses near the axis label. Bars may be oriented in either a horizontal or vertical direction. The choice of direction may make the graph more meaningful.

Try It Out

- Bar graphs are best used for representing categories that do not have continuous values. Have students prepare bar graphs representing the number of students in each grade in the school.

Using a Calculator

After you've made measurements, a calculator can help you analyze your data.

Add and Multiply Decimals

Suppose you're an astronaut. You may take 8 pounds of Moon rocks back to Earth. The table shows the weights of the rocks. Can you take them all? Use a calculator to find out.

Weight of Moon Rocks

Moon Rock	Weight of Rock on Moon (lb)
Rock 1	1.7
Rock 2	1.8
Rock 3	2.6
Rock 4	1.5

1. To add, press:

1 . 7 + 1 . 8 +

2 . 6 + 1 . 5 =

Display: 7.6

2. If you make a mistake, press the clear entry key (CE/C) once. Enter the number again. Then continue adding. (Note: If you press CE/C twice, it will clear all.)

3. Your total is 7.6 pounds. You can take the four Moon rocks back to Earth.

4. How much do the Moon rocks weigh on Earth? Objects weigh six times as much on Earth as they do on the Moon. You can use a calculator to multiply.

Press: 7 . 6 × 6 =

Display: 45.6

5. The rocks weigh 45.6 pounds on Earth.

Finding an Average

An average is a way to describe a group of numbers. For example, after you have made a series of measurements, you can find the average. This can help you analyze your data.

Add and Divide to Find the Average

The table shows the amount of rain that fell each month for the first six months of the year. What was the average rainfall per month?

Rainfall

Month	Rain (mm)
Jan.	102
Feb.	75
Mar.	46
Apr.	126
May	51
June	32

1. Add the numbers in the list.

$$\left.\begin{array}{r} 102 \\ 75 \\ 46 \\ 126 \\ 51 \\ +\ 32 \end{array}\right\} 6 \text{ addends}$$

$$432$$

2. Divide the sum (432) by the number of addends (6).

$$\begin{array}{r} 72 \\ 6\,\overline{)\,432} \\ -\ 42 \\ \hline 12 \\ -\ 12 \\ \hline 0 \end{array}$$

3. The average rainfall per month for the first six months was 72 mm of rain.

Using a Calculator

Helpful Hints Calculators are great tools but they have one fault. They always give an answer. However, if one pushes the wrong button… Try to get your students in the habit of always checking to see that the result shown on the calculator display is reasonable.

Try It Out

- Divide the class into groups of about six students. Have each group member trace an outline of his or her shoe on a sheet of paper and cut it out. Within groups measure the length of each shoe in centimeters. If placed end-to-end, how far will the shoe outlines reach? Use the calculator to find the total length.
- Record each group's total length on the chalkboard. Have the groups use calculators to find the total length of all the feet.

Finding an Average

Helpful Hints Scientists often find the average (mean) value for their data. In any experiment where multiple repetitions would be expected to give the same result, the average is used as the best estimate of that result. Of course, there are always errors due to human observation and experimental conditions. The smaller the errors the more uniform are the results.

Students should learn that experiments should be repeated to provide reliable answers. The repetition ideally is within the same working group. However, this is not always practical in the classroom. The results from different groups can be gathered and averaged.

Try It Out

- Provide students with data on the number of minutes spent in science class each day for a week. Have students find the average amount of time spent in science class daily.

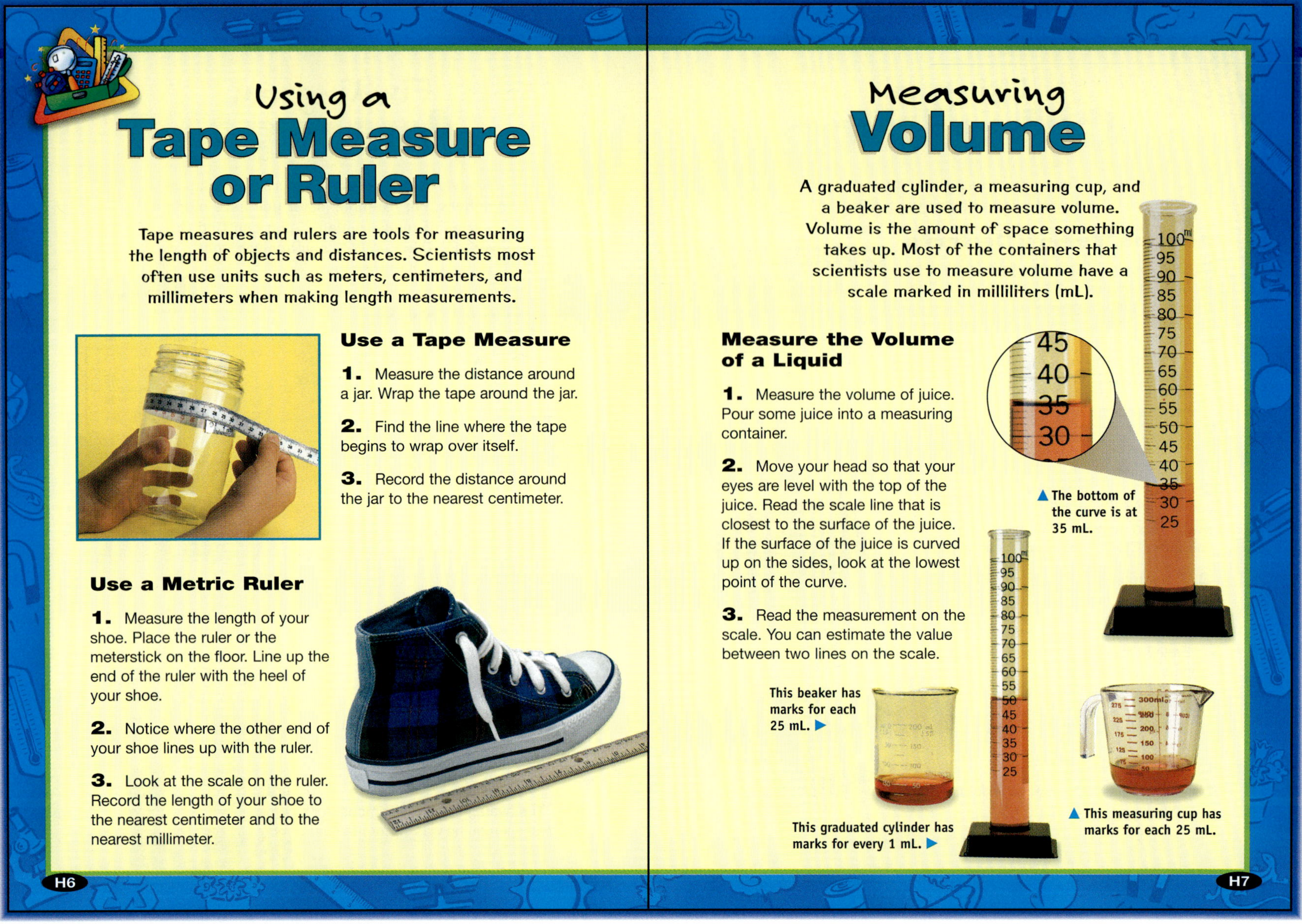

Using a
Tape Measure or Ruler

Tape measures and rulers are tools for measuring the length of objects and distances. Scientists most often use units such as meters, centimeters, and millimeters when making length measurements.

Use a Tape Measure

1. Measure the distance around a jar. Wrap the tape around the jar.

2. Find the line where the tape begins to wrap over itself.

3. Record the distance around the jar to the nearest centimeter.

Use a Metric Ruler

1. Measure the length of your shoe. Place the ruler or the meterstick on the floor. Line up the end of the ruler with the heel of your shoe.

2. Notice where the other end of your shoe lines up with the ruler.

3. Look at the scale on the ruler. Record the length of your shoe to the nearest centimeter and to the nearest millimeter.

H6

Measuring
Volume

A graduated cylinder, a measuring cup, and a beaker are used to measure volume. Volume is the amount of space something takes up. Most of the containers that scientists use to measure volume have a scale marked in milliliters (mL).

Measure the Volume of a Liquid

1. Measure the volume of juice. Pour some juice into a measuring container.

2. Move your head so that your eyes are level with the top of the juice. Read the scale line that is closest to the surface of the juice. If the surface of the juice is curved up on the sides, look at the lowest point of the curve.

3. Read the measurement on the scale. You can estimate the value between two lines on the scale.

▲ The bottom of the curve is at 35 mL.

This beaker has marks for each 25 mL. ▶

This graduated cylinder has marks for every 1 mL. ▶

▲ This measuring cup has marks for each 25 mL.

H7

Using a
Tape Measure or Ruler

Helpful Hints Tape measures often have ends that are ragged or deformed. Such tape measures may still be used by measuring from the one centimeter mark, and then subtracting one from the result. Occasionally, rulers suffer from the same problem.

Try It Out

- Measuring round or irregularly shaped objects is often a problem. Have your students measure the diameter of a ball. Challenge them to devise an accurate method. The easiest way to do it is to place the ball between two vertical planes, such as two books. Then measure the distance between the planes.

Measuring
Volume

Helpful Hints Containers that are graduated to measure volume always have a range of error. (In fact, the same can be said for all measuring instruments.) Usually, the smaller the diameter of the container, the more accurate it is. Graduated cylinders are much more accurate than measuring cups designed for the kitchen. Beakers that have graduations on the sides are only approximate.

Try It Out

- Have students use a measuring cup to find the volume of a liquid. Then have them use a graduated cylinder to determine the volume again. Have students discuss the reason for any difference.

Using a Thermometer

A thermometer is used to measure temperature. When the liquid in the tube of a thermometer gets warmer, it expands and moves farther up the tube. Different scales can be used to measure temperature, but scientists usually use the Celsius scale.

Measure the Temperature of a Cold Liquid

1. Take a chilled liquid out of the refrigerator. Half fill a cup with the liquid.

2. Hold the thermometer so that the bulb is in the center of the liquid. Be sure that there are no bright lights or direct sunlight shining on the bulb.

3. Wait a few minutes until you see the liquid in the tube of the thermometer stop moving. Read the scale line that is closest to the top of the liquid in the tube. The thermometer shown reads 21°C (about 70°F).

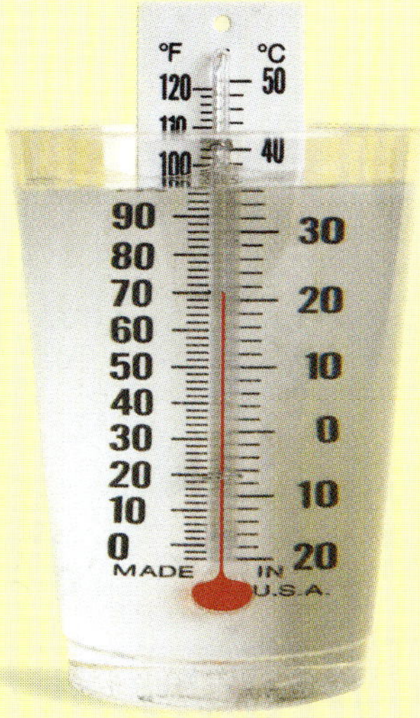

Using a Balance

A balance is used to measure mass. Mass is the amount of matter in an object. To find the mass of an object, place it in the left pan of the balance. Place standard masses in the right pan.

Measure the Mass of a Ball

1. Check that the empty pans are balanced, or level with each other. When balanced, the pointer on the base should be at the middle mark. If it needs to be adjusted, move the slider on the back of the balance a little to the left or right.

2. Place a ball on the left pan. Then add standard masses, one at a time, to the right pan. When the pointer is at the middle mark again, each pan holds the same amount of matter and has the same mass.

3. Add the numbers marked on the masses in the pan. The total is the mass of the ball in grams.

Using a Thermometer

Helpful Hints When using a thermometer to measure the temperature of a liquid, the thermometer should be read with the bulb still immersed in the liquid. Otherwise, the liquid in the bulb will begin to expand or contract immediately after it is removed.

When measuring air temperatures, students have a tendency to hold the bottom of the thermometer. In order not to affect the reading, they should keep their fingers well away from the bulb.

Try It Out

- Divide your class into groups. Give each group equal volumes of warm and cold water in plastic foam cups. Have each group measure the temperature of the water in both cups. Then have them predict the temperature of the water when combined. Have students try it. The resulting temperature will be halfway between the two.

Using a Balance

Helpful Hints Teach students to place the object they are measuring on the left-hand pan. Then they will not have a problem when they later encounter balances that have a mass that slides from left to right.

After the balance has been zero adjusted, it should not be moved. Another location might cause the pointer to move off zero.

Try It Out

- Do some paper towels absorb more water than others? Since water has mass, and so do paper towels, the balance is a good instrument to use in determining the answer. Have your students, in teams, design an experiment to solve the problem.

Making a Chart to Organize Data

A chart can help you keep track of information. When you organize information, or data, it is easier to read, compare, or classify it.

Classifying Animals

Suppose you are studying characteristics of different animals. You want to organize the data that you collect.

Look at the data below. To put this data in a chart, you could base the chart on the two characteristics listed—the number of wings and the number of legs.

Give the chart a title that describes the data in it.

Name categories, or groups, that describe the data you have collected.

Make sure the information is recorded correctly in each column.

Animals—Number of Wings and Legs

Animal	Number of Wings	Number of Legs
Flea	0	6
Snake	0	0
Bee	4	6
Spider	0	8
Dog	0	4
Bird	2	2
Cow	0	4
Butterfly	4	6

Next, you could make another chart to show animal classification based on number of legs only.

H10

Reading a Circle Graph

A circle graph shows a whole divided into parts. You can use a circle graph to compare the parts to each other. You can also use it to compare the parts to the whole.

A Circle Graph of Fuel Use

This circle graph shows fuel use in the United States. The graph has 10 equal parts, or sections. Each section equals $\frac{1}{10}$ of the whole. One whole equals $\frac{10}{10}$.

Estimated Fuel Use in the United States

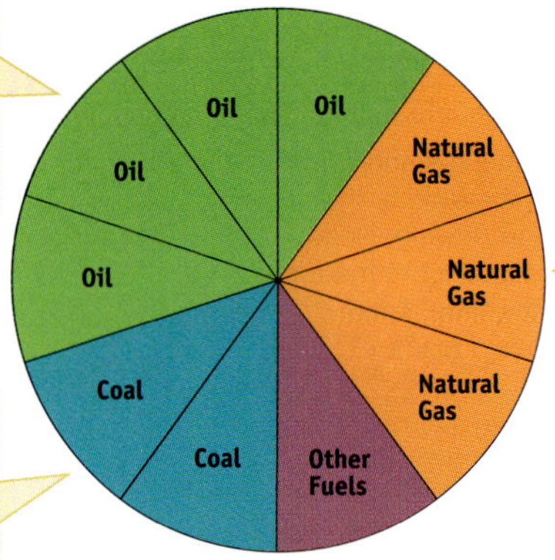

Of all the fuel used in the United States, 4 out of 10 parts, or $\frac{4}{10}$, is oil.

Of all the fuel used in the United States, 3 out of 10 parts, or $\frac{3}{10}$, is natural gas.

Of all the fuel used in the United States, 2 out of 10 parts, or $\frac{2}{10}$, is coal.

H11

Making a Chart to Organize Data

Helpful Hints When children do science experiments, they should always make data charts to record their observations. The chart might be kept by individual students, a working group, or you. In any case, the chart, or table, should have a title, columns for data, and column headers that tell what data is in each column. If a column in a chart contains measurements, the unit of measure should appear in the column header. This eliminates the need to write the unit after each measurement in the column.

Try It Out

- If you have a computer with a spreadsheet program, have students set up their data charts on the spreadsheet. If you aggregate data from teams following a science activity, you might consider having one or two students input the data as it is reported. Then duplicate the class data for each student.

Reading a Circle Graph

Helpful Hints Circle graphs make it easy to compare subsets of data. Because data has to be converted to degrees or fractions, circle graphs can be more difficult to prepare than bar graphs. At this age, the emphasis should be on interpreting circle graphs.

Try It Out

- Collect circle graphs from news magazines and newspapers. Distribute them and ask students to write descriptions of what they show. Discuss the advantages of circle graphs over a written paragraph.

Measuring
Elapsed Time

A calendar can help you find out how much time has passed, or elapsed, in days or weeks. A clock can help you see how much time has elapsed in hours and minutes. A clock with a second hand or a stopwatch can help you find out how many seconds have elapsed.

Using a Calendar to Find Elapsed Days

This is a calendar for the month of October. October has 31 days. Suppose it is October 22 and you begin an experiment. You need to check the experiment two days from the start date and one week from the start date. That means you would check it on Wednesday, October 24, and again on Monday, October 29. October 29 is 7 days after October 22.

Monday, Tuesday, Wednesday, Thursday, and Friday are weekdays. Saturday and Sunday are weekends.

October

Sunday	Monday	Tuesday	Wednesday	Thursday	Friday	Saturday
	1	2	3	4	5	6
7	8	9	10	11	12	13
14	15	16	17	18	19	20
21	22	23	24	25	26	27
28	29	30	31			

Last month ended on Sunday, September 30.

Next month begins on Thursday, November 1.

Using a Clock or a Stopwatch to Find Elapsed Time

You need to time an experiment for 20 minutes.

It is 1:30 P.M.

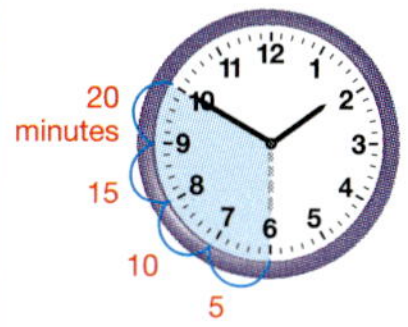

Stop at 1:50 P.M.

You need to time an experiment for 15 seconds. You can use the second hand of a clock or watch.

60 seconds = 1 minute

Start the experiment when the second hand is on number 6.

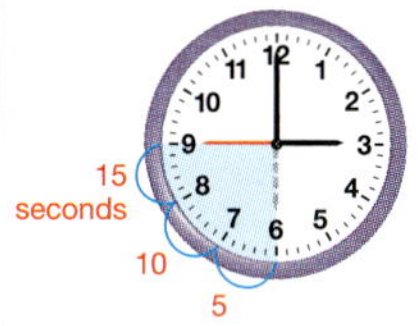

Stop when 15 seconds have passed and the second hand is on the 9.

You can use a stopwatch.

Press the reset button on a stopwatch so that you see 0:00$_{00}$.

Press the start button. When you see 0:15$_{00}$, press the stop button.

Measuring
Elapsed Time

Helpful Hints Estimating time intervals is difficult for many people. In many science experiments, an accurate measurement of how long an event took to occur is an important piece of data. Emphasize with students that finding elapsed time is part of data collection in science.

Try It Out

- Use your classroom clock to determine the time elapsed since the school day started, until recess, and so on. Ask students which is easier for figuring elapsed time, a clock with a circular dial or a digital clock?
- How much time must elapse before your next school holiday? Students could number, in reverse order, days on a calendar from that date.

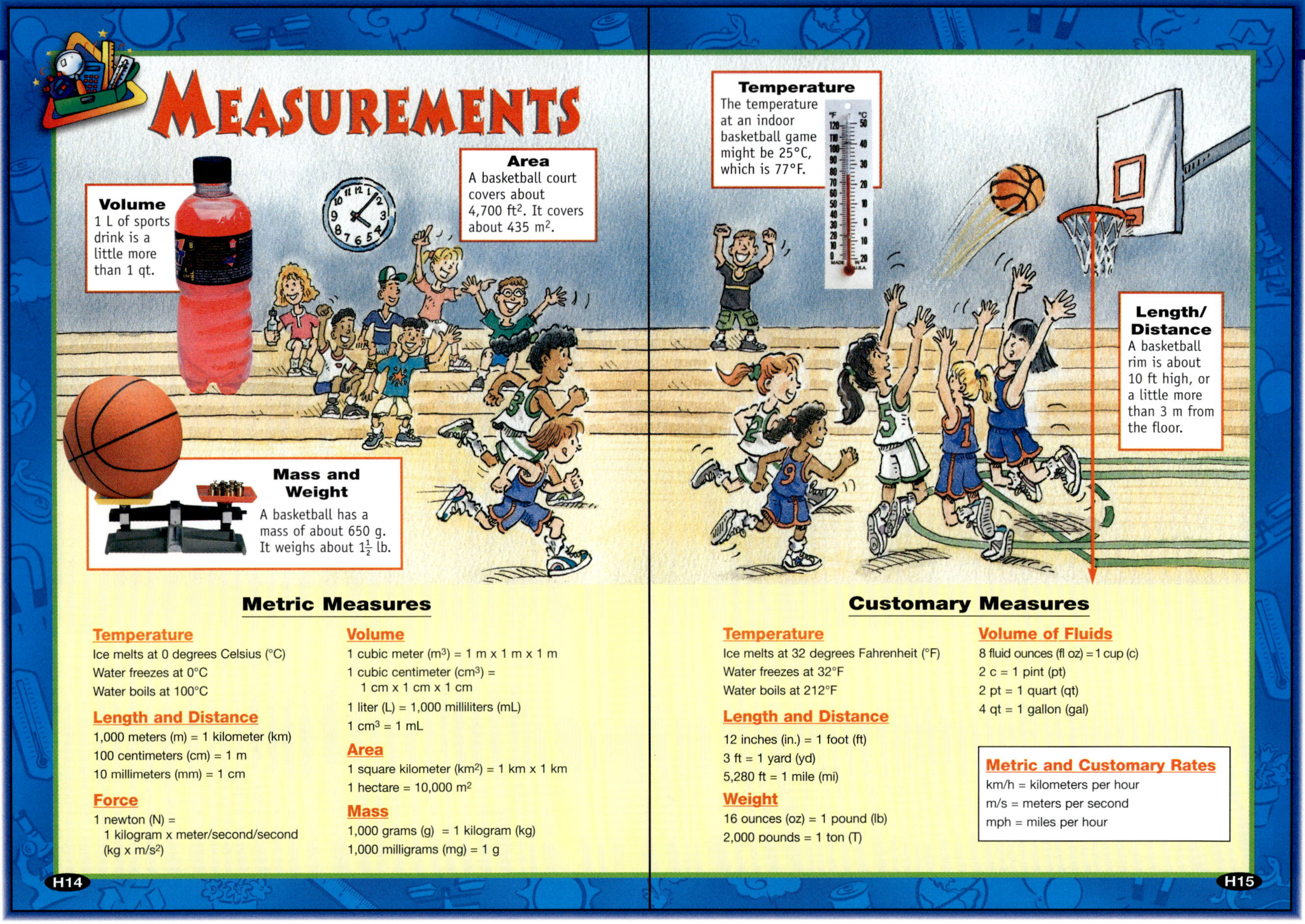

Measurements

Volume
1 L of sports drink is a little more than 1 qt.

Area
A basketball court covers about 4,700 ft^2. It covers about 435 m^2.

Mass and Weight
A basketball has a mass of about 650 g. It weighs about $1\frac{1}{2}$ lb.

Temperature
The temperature at an indoor basketball game might be 25°C, which is 77°F.

Length/ Distance
A basketball rim is about 10 ft high, or a little more than 3 m from the floor.

Metric Measures

Temperature
Ice melts at 0 degrees Celsius (°C)
Water freezes at 0°C
Water boils at 100°C

Length and Distance
1,000 meters (m) = 1 kilometer (km)
100 centimeters (cm) = 1 m
10 millimeters (mm) = 1 cm

Force
1 newton (N) =
1 kilogram x meter/second/second (kg x m/s^2)

Volume
1 cubic meter (m^3) = 1 m x 1 m x 1 m
1 cubic centimeter (cm^3) =
1 cm x 1 cm x 1 cm
1 liter (L) = 1,000 milliliters (mL)
1 cm^3 = 1 mL

Area
1 square kilometer (km^2) = 1 km x 1 km
1 hectare = 10,000 m^2

Mass
1,000 grams (g) = 1 kilogram (kg)
1,000 milligrams (mg) = 1 g

Customary Measures

Temperature
Ice melts at 32 degrees Fahrenheit (°F)
Water freezes at 32°F
Water boils at 212°F

Length and Distance
12 inches (in.) = 1 foot (ft)
3 ft = 1 yard (yd)
5,280 ft = 1 mile (mi)

Weight
16 ounces (oz) = 1 pound (lb)
2,000 pounds = 1 ton (T)

Volume of Fluids
8 fluid ounces (fl oz) = 1 cup (c)
2 c = 1 pint (pt)
2 pt = 1 quart (qt)
4 qt = 1 gallon (gal)

Metric and Customary Rates
km/h = kilometers per hour
m/s = meters per second
mph = miles per hour

H14 H15

Measurements

It is usually not a good idea to ask students to convert values from one measuring system to another. When metric measurements are required, use metric tools; similarly, when customary measurements are needed, use the appropriate instruments. However, some relational benchmarks are useful. For example:

1 cm . . . . is a generous . . . . 1/2 inch
1 meter . . . . is a generous . . . . 1 yard
1 liter . . . . is a generous . . . . 1 quart
1 kilogram . . . . . . is a generous . . . . . . 2 pounds
1 kilometer . . . . . is a generous . . . . 1/2 mile

Room temperature is about 20˚C.
Hot tap water is usually about 40˚C.

If conversions are necessary, use a simple graph to do it. For a temperature conversion, make a graph with Celsius temperatures on one axis and Fahrenheit on the other. Locate and mark two points using these temperatures as coordinates: (0˚C, 32˚F) and (100˚C, 212˚F). Then draw a straight line through both points. To convert from one temperature scale to another, read across (or up) from one axis to the line and then down (or across) to the other axis. The same technique may be used with length, mass, or volume. All that is needed are two points to establish the line.

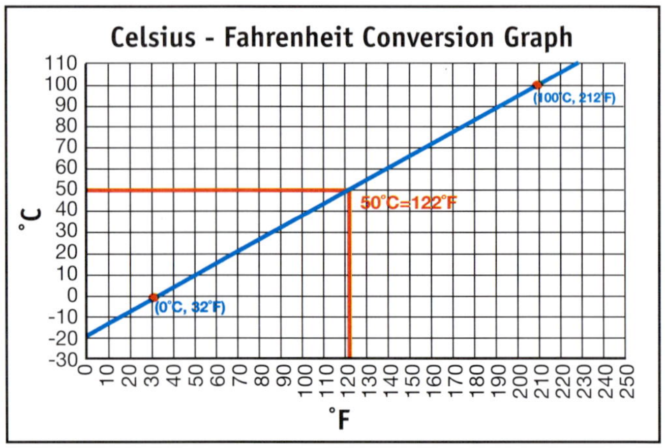

GLOSSARY

Pronunciation Key

Symbol	Key Words
a	c**a**t
ā	**a**pe
ä	c**o**t, c**a**r
e	t**e**n, b**e**rry
ē	m**e**
i	f**i**t, h**e**re
ī	**i**ce, f**i**re
ō	g**o**
ô	f**a**ll, f**o**r
oi	**oi**l
o͝o	l**oo**k, p**u**ll
o͞o	t**oo**l, r**u**le
ou	**ou**t, cr**ow**d
u	**u**p
ʉ	f**u**r, sh**i**rt
ə	**a** in **a**go
	e in ag**e**nt
	i in penc**i**l
	o in at**o**m
	u in circ**u**s
b	**b**ed
d	**d**og
f	**f**all

Symbol	Key Words
g	**g**et
h	**h**elp
j	**j**ump
k	**k**iss, **c**all
l	**l**eg
m	**m**eat
n	**n**ose
p	**p**ut
r	**r**ed
s	**s**ee
t	**t**op
v	**v**at
w	**w**ish
y	**y**ard
z	**z**ebra
ch	**ch**in, ar**ch**
ŋ	ri**ng**, dri**nk**
sh	**sh**e, pu**sh**
th	**th**in, tru**th**
th	**th**en, fa**th**er
zh	mea**s**ure

A heavy stress mark (ʹ) is placed after a syllable that gets a heavy, or primary, stress, as in **picture** (pikʹchər).

A

adaptation (ad əp tāʹshən) A part or behavior that makes a living thing better able to survive in its environment. (C54) The spider's behavior of spinning a web to catch an insect, such as a bee, is an *adaptation* that helps the spider get food

air (er) The invisible, odorless, and tasteless mixture of gases that surrounds Earth. (E10) *Air* consists mainly of the gases nitrogen and oxygen.

air mass (er mas) A large body of air that has about the same temperature, air pressure, and moisture throughout. (E62) When warm and cold *air masses* meet, the weather changes.

air pressure (er preshʹər) The push of the air in all directions against its surroundings. (E31) You can see the effect of *air pressure* when you blow up a balloon.

amphibian (am fibʹē ən) A vertebrate that usually lives in water in the early part of its life; it breathes with gills and then later develops lungs. (C19) Frogs, toads, and salamanders are *amphibians*.

anemometer (an ə mämʹət ər) A device used to measure the speed of the wind. (E39) The *anemometer* showed that the wind was blowing at 33 km/h.

atmosphere (atʹməs fir) The blanket of air that surrounds Earth, reaching to about 700 km above the surface. (E12) Earth's *atmosphere* makes it possible for life to exist on the planet.

atom (atʹəm) The smallest part of an element that still has the properties of that element. (B30) Water forms when *atoms* of the elements hydrogen and oxygen combine in a certain way.

axis (akʹsis) An imaginary straight line from the North Pole, through Earth's center, to the South Pole. (E78) Earth makes one complete turn on its *axis* in about 24 hours.

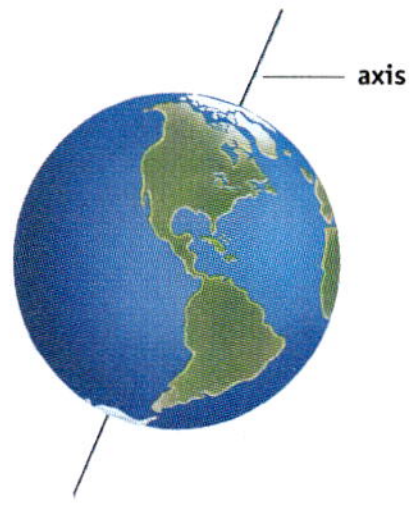

B

barometer (bə rämʹət ər) A device used to measure air pressure. (E30) Scientists use a *barometer* to gather information about the weather.

bay (bā) Part of a sea or lake extending into the land. (A14) The ship sailed through the *bay* into the Atlantic Ocean.

behavior (bē hāvʹyər) The way in which a living thing acts or responds to its environment. (C55) Purring, washing themselves, and hunting mice are three common *behaviors* of cats.

bird (bʉrd) A vertebrate that has wings, is covered with feathers, and hatches from a hard-shell egg. (C21) A *bird* is the only organism in the animal kingdom that has feathers covering its body.

boiling (boilʹiŋ) The rapid change of state from a liquid to a gas. (B40) When water is *boiling*, bubbles of water vapor form.

C

carbon dioxide (kärʹbən dī äksʹīd) A colorless, odorless gas. (E10) Plants use *carbon dioxide* from the air in the process of making food.

chemical change (kemʹi kəl chānj) A change in matter that results in one or more different kinds of matter forming. (B56) A *chemical change* occurs when matter, such as paper, burns and forms gases and ash.

chemical formula (kemʹi kəl fôrʹmyo͞o lə) A group of symbols that shows the kinds and number of atoms in a single unit of a compound. (B35) The *chemical formula* for carbon dioxide is CO_2.

chemical property (kemʹi kəl präpʹər tē) A characteristic of a substance that can only be seen when the substance changes and a new substance is formed; describes how matter reacts with other matter. (B13, B56) A *chemical property* of iron is that iron can combine with oxygen to form rust.

chemical reaction (kemʹi kəl rē akʹshən) The process in which one or more substances are changed into one or more different substances. (B57) A *chemical reaction* takes place when burning wood changes to ash.

chemical symbol (kemʹi kəl simʹbəl) One or two letters that stand for the name of an element. (B30) The *chemical symbol* for gold is *Au*.

circuit breaker (sʉrʹkit brākʹər) A switch that opens or closes a circuit by turning off or on. (D52) When a circuit overheats, the *circuit breaker* switches off and the lights go out.

cirrus cloud (sirʹəs kloud) A thin, feathery cloud made up of ice crystals high in the sky. (E57) *Cirrus clouds* often look like wisps of hair.

climate (klīʹmət) The average weather conditions of an area over a long period of time. (E84) Some regions have a hot, rainy *climate*.

cloud (kloud) A mass of tiny droplets of water that condensed from the air. (E46) A dark *cloud* blocked the sunlight.

cold front (kōld frunt) The leading edge of a cold air mass that forms as the cold air mass moves into a warm air mass. (E62) Thunderstorms often occur along a *cold front*.

compass (kumʹpəs) A device containing a magnetized needle that moves freely and is used to show direction. (D23) The north pole of the needle in a *compass* points toward Earth's magnetic north pole.

compound (käm′pound) Matter made up of two or more elements chemically combined. (B33) Salt is a *compound* made up of sodium and chlorine.

condensation (kän dən sā′shən) The change of state from a gas to a liquid. (B42) Drops of water form on the outside of a very cold glass because of the *condensation* of water vapor in the air.

condense (kən dens′) To change from a gas to a liquid. (E46) Water vapor from the air *condenses* on a cold window.

conductor (kən duk′tər) A material through which electricity moves easily. (D42) Copper wire is a good *conductor* of electricity.

conifers (kän′ə fərz) Cone-bearing plants. (C37) Pines and fir trees are examples of *conifers*.

conservation (kän sər vā′shən) The preserving and wise use of natural resources. (A31) The *conservation* of forests is important to both humans and wildlife.

controlled experiment (kən-trōld′ ek sper′ə mənt) A test of a hypothesis in which the setups are identical in all ways except one. (S7) In the *controlled experiment*, one beaker of water contained salt.

cumulus cloud (kyo͞o′myo͞o ləs kloud) A large puffy cloud. (E55) White *cumulus clouds* can often be seen in an otherwise clear summer sky.

D

delta (del′tə) A flat, usually triangular plain formed by deposits of sediment where a river empties into the ocean. (A12) The largest *delta* in the United States is at the mouth of the Mississippi River.

density (den′sə tē) The property that describes how much matter is in a given space, or volume. (B9, B11) The *density* of air varies with its temperature.

dicot (dī′kät) A flowering plant that produces seeds that have two sections. (C38) A trait of a *dicot* is that the veins of its leaves form a branching pattern.

E

electric cell (ē lek′trik sel) A device that changes chemical energy to electrical energy. (D60) A battery in a flashlight consists of one or more *electric cells*.

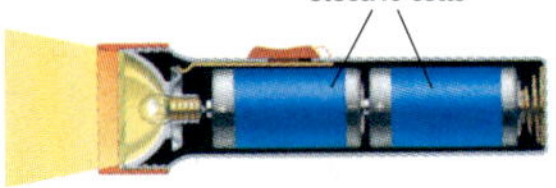

electric charge (ē lek′trik chärj) The electrical property of particles of matter; an electric charge can be positive or negative. (D30) Rubbing a balloon with a wool cloth causes negative *electric charges* to move from the wool to the balloon.

electric circuit (ē lek′trik sur′kit) A path along which an electric current can move. (D41) We made an *electric circuit*, using a battery, wires, and a light bulb.

electric current (ē lek′trik kur′ənt) A continuous flow of electric charges. (D41) *Electric current* in wires allows you to run electric appliances, such as an iron or refrigerator, in your home.

electric discharge (ē lek′trik dis′chärj) The loss or release of an electric charge. (D33) A bolt of lightning is an *electric discharge*.

electromagnet (ē lek′trō mag nit) A magnet made when an electric current passes through a wire coiled around an iron core. (D70) A large *electromagnet* can be strong enough to lift heavy metal objects such as cars.

element (el′ə mənt) Matter made up of only one kind of atom. (B30) Iron, oxygen, and aluminum are three examples of *elements*.

energy (en′ər jē) The ability to cause change. (B39) Most automobiles use *energy* from gasoline to move.

environment (en vī′rən mənt) Everything that surrounds and affects a living thing. (C44) Desert animals and forest animals live in very different *environments*.

equator (ē kwāt′ər) An imaginary line circling the middle of Earth, halfway between the North Pole and the South Pole. (E78) The *equator* divides Earth into the Northern Hemisphere and the Southern Hemisphere.

erosion (ē rō′zhən) The gradual wearing away and removing of rock material by forces such as moving water, wind, and moving ice. (A10) Ocean waves cause *erosion* of the seashore.

evaporate (ē vap′ə rāt) To change from a liquid to a gas. (E46) Some of the water boiling in the pot *evaporated*.

evaporation (ē vap ə rā′shən) The change of state from a liquid to a gas. (B40) Under the hot sun, water in a puddle changes to water vapor through the process of *evaporation*.

exoskeleton (eks ō skel′ə tən) A hard outer structure, such as a shell, that protects or supports an animal's body. (C15) A lobster has a thick *exoskeleton*.

extinct (ek stiŋkt′) No longer living as a species. (C58) Traces of some *extinct* species can be found in fossils.

F

ferns (furnz) Spore-forming plants that have roots, stems, and leaves. (C36) *Ferns* that grow in tropical places have very tall fronds.

filament (fil′ə mənt) A long, thin coil of wire that glows when electricity passes through it. (D48) The *filament* in an incandescent light bulb gives off light.

fish (fish) A vertebrate that lives in water and has gills used for breathing and fins used for swimming. (C18) Sharks and tuna are kinds of *fish*.

flash flood (flash flud) A sudden, violent flood. (E67) Heavy rains caused *flash floods* as the stream overflowed.

fog (fôg) A cloud that touches Earth's surface. (E46) Traffic accidents often increase where *fog* is heavy.

fossil fuel (fäs′əl fyo͞o′əl) A fuel that formed from the remains of once-living things and that is nonrenewable. (A47) Oil is a *fossil fuel*.

freezing (frēz′iŋ) The change of state from a liquid to a solid. (B42) Water turns to ice by *freezing*.

front (frunt) The place where two air masses meet. (E62) Forecasters watch the movement of *fronts* to help predict the weather.

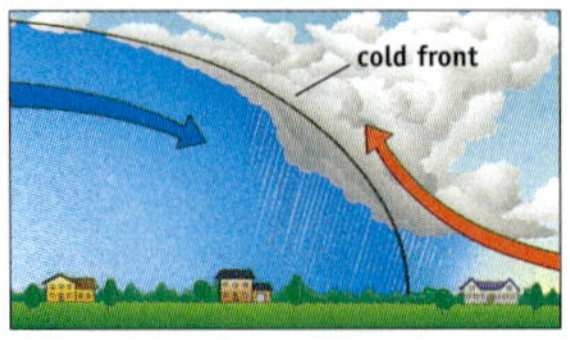

fuse (fyo͞oz) A device in a circuit that contains a metal strip, which melts when the circuit is overheated, thus breaking the circuit. (D52) The *fuse* blew because too many appliances were connected to the same electric circuit.

G

gas (gas) The state of matter that has no definite shape or volume. (B29) Helium is a very light *gas* that is used to fill some balloons.

generator (jen′ər āt ər) A device that changes energy of motion into electrical energy. (D58) The huge *generator* uses water power to produce electricity.

gill (gil) A feathery structure on each side of a fish's head that lets the fish breathe underwater. (C18) A fish takes in oxygen through its *gills*.

glacier (glā′shər) A huge mass of slow-moving ice that forms over land; glaciers form in areas where the amount of snow that falls is more than the amount of snow that melts. (A22) As it moves, a *glacier* changes the surface beneath it.

greenhouse effect (grēn′hous e fekt′) The process by which heat from the Sun builds up near Earth's surface and is trapped by the atmosphere. (E15) Some scientists fear that air pollution may increase the *greenhouse effect* and raise temperatures on Earth.

H

hazardous waste (haz′ər dəs wāst) A waste material that dirties the environment and that can kill living things or cause disease. (A65) Some chemicals used to kill insects become *hazardous wastes*.

headland (hed′land) A piece of land that extends out into the water and usually slows down the flow of water that passes it. (A14) The lighthouse stood on a *headland* overlooking the bay.

high-pressure area (hī presh′ər er′ē ə) An area of higher air pressure than that of the surrounding air. (E33) Winds move from *high-pressure areas* to low-pressure areas.

horsetails (hôrs tālz) Plants that reproduce by spores and have underground stems. (C36) *Horsetails* are also known as scouring rushes because of the tough tip at the end of their bamboo-like stem.

humidity (hyo͞o mid′ə tē) The amount of water vapor in the air. (E47) Tropical climates have warm temperatures and high *humidity*.

hurricane (hur′i kān) A large, violent storm accompanied by strong winds and, usually, heavy rain. (E70) The winds of the *hurricane* blew at over 125 km/h.

hypothesis (hī päth′ə sis) An idea about or explanation of how or why something happens. (S6) The *hypothesis* about the expanding universe has been supported by evidence gathered by astronomers.

I

ice age (īs āj) A period of time when glaciers covered much of Earth's land. (E89) During the last *ice age,* glaciers covered parts of North America.

incineration (in sin ər ā′shən) Burning to ashes. (A60) You can get rid of trash by *incineration*.

instinctive behavior (in stiŋk′tiv bē hāv′yər) A behavior that a living thing does naturally without having to learn it. (C56) For a mother bird, feeding her young is an *instinctive behavior*.

insulator (in′sə lāt ər) A material through which electricity does not move easily. (D42) Rubber can prevent an electric shock because rubber is a good *insulator*.

invertebrate (in vur′tə brit) An animal that does not have a backbone. (C15) *Invertebrates* include jellyfish, sponges, insects, and worms.

L

landfill (land′fil) An area where trash is buried and covered over with dirt. (A59) In some places, towns decide to build recreation areas, such as parks, on the sites of old *landfills*.

learned behavior (lurnd bē hāv′yər) A behavior that an organism is taught or learns from experience. (C56) Sitting on command, catching a ball, and jumping through a hoop are examples of *learned behavior* for a dog.

lines of force (līnz uv fôrs) The lines that form a pattern showing the size and shape of a magnetic force field. (D19) Iron filings sprinkled over a magnet form *lines of force* that show the strength and the direction of the magnet's force.

liquid (lik′wid) The state of matter that has a definite volume but no definite shape. (B29) A *liquid,* such as water or milk, takes the shape of its container.

litter (lit′ər) The trash that is discarded on the ground or in water rather than being disposed of properly. (A66) The children cleaned up the park by removing all the *litter* they could find.

liverworts (liv′ər wurts) Nonseed plants that lack true roots, stems, and leaves. (C36) The logs by the stream were covered with mosslike *liverworts*.

lodestone (lōd′stōn) A naturally magnetic mineral found at or near Earth's surface. (D22) A piece of *lodestone* will attract iron.

low-pressure area (lō presh′ər er′ē ə) An area of lower air pressure than that of the surrounding air. (E33) Storms are more likely to occur in *low-pressure areas*.

M

magnet (mag′nit) An object that has the property of attracting certain materials, mainly iron and steel. (D11) The girl used a horseshoe *magnet* to pick up paper clips.

magnetic field (mag net′ik fēld) The space around a magnet within which the force of the magnet can act. (D20) The magnet attracted all the pins within its *magnetic field*.

magnetism (mag′nə tiz əm) A magnet's property of attracting certain materials, mainly iron and steel. (D11) *Magnetism* keeps kitchen magnets attached to a refrigerator door.

mammal (mam′əl) A vertebrate, such as a cat, that has hair or fur and feeds its young with milk. (C22) Dogs, cats, rabbits, deer, bats, horses, mice, elephants, whales, and humans are all *mammals*.

mass (mas) The amount of matter that something contains. (B10) A large rock has more *mass* than a small rock that is made of the same material.

matter (mat′ər) Anything that has mass and takes up space. (B10) Rocks, water, and air are three kinds of *matter*.

melting (melt′iŋ) The change of state from a solid to a liquid. (B40) As the temperature of the air rises, snow and ice change to liquid water by the process of *melting*.

metric system (me′trik sis′təm) A system of measurement in which the number of smaller parts in each unit is based on the number 10 and multiples of 10. (B20) Centimeters, meters, and kilometers are units of length in the *metric system*.

mineral (min′ər əl) A solid, found in nature, that has a definite chemical makeup. (A41) Salt, coal, diamond, and gold are some examples of *minerals*.

mixture (miks′chər) Matter that is made up of two or more substances that can be separated by physical means. (B50) This salad contains a *mixture* of lettuce, cucumbers, celery, and tomatoes.

molt (mōlt) To shed an outer covering such as hair, outer skin, horns, or feathers at certain times. (C30) Snakes and insects *molt*.

monocot (män′ō kät) A flowering plant that produces seeds that are in one piece. (C38) About one third of all flowering plants are *monocots*.

mosses (môs′əs) Small nonseed plants that lack true roots, stems, and leaves. (C35) The leaflike part of *mosses* grows only a few centimeters above ground.

N

natural resource (nach′ər əl rē′sôrs) Any useful material from Earth, such as water, oil, and minerals. (A31) One reason that trees are an important *natural resource* is that their wood is used to build houses and to make paper.

nitrogen (nī′trə jən) A colorless, odorless, tasteless gas that makes up about four fifths of the air. (E10) *Nitrogen* is used by plants for growth.

nonrenewable resource (nän ri no͞o′ə bəl rē′sôrs) A natural resource that can't be replaced once it's removed. (A42) Minerals are classified as a *nonrenewable resource* because there's a limited amount of them.

nonseed plants (nän sēd plants) Plants that do not reproduce with seeds. (C35) Ferns are *nonseed plants*.

Northern Hemisphere (nôr′*th*ərn hem′i sfir) The half of Earth north of the equator. (E79) Canada is in the *Northern Hemisphere*.

north pole (nôrth pōl) One of the ends of a magnet where the magnetic force is strongest; it points to the north when the magnet moves freely. (D13) *North poles* of magnets repel each other.

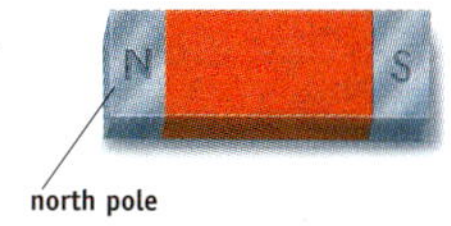

O

ore (ôr) A mineral or rock that contains enough of a metal to make mining that metal profitable. (A41) Gold, aluminum, copper, and tin come from *ores*.

organism (ôr′gə niz əm) A living thing that can be classified as belonging to one of several kingdoms. (C8) Animals and plants are *organisms*.

oxygen (äks′i jən) A colorless, odorless, tasteless gas that makes up about one fifth of the air. (E10) *Oxygen* is essential to life.

P

packaging (pak′ij iŋ) The wrapping and containers in which items are transported or offered for sale. (A75) *Packaging* protects products from damage but adds to their cost.

parallel circuit (par′ə lel sʉr′kit) An electric circuit having more than one path along which electric current can travel. (D51) Because the circuits in a home are *parallel circuits*, you can switch off one light and others will stay on.

physical change (fiz′i kəl chānj) A change in size, shape, or state of matter in which no new matter is formed. (B48) Cutting an apple in half and freezing water into ice cubes are *physical changes*.

physical property (fiz′i kəl präp′ər tē) A characteristic of a material or object that can be seen or measured without changing the material into a new substance. (B12) One *physical property* of a ball is its round shape.

polar climate (pō′lər klī′mət) A very cold climate that does not receive much energy from the Sun. (E85) The Arctic has a *polar climate*.

pollutant (pə lo͞ot′ ′nt) A substance that causes pollution. (A65) The exhaust gases from cars add *pollutants* to the air.

pollution (pə lo͞o′shən) The dirtying of the environment with waste materials or other unwanted substances. (A65) Water *pollution* can cause disease or even death in living things.

precipitation (prē sip ə tā′shən) Any form of water that falls from clouds to Earth's surface. (E46) Rain, snow, and hail are forms of *precipitation*.

property (präp′ər tē) A characteristic that describes matter. (B12) Hardness is a *property* of steel.

R

rain gauge (rān gāj) A device for measuring precipitation. (E47) The *rain gauge* at the weather station showed that 2 cm of rain had fallen in 24 hours.

recycle (rē sī′kəl) To process and reuse materials. (A72) Discarded newspapers are *recycled* to make new paper.

relative humidity (rel′ə tiv hyo͞o mid′ə tē) The amount of water vapor present in the air at a given temperature compared to the maximum amount that the air could hold at that temperature. (E47) A *relative humidity* of 95 percent on a warm day can make you feel sticky and uncomfortable.

renewable resource (ri no͞o′ə bəl rē′sôrs) A resource that can be replaced. (A42) Water is a *renewable resource* because rain increases the supply of water.

reptile (rep′təl) A vertebrate, such as a lizard or a crocodile, that has dry scaly skin and lays eggs that have a leathery shell. (C20) *Reptiles* can be found in both deserts and rain forests.

river system (riv′ər sis′təm) A river and all the waterways, such as brooks, streams, and rivers, that drain into it. (A11) The Mississippi River and the many waterways feeding into it make up the largest *river system* in the country.

rock (räk) A solid material that is made up of one or more minerals and that may be used for its properties. (A41) Granite is a hard *rock* used in construction.

S

sand dune (sand do͞on) A mound, hill, or ridge of sand formed by the wind. (A21) *Sand dunes* are common in the desert.

savanna (sə van′ə) A broad, grassy plain that has few or no trees. (C48) Nearly half of Africa is covered by *savannas*.

sediment (sed′ə mənt) Sand, soil, and rock carried by water, wind, or ice. (A12) The rushing water of the river deposited *sediment* along the riverbanks.

seed plants (sēd plants) Plants that reproduce with seeds. (C35) Corn and wheat are *seed plants*.

series circuit (sir′ēz sʉr′kit) An electric circuit in which the parts are connected in a single path. (D50) Electric current can follow only one path in a *series circuit*.

soil (soil) Loose material that covers much of Earth's land surface and is made up of three layers—topsoil, subsoil, and partly weathered rock. (A30) Plants, insects, and worms live in *soil*.

solar cell (sō′lər sel) A device that changes sunlight into electrical energy. (D64) *Solar cells* used in power plants can produce electricity without polluting the air.

solar energy (sō′lər en′ər jē) The clean and relatively low-cost energy from the Sun. (A50, D64) *Solar energy* is used to heat water in some homes.

solid (säl′id) Matter that has a definite volume and a definite shape. (B29) A *solid*, such as a rock, a wooden block, or an ice cube, has a definite volume and shape.

solution (sə lo͞o′shən) A mixture in which the particles of different substances are mixed evenly. (B51) Stirring sugar into water makes a *solution*.

Southern Hemisphere (su*th*′ərn hem′i sfir) The half of Earth south of the equator. (E79) The island continent Australia is in the *Southern Hemisphere*.

south pole (south pōl) One of the ends of a magnet where the magnetic force is strongest; it points to the south when the magnet moves freely. (D13) The *south pole* of one magnet attracts the north pole of another magnet.

standard unit (stan′dərd yo͞on′it) A unit of measure that everyone agrees to use. (B19) Scientists use the gram as the *standard unit* of mass.

state of matter (stāt uv mat′ər) Any of the three forms that matter may ordinarily take: solid, liquid, and gas. (B29) When ice melts, it changes to a liquid *state of matter.*

static electricity (stat′ik ē lek-tris′i tē)) Electric charges that have built up on the surface of an object. (D31) Walking across a carpet on a cold, dry day can produce *static electricity*.

stratus cloud (strāt′əs kloud) A low, flat cloud that often brings drizzle. (E55) Large sheets of very dark *stratus clouds* covered the sky on the rainy morning.

substance (sub′stəns) A class of matter made up of elements and compounds. (B34) Salt and sugar are *substances*.

switch (swich) A device that completes or breaks the path a current can follow in an electric circuit. (D41) In order to turn on the light, you must press the *switch* to complete the circuit.

T

temperate climate (tem′pər it klī′mət) A climate that generally has warm, dry summers and cold, wet winters. (E85) Most regions of the United States have a *temperate climate*.

theory (thē′ə rē) A hypothesis that is supported by a lot of evidence and is widely accepted by scientists. (S9) The big-bang *theory* offers an explanation for the origin of the universe.

thunderstorm (thun′dər stôrm) A storm that produces lightning and thunder and often heavy rain and strong winds. (E66) When the weather is hazy, hot, and humid, *thunderstorms* are likely to develop.

tornado (tôr nā′dō) A violent, funnel-shaped storm of spinning wind. (E72) The wind speed at the center of a *tornado* can be twice that of hurricane winds.

tropical climate (träp′i kəl klī′mət) A hot, rainy climate. (E85) Areas that are near the equator have a *tropical climate* because they receive the greatest amount of energy from the Sun.

troposphere (trō′pō sfir) The layer of the atmosphere closest to the surface of Earth. (E12) The *troposphere* reaches about 11 km above the surface of Earth and is the layer of the atmosphere in which weather occurs.

V

variable (ver′ē ə bəl) The one difference in the setups of a controlled experiment; provides a comparison for testing a hypothesis. (S7) The *variable* in an experiment with plants was the amount of water given each plant.

vertebra (vʉr′tə brə) One of the bones that together make up the backbone. (C14) Each knob in your backbone is a *vertebra*.

vertebrate (vʉr′tə brit) An animal that has a backbone. (C14) Reptiles and birds are *vertebrates*.

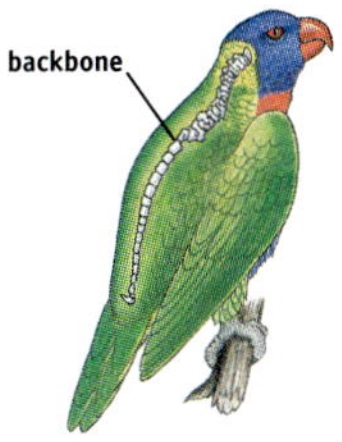

voltage (vōl′tij) The force of an electric current, measured in volts. (D63) Electric currents of high *voltage* travel through long-distance power lines.

volume (väl yo͞om) The amount of space that matter takes up. (B10) A baseball has a greater *volume* than a golf ball does.

W

warm front (wôrm frunt) The leading edge of a warm air mass that forms as the warm air mass moves forward into a cold air mass. (E63) Light rain often falls along a *warm front*.

water cycle (wôt′ər sī′kəl) The movement of water into the air as water vapor and back to Earth's surface as rain, snow, or hail. (E46) The *water cycle* is powered by energy from the Sun.

water vapor (wôt′ər vā′pər) Water that is in the form of a gas. (E10) *Water vapor* from the air forms drops of water on cold glass surfaces.

weather (we*th*′ər) The condition of the atmosphere at a certain place and time. (E13) The *weather* today in Chicago is snowy.

weather forecaster (we*th*′ər fôr′kast ər) A person who makes weather predictions or reports weather conditions. (E61) The *weather forecaster* predicted rain for the next three days.

weather satellite (we*th*′ər sat′'l īt) A human-made device in space that takes pictures of Earth and collects information about the weather. (E54) The *weather satellite* sent back pictures of clouds to weather stations in different locations on the ground.

weathering (we*th*′ər iŋ) The physical and chemical processes by which rock is broken down into smaller pieces. (A10) Cracks in rock produced by freezing rainwater or the growth of plant roots are examples of *weathering*.

wind (wind) The movement of air over Earth's surface. (E21) The strong *wind* lifted the kite high above the houses.

windsock (wind′säk) A device used to show wind direction, consisting of a cloth bag that is open at both ends and hung on a pole. (E38) The *windsock* showed that the wind was blowing from the north.

wind vane (wind vān) A device, often shaped like an arrow, used to show the direction of the wind. (E38) The *wind vane* on the roof of the weather station showed that the wind was blowing from the southwest.

INDEX

A

B

C

***Activity**
Bold heads indicate Teaching Guide material.

G

H

I

J

K

L

*Activity
Bold heads indicate Teaching Guide material.

*Activity
Bold heads indicate Teaching Guide material.